# Akiva

*The Jewish Publication Society expresses its gratitude for the generosity of the following sponsors of this book:*

RABBI BARRY AND DEBBY SCHWARTZ

IN MEMORY OF MIRYOM & BEN SHUMAN

UNIVERSITY OF NEBRASKA PRESS

*Lincoln*

# Akiva

## Life, Legend, Legacy

### REUVEN HAMMER

THE JEWISH PUBLICATION SOCIETY

*Philadelphia*

All rights reserved. Published by the University of
Nebraska Press as a Jewish Publication Society book.
Manufactured in the United States of America.

∞ Library of Congress Cataloging-in-Publication Data

Hammer, Reuven, author.
Akiva: life, legend, legacy / Reuven Hammer.
pages   cm
"Published by the University of Nebraska Press
as a Jewish Publication Society book."
Summary: "Reuven Hammer traces the life of
the great and legendary Sage, from youth to a
martyr's death, and his many contributions to
Rabbinic Judaism"—Provided by publisher.
Includes bibliographical references and index.
ISBN 978-0-8276-1215-0 (hardback: alk. paper)
ISBN 978-0-8276-1248-8 (epub)
ISBN 978-0-8276-1249-5 (mobi)
ISBN 978-0-8276-1275-4 (pdf)
1. Akiba ben Joseph, approximately
50–approximately 132. 2. Tannaim—Biography.
3. Jews—History—Bar Kokhba Rebellion,
132–135. 4. Martyrdom—Judaism. I. Title.
BM755.A6H36 2015
296.1'20092—dc23
[B]
2015020052

Set in Garamond by M. Scheer.
Designed by Rachel Gould.

*To my wife, Raḥel, to whom I owe so much*
*—in joyous celebration of our sixtieth*
*wedding anniversary.*
*As Akiva said, "Mine and yours are hers."*

# CONTENTS

# AUTHOR'S NOTE

I have always been intrigued by the figure of Rabbi Akiva and the stories told about his life and death, so it was only natural for me to consider writing a book about him. I recall that one of my college projects was to work on the development and the script of a film strip about his life. It was, needless to say, a simple and uncritical retelling of the well-known fable. Much later, in translating *Sifre Deuteronomy* and in compiling an anthology of tannaitic midrashim, I was fascinated by Akiva's interpretations and teachings. None of that, however, really included the critical study of his life that writing this volume has required. It has been an intriguing journey to uncover the various elements that went into the legends about Akiva and to begin to appreciate the man behind the legends. Stories about him are filled with drama, but the reality behind them is even more fascinating, as I hope readers will discover.

Akiva is a compelling figure, perhaps the most interesting of all the early Sages. One of the reasons for this is that Rabbinic literature contains such full and colorful accounts of his life. The problem, of course, is that these stories are a complicated mixture of fact and fiction, a mixture that in the popular mind is seldom differentiated. Even books of Jewish history, to say nothing of fiction, frequently take all of these stories at face value and indeed even elaborate on them.

The task I set for myself in writing this book was to separate history and legend and to see to what extent it is possible to determine what we know about the real Akiva, as well as to appreciate what the tellers of the legend were trying to teach.

In order to do that and write a volume that would be accessible to a wide audience it was necessary to review primary and secondary sources, to see what past as well as contemporary scholars had to say on the subject. The result of this was that, in the end, I felt that I knew both more and less than I had known before. The certainty I had felt about Akiva previously was greatly diminished. Ironically, I may know less about the real Akiva than I thought I knew before, but I now have an increased admiration for his true accomplishments—and also an increased realization of how baffling some of his concepts and actions may seem to modern readers.

I want to express my deep appreciation to my wife Raḥel for her great help and patience with this work, as with all my previous books. I am also indebted to the librarians of various institutions, among them the Hebrew Union College in Jerusalem and the National Library on the campus of the Hebrew University in Jerusalem. A special thank-you goes to my daughter, Rina Saper, an information specialist, for her help in obtaining many of the articles needed for this work. It should be noted that in citing biblical texts I use the New Jewish Publication Society translation (NJPS) except where translating passages in which a different translation is required to convey the way in which the Sages understood and interpreted the verse. My sincere appreciation to the staff of The Jewish Publication Society, especially to Barry Schwartz and Carol Hupping for their wise guidance and efforts in bringing this work to fruition. Their questions and prodding led me to deeper and better understandings.

# PREFACE

I consider it a privilege to be writing a book about Akiva ben Yosef for The Jewish Publication Society, not only because of the significance of the subject, but because the first important work on Akiva in English was written some eighty years ago by my esteemed teacher and mentor Louis Finkelstein of blessed memory and reprinted by JPS in 1962 (*Akiba: Scholar, Saint and Martyr*). It is important, however, to make it clear that this volume is not intended in any way as an update or revision of Professor Finkelstein's monumental work. His book remains an outstanding study that still stands on its own merits. More importantly, his work and mine are fundamentally different in their aims. Professor Finkelstein, with his encyclopedic knowledge and breadth of vision, took all the sources, integrated them, and created a full-fledged biography of the great Sage, placing the sources in historical contexts according to his understanding. My work, on the other hand, makes no such attempt, since current scholarship places a great emphasis on differentiating between the reliability of various sources.

Over the past half-century much progress has been made in understanding the history of the period between the end of the Great Revolt and that of the Bar Kokhva Rebellion (73 CE–135 CE) as well as in the way in which the Rabbinic sources concerning that period are to be understood. Modern scholarship and new, more sophisticated interpretation of the Rabbinic sources have changed our perspective on many aspects of Rabbi Akiva's life and legacy. Not all scholars agree on all of these matters concerning Akiva, as is to be expected. Some seek ways to verify the historicity of at least part of what appears in these writings; others feel that the most we can say is that these sources tell us what their writers believed and wanted us to know.

As long ago as the beginning of the last century, the great scholar Louis Ginzberg wrote that "a full history of Akiva, based upon authentic sources, will probably never be written, although he, to a degree beyond any other, deserves to be called the father of Rabbinic Judaism."[1] Some three-quarters of a century later another esteemed scholar of Rabbinics, Judah Goldin, claimed that it is not possible "to write a biography in the serious sense of the word" of any of the talmudic Sages.[2] The reasons are many, among them that none of the sources, even the oldest of them, is contemporaneous with the life of their subjects, that the sources contradict one another, and that they do not always contain accurate transcriptions of the original material. There is even some doubt as to the authorship of many of these sayings and traditions.

As time has progressed scholars have become ever more skeptical about the reliability of Rabbinic writings, to the point where some feel that nothing can be known with absolute certainty about any of the Rabbinic figures. A recent article by Rutgers University professor Azzan Yadin-Israel made the case that there is virtually nothing we can know about Akiva as a youth.[3] Avigdor Shinan of the Hebrew University, Jerusalem, contends that we actually know nothing of the history of Akiva except what the writers of the sources wanted us to learn about his life.[4]

In this volume I have carefully weighed and sifted through this scholarship in order to create a more nuanced understanding of the man, to differentiate between those sources that are clearly later legends and the earlier ones, which are closer to the facts, as nearly as they can be determined. I have endeavored to differentiate between the more reliable, factual traditions and the later, fanciful stories and to relate whatever can be gleaned from them, leaving the rest to our imagination. And so this work is not and could not be a full and detailed biography of Akiva, since it deals only with those parts of his life about which there is reasonably reliable information.

I have also striven to elucidate Akiva's methodology and ideology wherever possible, for when all is said and done, it was Akiva's unceasing work in preserving and molding Jewish Law and legend that made him the outstanding figure he was and that had such a great impact on the development of Rabbinic Judaism.

The sources that tell of Akiva's life, especially those concerning the start of his Jewish learning and of his late years and his death, are found primarily first in early tannaitic literature and then in later talmudic and aggadic works. The earlier writings were all composed in the Land of Israel. They include the Mishnah—the compilation of mainly legal discussions and conclusions by the Sages who lived before the year 200 CE, as compiled by Rabbi Judah the Prince; the Tosefta, material by those same Sages that was not included in the Mishnah; tannaitic midrashim, expositions of the texts of four books of the Torah—the *Mekhilta* (Exodus), the *Sifra* (Leviticus), *Sifre Numbers*, and *Sifre Deuteronomy*; *Avot de-Rabbi Natan*, material connected to the section of the Mishnah known as *Avot* (the Fathers); the minor tractate *Semahot*, concerning death and mourning—all produced in their final form between the third and fourth centuries CE. The somewhat later works from the Land of Israel include the Jerusalem Talmud (c. 500 CE), *Genesis Rabbah*, and others. The major work from Babylonia is the Babylonian Talmud, completed around 600 CE.

I have attempted to separate these sources by chronology. I view the earlier ones from the Land of Israel as more reliable, since they are closer to Akiva in both time and place. By comparing these to the Babylonian Talmud, one can see the way in which the earlier sources served as a basis for the later ones and that these later writings added much legendary material and often changed what had come before. This does not mean that everything in the early material is necessarily factual. Even there, literary forms and fictional fantasies had sometimes been imposed on whatever facts were known. On the other hand, material is sometimes found in later sources, especially in casual asides, that seem to reflect ancient traditions and should be taken seriously.

Legal matters are thought to be more reliable than historical ones, since the Sages made every possible attempt to memorize and pass on those teachings and traditions exactly as received from one generation to another. Nevertheless, even there caution is advised, since we sometimes find the same laws or sayings ascribed in different places to different Sages. Furthermore, early manuscripts do not always read the same as later, printed texts.

## DEALING WITH LEGENDS

Some of the most important people in human history have turned into legends, legends that, through the years of telling and retelling, have become fact and reality. The heroes in Homer and in the great Greek dramas may have been based on real people, but to know what they really were like, what they really did and said, is impossible. They live through the legends that they generated. Similarly important religious figures such as Abraham, Moses, and King David are known to us only through the literature that brings them to life. The same is true of the very early central figures in Christianity and Islam. The separation between fact and fiction, between life and legend, is murky indeed. This is also the case of the great Sages of Israel, be it Yohanan ben Zakkai, Hillel, and Shammai or the subject of this book, Akiva ben Yosef, whose lives are known to us exclusively through the Rabbinic literature in which stories are told of their actions and teachings and where sayings are recorded in their names.

The legend of Akiva has become part and parcel of Jewish lore, so much so that it has influenced Jewish life and even Jewish Law and practice. His story has been told and retold in many forms from ages past to this very day, in poetry, song, and fiction, as well as in numerous scholarly tomes and articles. With the possible exception of Hillel, Akiva is the most well-known of all the early masters, a beloved figure representing the best features of Rabbinic leadership and the willingness to give one's all, including life itself, for the sake of God and Torah. It is no wonder that his name has become associated with so many Jewish institutions and movements.

Yet there is no doubt that it is easier to tell Akiva's story in fiction than in historical prose, since the sources we have for him are incomplete and are spread over several centuries, none of which is closer than a few hundred years after his death. Worst of all, they often contradict one another. So "the story" that is woven so deeply in our consciousness is really a simplification and an amalgamation of those sources, sewn and patched together in a way that has become an appealing legend. In the end it is more an idealization of a Rabbinic Sage than it is a reliable story about Akiva the actual man. His legend will undoubtedly live on, as do so many fascinating legends. And with the tools now available to us we can begin to understand how the legends about him were created and what they were intended to achieve. Legend aside, the search for truth and honesty compels us to be willing to make distinctions and to appreciate Akiva for what he was and what he accomplished, as well as for what he has become in Rabbinic legend.

Here in this volume I've striven to separate fact from fiction concerning his life and have tried to discern his basic beliefs and his contribution to Rabbinic Judaism, as far as that is possible. I have made copious use of the many scholarly works published on the subject over the past several decades and have indicated in the text, and more completely in the endnotes, the names of the scholars and their works that I have used to help me create my own ideas. I of course take full responsibility for whatever I have written and hope that it will serve to shed light on the life and work of one of the greatest and most unusual of our Sages, Akiva ben Yosef.

# ABBREVIATIONS

| | |
|---|---|
| ARN-A | *Avot de-Rabbi Natan* A |
| ARN-B | *Avot de-Rabbi Natan* B |
| *Avot* | *Pirke Avot* |
| Deut. | Deuteronomy |
| Exod. | Exodus |
| Gen. | Genesis |
| *Gen. R.* | *Genesis Rabbah* |
| *Deut. R.* | *Deuteronomy Rabbah* |
| *Eccles. R.* | *Ecclesiastes Rabbah* |
| *Exod. R.* | *Exodus Rabbah* |
| Ezek. | Ezekiel |
| Isa. | Isaiah |
| JE | *Jewish Encyclopedia* |
| Jer. | Jeremiah |
| *Lam. R.* | *Lamentations Rabbah* |
| Lev. | Leviticus |
| *Lev. R.* | *Leviticus Rabbah* |
| *Mekh.* | *Mekhilta de-Rabbi Yishmael* |
| Neh. | Nehemiah |
| Num. | Numbers |
| Prov. | Proverbs |
| Ps. | Psalm |
| *Sifre D.* | *Sifre Deuteronomy* |
| *Sifre N.* | *Sifre Numbers* |
| Song | Song of Songs |

| | |
|---|---|
| *Song R.* | *Song of Songs Rabbah* |
| T. | Tosefta |
| *TK* | *Tosefta Kifshuta* |
| Y. | Jerusalem Talmud (Talmud Yerushalmi, Jerusalem Talmud) |

# TIMELINE

All dates are CE. The dates relating to Akiva are approximate and reflect an effort to reconstruct the timing of these events from the available sources.

| | |
|---|---|
| 50 | Akiva's birth |
| 66 | Great Revolt begins |
| 70 | Destruction of Second Temple in Jerusalem, death and exile of thousands of Judeans, consolidation of complete Roman rule over Judea |
| 70 | Rabban Yohanan ben Zakkai establishes the Sanhedrin, the Rabbinic court, in Yavneh, the new center of Jewish learning |
| 73 | Fall of Masada and the end of the Great Revolt |
| mid-70s | Akiva marries |
| 78 | Akiva begins his studies, attending academies at Lod, Yavneh, and elsewhere |
| 80 | Rabban Gamliel II heads the Sanhedrin |
| 93 | Akiva ordained by Rabbi Joshua and founds his own academy at B'nai Brak |
| 93 | Akiva is appointed by Rabban Gamliel II as judge, member of a delegation to Rome, and manager of programs to help the needy. Akiva begins to gather and organize oral traditions, creating the early form of the Mishnah and collections of Midrash |
| 115–117 | Kitos War |

# Akiva

# One

## AKIVA'S EARLY LIFE

Akiva ben Yosef may be the most well-known and beloved of the early Rabbinic Sages, the Tannaim,[1] but his life is largely a mystery and will probably always remain so. As the Talmud scholar Louis Ginzberg famously wrote, "A full history of Akiva, based upon authentic sources, will probably never be written, although he, to a degree beyond any other, deserves to be called the father of Rabbinical Judaism."[2] Akiva ben Yosef was "the man who marked out a path for Rabbinical Judaism for almost two thousand years."[3] His contribution to Rabbinic Judaism was so great that tradition designated him as one of the two "Fathers of the world," the other being his contemporary rival, Rabbi Ishmael.[4] In an early midrash Akiva was termed one of three without whom "the Torah would have been forgotten in his time." The others were Shaphan, the scribe who brought the newly discovered book of Deuteronomy to King Josiah in the sixth century BCE (2 Kings 22:14), and Ezra, the scribe who returned from the Babylonian exile and held a public ceremony affirming the divinity and authority of the Torah in the fifth century BCE (Nehemiah 8–9).[5]

When the Talmud wanted to prove the importance of Rabbi Judah the Prince, who was said to have been the greatest sage since Moses himself,[6] it stated that he had been born on the very day that Akiva died,[7] thus indicating that Akiva could be replaced only by one as great as that. Yet of Akiva's early life, we know virtually nothing. The sources, even those that are clearly legendary, tell nothing of him until he was a mature man. We do not even know when he was born.

The generally accepted assumption is that he died at an advanced age during the Bar Kokhva Rebellion and the Hadrianic persecution, somewhere around the year 132 CE,[8] although, as we shall see in chapter 8, the sources concerning that are far from clear. Avot de-Rabbi Natan B (ARN-B, in chapter 12), considered by many to be an early tannaitic work, posits that Akiva lived 120 years, in which case he would have been born around 12 CE and begun his studies in 52 CE. This is impossible, since that is prior to the destruction of the Temple and to the founding of the schools in Yavneh and Lod (Lydda) where Akiva studied. Obviously, then, 120 years is a schematic figure, taken from the biblical life of Moses, and is, in biblical symbolic terms, the life span of worthy individuals. If we assume that Akiva lived a long life, he would have been eighty or so when he died; therefore his birth would have been somewhere around the year 50 CE (the second half of the first century CE), some twenty years before the destruction of the Second Temple and the beginning of the Roman exile.

Akiva was born and lived most of his life near Lod in the lowlands of Judea, far from the metropolis of Jerusalem and the seat of religious studies. The name Akiva, which was not uncommon at the time,[9] is a variation of Akavya. The Hebrew root is the same as in the name Yaakov (Jacob), meaning the heel, the curved part of the foot, or possibly "to follow after."[10] In most Hebrew sources it is spelled in the Aramaic fashion with an *alef* at the end, but in the Jerusalem Talmud the form is the Hebrew one, ending with a *heh*.

Aside from the fact that his father's name was Yosef, the sources tell us nothing about the members of his family or their background. Nothing is known of his mother or any siblings. It would have been unusual for a family to have only one child, unless the mother died prematurely or could not have any other children. Of course the argument from silence is hardly conclusive, since Rabbinic sources make no attempt at writing complete biographies of the Sages and show little interest in telling such stories unless they contribute to some important ethical or legal teaching. Either Akiva grew up in a normal family, surrounded by mother and father and brothers and sisters, none of whom was considered important enough to be mentioned, or else he was an only child, possibly without a mother to tend to him through his adolescent years. All of that can only be left to our imagination.

Concerning the socioeconomic status of his family, again the sources are silent. There are, however, a few clues that lead to the conclusion that they were neither well educated nor wealthy. He had no scholars in his family background, a fact he himself admitted. In the Jerusalem Talmud, one of the earliest works that contains his sayings, Akiva remarks that when Rabban Gamliel II was forced to step down as head of the academy in Yavneh, he, Akiva, was not appointed in Gamliel's place because others, who were not greater than he in learning, had greater ancestors. "Happy is the man whose ancestors earn him merit," he said. "Happy is the man who has a peg upon which he can raise himself."[11]

In an offhand remark found in the Babylonian Talmud that has the ring of truth to it, Akiva recalls that in his youth he was an *am ha-aretz* (an ignorant peasant), something there was no reason for him to say were it not a fact. "When I was an *am ha-aretz*, if I encountered a scholar, I would have bitten him like an ass!"[12] Although in the original meaning of the term an *am ha-aretz* was simply a country person, it had come to mean illiterate and therefore ignorant.

Again, all the sources, early and late, insist that he began to learn to read at the age of forty. Forty may be an exaggeration, as was 120, but the meaning is clear: he was a mature individual, even married with a child, yet probably unlettered, when he began his studies.[13]

Looking back at his early years, remembering what he had done in his youth, Akiva once remarked to his students, "I give thanks to You, O Lord my God, that You have set my portion among those who sit in the house of study and not among those who loiter at street corners in the marketplace!"[14] That is what he had been—and what he might still have been had not something occurred that changed his life.

As for his financial standing, again the same early sources in Avot de-Rabbi Natan note Akiva's lack of resources when he began to study. "In the future judgment, Rabbi Akiva will put all the poor in a guilty light. For if they are asked, 'Why did you not study Torah?' and they will say, 'Because we were poor,' they shall be told, 'Indeed, was not Rabbi Akiva even poorer and in wretched circumstances!'"[15] Akiva was forced to depend first on his own labors and then on his wife's help during that period of time. Had his family been better off, it would be expected that they would have helped him, but at no time is there any mention of them in that regard. All of these things together indicate that Akiva's background, if not one of profound poverty, was at the very least of a family without status and without learning. The chances of a person from such a background becoming one of the foremost Sages of Israel, famous, influential, and beloved, would seem to have been nil, and yet, as is well-known, that is what happened.[16]

The section of Judea where Akiva was born and in which he grew up and lived much of his life was in the lowlands, not far from the coast of the Mediterranean Sea[17] near the city of Lod.[18] Unlike the hill country that led from there up to Jerusalem, it was fertile agricultural land and was populated and owned by prosperous farmers. If, as seems likely, Yosef was not one of them, this family might have belonged to the landless poor, to those who worked either as day laborers or as tenant farmers. According to a third-century source (Tractate Semahot, 9, usually appended to the Babylonian Talmud), when Akiva's father died, others bared their shoulders as a sign of mourning, but Akiva did not. Since the law was that one does not perform that act of mourning if parents "were not worthy," this may be another indication of low status of his family.

Tenant farmers lived a life of uncertainty and penury. Much of what they produced had to be given to their landlord. If that were the case for Akiva's family, then Yosef would have had little time for his son and would have had little to teach him except for the skills needed to eke out a living as a landless peasant. Illiterate himself, it would never have occurred to him to bother to attain schooling for his child, nor was such schooling easily available at that time for country folk without independent means.

Akiva's childhood and early adulthood, when he was an ignorant peasant, an *am ha-aretz*, took place, then, in the final years of the Second Temple, which was destroyed in the year 70 CE. In that prewar period, living in the lowlands, far from the metropolis of Jerusalem and the center of religious and political intrigue, he would have been ignorant of the major currents of Jewish thought and practice that flourished at that time. All that we know for certain in that regard is that he hated the Pharisaic Sages with a passion.[19]

## THE PHARISEES AND OTHER SECOND TEMPLE SECTS

The Second Temple period was a time when the books of the Torah were consolidated and became the accepted constitution of the Jewish people. But the interpretation of the Torah became a matter of conflict, and different sects emerged, each contending that its interpretation was the correct one. The three major sects, as described by the Jewish historian Josephus, were the Pharisees, the Sadducees, and the Essenes, although other groups, such as the Dead Sea Sect, also existed. In general the divisions reflected socioeconomic differences as well as religious distinctions. The Sadducees constituted the wealthy classes, including the priest-hood, and taught a conservative approach to religion, stressing the literal interpretation of the Torah and rejecting any ideas or laws that were not found in the written text. The Pharisees, although a small sect themselves, were favored by the plebian masses. They represented the urban population and taught a progressive approach to Judaism, interpreting the Torah in such a way as to allow for new ideas and new developments and including oral traditions as well as written ones. There were significant divisions within the Pharisaic ranks: the more liberal School of Hillel and the more rigid School of Shammai.[20] Even here there were socioeconomic divisions: the Shammaites included people of greater wealth such as landowners in the fertile lowlands, while the Hillelites were generally the poorer classes, townsfolk or farmers of the hilly countryside.[21]

Most Jews seemed to favor the Pharisees, even though they did not actually belong to that sect or follow all their strict observances. "They observed the Sabbath and holidays, heard the scriptural lessons in synagogue on Sabbath, abstained from forbidden foods . . . circumcised their sons on the eighth day, and adhered to the 'ethical norms' of folk piety."[22] However, the Pharisees themselves described another group whom they called *amei ha-aretz*, literally "people of the land" or country people, but in essence meaning ignorant and boorish. This was not a sect or organized group, but a term that described those individuals who were not careful in their observance and therefore not to be trusted, and it was generally applied to small landowners and tenant farmers.[23] One definition of an *am ha-artez* was "whoever has sons and does not rear them to study Torah."[24] As *amei ha-aretz*, Akiva's family would not have been particularly scrupulous about matters of ritual purity or of tithes. It is doubtful if they would have identified with any of the religious movements that flourished at that time.

During the time of the Great Revolt (66–73 CE), Roman armies swept through the lowlands where Akiva lived, but there were no great battles or devastation such as occurred in Jerusalem or in the Galilee, where the fighting was fierce. If any of this made an impression upon the young Akiva, it is never recorded that he ever spoke of it or alluded to it in his teachings. His negative attitude to the Romans, however, especially in his later years, may have been influenced by what he saw and experienced at that time.

Prior to the Great Revolt, extremist freedom fighters had roamed freely through the villages of Judea, where Akiva lived, operating there unhindered.[25] What impression had they made on the young man? There is nothing to indicate that he took part in the uprising in any way, but he could hardly have been ignorant of what was going on around him. Unlike some of the Pharisaic leaders of that time, such as Yohanan ben Zakkai, who counseled acquiescence to the Romans, fifty years later during the years of the Hadrianic decrees and the Bar Kokhva Rebellion, Akiva never did any such thing. If the opinions of his pupil Shimon bar Yohai are anything like his teacher's, Akiva had nothing but disdain for the Romans and welcomed the possibility of their overthrow. For Akiva, Rome was Edom, the enemy of Israel, as Esau had been the enemy of Jacob. He was one of those who felt that "the voice of Jacob" was the cry of oppressed Jews against "the hands of Esau"—the Romans who killed so many Jews at the time of the revolt.[26]

To an unlearned youth, any Pharisaic Sages who appeared in his area would have been perceived as arrogant men who despised people like himself and made extravagant demands for strictness of observance and payment of all sorts of tithes the poor could hardly afford. His attitude might have been similar to that expressed in Christian scripture as the way Galilean peasants thought of the Pharisees a few generations earlier. Of course the Christian scripture cannot be taken as unprejudiced, since its intent is to show that the teachings of Jesus were superior and more loving than those of the Pharisees. Nevertheless even within Rabbinic writings there are descriptions of some within the Pharisaic group who were haughty and overbearing. "The plague of Pharisees brings destruction upon the world," says the Mishnah.[27] And an early teaching cites seven types of Pharisees and describes their faults, while also quoting King Jannai as saying, "Fear not the Pharisees and the non-Pharisees but the hypocrites who are the Pharisees because their deeds are the deeds of Zimri but they expect a reward like Phineas."[28] An unlettered youth would hardly have made a distinction between a true Pharisee and the hypocritical imitators.

Akiva experienced the Great Revolt against the Romans, ending in the destruction of the Second Temple, the razing of Jerusalem, the deaths of thousands upon thousands of Judeans, the exile and slavery of thousands more, and the armies of Rome. Only after that, in the postwar period, did he begin to study and change his way of life.

### FROM TEMPLE WORSHIP TO TORAH STUDY

When the Great Revolt was over, much of Judea recovered swiftly. Landowners there had capitulated and were permitted to retain their land and continue farming.[29] Nevertheless everything in Jewish life changed radically, beginning with the way in which Jews governed themselves. All power was now in the hands of the Romans, who retained Caesarea as their capital. Jerusalem ceased to exist as far as Jews were concerned. The Sanhedrin that had sat there no longer functioned. With the disappearance of the Temple and the cessation of the cult, the power of the priesthood also vanished. The Sadducean group no longer existed. The Essenes and other sects had also vanished. The Sages—the leaders of Pharisaic Judaism—remained the only influential source of religious teaching. Under the leadership of Yohanan ben Zakkai they assumed whatever political power they could, and the seat of power transferred from devastated Jerusalem to the center of learning and jurisprudence that Ben Zakkai had established in Yavneh,[30] south of Jaffa, not far from where Akiva lived.

For all intents and purposes, Yavneh became the new Jerusalem, the center of the Rabbinic court and the source of Jewish learning. Ben Zakkai went so far as to name his court the Sanhedrin.[31] There was increased activity and more public learning now in that area than before. Perhaps that began to make a difference to Akiva's attitude. Otherwise how are we to understand the metamorphosis that changed this youth, who hated men of learning, into one who desired to enter into the circle of the learned? The Pharisees' attitude toward people like Akiva and his father was characterized by the distinguished historian Salo Baron as ambivalent, "at once cherished as ardent followers and despised as ritually unreliable illiterates."[32] No wonder Akiva would have torn apart any Sage from that group. But the Pharisees no longer existed as a sect. Instead there were learned men, Sages, now known as Rabbis, who sought to spread the knowledge of the Torah and of Jewish practice among the masses, creating a Judaism that could outlive the loss of the central sanctuary, the Temple, the sacrificial worship, and the Priesthood, a Judaism that could exist even without independence and self-government. These Sages became the predominant religious leaders of Judea and played an ever more important role in the life of the nation. Torah study became the center of religious life, and teachers roamed the land eager to impart such knowledge. The disputes that had led to divisions and the creation of sects that did not recognize one another's legitimacy had disappeared. Now there were differences of opinion and discussions and disputes, but the overwhelming desire was for inclusiveness and for respect for differences.[33] This new emphasis on the study of Torah[34] together with the increased importance of prayer transformed Judaism and enabled it to survive the crises of the destruction of the Temple.

Perhaps Akiva encountered these Sages, heard their public lessons, which took place in the open where anyone could listen, and began to feel the need for something more in his life. Without learning, without skills, without resources, what kind of a life could he look forward to? Scratching out a poor living as his father had done, perhaps finding a wife, if he could even afford one. For a young man of intelligence—and his subsequent history surely proves that he was extraordinarily gifted—such a life must have been unbearably frustrating.

Both fact and fiction are replete with tales of young people with brilliant, unrecognized potential who were discovered by a teacher or some other person who was able to discern the hidden talent and help the otherwise unknown youth to realize himself and achieve greatness. The Akiva of legend has been provided with such a person in the unlikely character not of a teacher or professional, but of a young woman with whom Akiva falls in love—his future wife. But is this fact or fiction?

# *Two*

## BECOMING A SAGE

The period of time following the defeat of the Great Revolt in 73 CE, the time when Akiva's life changed drastically, was an age of uncertainty. The Jews of the Roman colony of Judea had experienced a tragedy of enormous proportions, and Judaism itself and its very future stood at the crossroads. Could it survive the second destruction of the Jerusalem Temple, its cultic center? The changes that would have to be made were revolutionary, and the circumstances were difficult. The old order and the old commonplaces, the various "philosophies" of Judaism, no longer held. The Romans taunted the Jews over their defeat and interpreted it as the defeat of the God of Israel as well.[1] Even more difficult to deal with was the accusation by the Jewish-Christian messianic sect, which claimed to be the continuation of ancient Israel, that the Jews—the deniers—had been defeated because of their refusal to acknowledge the new messiah.

### THE SAGES

After the loss of political independence, the study of Torah became the basic source of Jewish identity. Even an *am ha-aretz* like Akiva would have been exposed to it and would have heard public lessons, arousing his curiosity. With an intelligence such as his, his interest could not help but be piqued by the preaching of these popular teachers, whose only aim was to arouse interest in the Torah and encourage observance of its ways of lovingkindness. Unlike the Pharisaic teachers he had scorned and even hated as a child, this was a different type of sage, and as Akiva matured he would have been able to gradually overcome his prejudices and to imagine a different life for himself. It cannot have been easy for a man of his age to begin to study and to apply himself to difficult biblical texts. Somehow he found the courage to embark on a journey that would lead him far from whatever work he had and make him, like Moses, the shepherd not of sheep but of a much more significant flock.

The Sages, who were the heirs of the Pharisees in many ways but not identical with them,[2] attempted to fill the void left by the loss of the Temple and the cult with religious reforms—new interpretations of ancient laws, new readings of the old texts, and new forms of religious observance. It was also a time of renewal and of the beginnings of Rabbinic Judaism, which became the dominant force within Judaism. The loss of the Temple led to a reinvigorated approach to teaching and studying Torah in the newly founded academies that sprang up throughout the country. The center of Judaism shifted from the Temple to the house of study, for it was important that literacy and the study of Torah become the heritage of every Jew.

The Rabbinic Sages, with no power except that of their own teaching, were able to kindle a spark of hope that attracted the masses and kept them loyal to Judaism, despite the defeat that had overtaken them. One of their tasks was to prevent the tragedy from overwhelming the people. Thus they opposed too much mourning and tried to keep it to a minimum. They also attempted to teach that the loss of the Temple did not interfere with the relationship between God and Israel and did not prevent them from attaining forgiveness from sin. In effect they strove to attain normalization of life and continuity of religious practice, turning people toward a more personal relationship to God and tradition through immersion in study. Let it be clear, however, that these Sages did not control the community nor dictate its actions and practices. There were those who followed them dutifully and those who did not. They were a relatively small and elite group with great influence, which would later determine the future of Judaism, but they never enjoyed the total allegiance of the entire Jewish population.

It was Yohanan ben Zakkai himself, now established at Yavneh, who had said to his pupil Rabbi Joshua, later to become one of Akiva's teachers, that one need not be grieved over the destruction of the Temple where atonement had been made for Israel, since "we have another atonement as effective as it, and what is it? Acts of lovingkindness, as it is said, 'For I desire lovingkindness and not sacrifice' (Hosea 6:6)."[3] Teachings such as this could open the heart and mind of one such as Akiva and encourage him to desire to enter the world of the Sages.

### AKIVA'S TURNING POINT

After the Great Revolt the coastal region where Akiva lived became an important center of Jewish learning. The leading Sages were there, either in the official court founded by Rabban Yohanan ben Zakkai in Yavneh or in the numerous academies of study that individual Sages founded for the benefit of the general public. In Akiva's own town of Lod there was a major academy headed by the great Sage Rabbi Eliezer ben Hyrkanus and his contemporary Rabbi Joshua. Scholars also taught in public places there, for the general populace.[4]

What would cause a poor young man lacking in learning to seek to study with the Sages? If the sources reveal very little about Akiva's early life, they provide a plethora of stories in answer to that question, stories with many variations and contradictions. These can be found in tannaitic works and the Jerusalem Talmud created in the Land of Israel, edited sometime between the third and fifth centuries, and in the sixth-century Babylonian Talmud, in which the most well-known and most romantic stories of Akiva can be found. The earlier tales relating traditions from the Land of Israel are much simpler and much more convincing.

We cannot be certain of Akiva's exact age when he decided that he wanted to study Torah. The oldest reference is also the shortest. *Sifre Deuteronomy*, a tannaitic work edited around 300 CE, states simply that he began to learn at age 40, a third of his lifetime, which here is said to have been 120 years.[5] There is no explanation whatsoever of this fact. To understand this source it is important to realize that it is actually part of a commentary on Deuteronomy 34:7, "Moses was a hundred and twenty years old when he died." The commentary states, "He [Moses] was one of four who died at the age of one hundred and twenty, and these were Moses, Hillel the elder, Rabban Yohanan ben Zakkai, and Rabbi Akiva." The midrash then divides the lives of each into three equal sections of forty years each. Of Ben Zakkai it says, "Rabban Yohanan ben Zakkai was a merchant for forty years, served the Sages for forty years, and led Israel for forty years." Concerning Akiva the text states, "Rabbi Akiva began to study Torah when he was forty years old, served the Sages for forty years, and led Israel for forty years."

Obviously the whole matter of the length of their lives and of the three time periods is merely schematic and offers us no factual information. Since, according to the text, Moses lived to 120, ascribing that length of life to others is a way of saying that they were comparable to that great leader and of immense importance to Judaism. It is a reasonable assumption, therefore, that the second period of Akiva's life, when he began to study and "served the Sages" (in other words, was still a student and not an ordained rabbi), began when he was a mature person, probably sometime in his twenties. Note that this account tells us nothing of what he did before then, in the first third of his life.

One manuscript of the *Sifre* has a different reading, which fills in this lacuna: "Rabbi Akiva studied Torah forty years, served the Sages for forty years, and led Israel for forty years."[6] At least one scholar has contended that this is the more accurate reading and that Akiva did not come to Torah late, but had always studied it. If that is so, all the sources that say he was ignorant before forty would be later additions and false.[7] "Studied Torah forty years," however, is a strange phrase. No one begins to study from birth, therefore the authenticity of this reading remains suspect, especially since it stands in contradiction to all other sources. One possibility is that it implies that his period of study when he was a student and not yet a Sage ended at age forty. A somewhat later version of the *Sifre* midrash found in the fifth-century *Genesis Rabbah*, fills in the text differently: "Rabbi Akiva was an ignoramus forty years, learned Torah forty years, and served Israel forty years."[8] The impression left by all of these statements is simply that he began his studies as a mature man and not as a child.

None of these sources deals with the question of what caused Akiva to desire to become a Sage. That would have been beyond the scope of any midrash based on Moses's life span. Assuming that he had not learned Torah before then, the question remains, what caused this change? Was it a sudden call, a flash of inspiration, or a gradual realization that something was missing in his life? Was it caused by some external event? For Moses there was the burning bush. For Paul there was the road to Damascus. Nothing quite so dramatic is recorded in any of the Akiva sources, early or late. In the earliest texts all we have is a drip of water or a piece of rope.

The question "What were the beginnings of Rabbi Akiva?" occupied the thoughts of many over the generations. The oldest story that specifically addresses this question is found in two versions of an early tannaitic source, *Avot de-Rabbi Natan* (ARN):[9]

> What were the beginnings of Rabbi Akiva? It is said that he was forty years old and had not yet studied a thing. One time he stood by the mouth of a well. "Who hollowed out this stone?" he wondered. He was told: "It is the water which falls upon it every day, continually." . . .
>
> Thereupon Rabbi Akiva drew the inference with regard to himself: If what is soft wears down the hard, all the more shall the words of Torah, which are as hard as iron, hollow out my

heart, which is flesh and blood! Forthwith he turned to the study of Torah.[10]

A variant of the story is found in *Avot de-Rabbi Natan* B (ARN-B), based on a manuscript found in the Cairo Geniza and published for the first time by Solomon Schechter in 1887. He considered it an earlier version than ARN-A:[11]

> Rabbi Akiva wanted to learn Torah. He went and sat near a well in Lod. He saw the hollowed out stone on the well and said, "Who hallowed out this stone?" They said to him, "It is the rope." He said to them, "Can it do that?" They said to him, "Yes because it continuously wears against it." . . . He said, "Is my heart harder than stone? I will go and learn one portion of the Torah."[12]

It is worth comparing the two versions. According to ARN-A, Akiva had never learned anything and was truly illiterate. ARN-B simply says that he wished to learn Torah and implies in the continuation of the text that he already knew how to read. A speaks of the power of water, B uses a rope. Both have the image of a well, and both, in a section not translated above, quote an appropriate verse from the book of Job: "Water wears away stone" (Job 14:19).

The texts continue, relating how he then began to learn together with his son. ARN-A states:

> He went together with his son and they appeared before an elementary teacher. Said Rabbi Akiva to him: "Master, teach me Torah."
>
> Rabbi Akiva took hold of one end of the tablet and his son the other end of the tablet. The teacher wrote down *alef bet* for him and he learned it; *alef tav*, and he learned it; the book of Leviticus,[13] and he learned it. He went on studying until he learned the whole Torah.[14]

ARN-B implies that Akiva could already read:

He went to the school and started reading the tablet together with his son. He learned Scripture, the Aramaic translation, *Midrash Halakhot* [laws connected to biblical texts], stories and parables—he learned everything![15]

Both of these sources demonstrate a familiarity with the *Sifre* text, accepting that Akiva was forty when he began to study and dividing his life into three time periods. *ARN-A* also states later on, "He was forty years old when he went to study Torah. At the end of thirteen years he taught Torah to the masses."[16] *ARN-B*, echoing *Sifre* more exactly, says, "When he was forty years old he went to the school. When he was forty years old he learned everything, and forty years he taught Israel."[17]

What is of greatest importance here is the fact that the teller ascribes the decision to learn and study not to any specific person's influence on Akiva, but to something within himself, some realization and inner drive to change his life. Furthermore, according to this story, Akiva was already a married man with at least one child, who was old enough to begin to learn to read or simply to learn together with his father.

Undoubtedly these charming tales are a literary invention rather than an exact record of what actually happened. In *ARN-A*, Akiva's reasoning is that of a Sage, based upon the principle of inference from major to minor, something that at this stage of his life he would hardly have been familiar with. In other words, it was accepted that Akiva had not studied Torah and had no thoughts of becoming a Sage until he was a mature man. The answer to what motivated him was basically that he came to it from his own inner urgings, by some realization that he possessed the ability to learn Torah, if only he had the will to persist.

Based on this early source, it seems likely that Akiva, whose innate intelligence cannot be doubted, was dissatisfied with his life as a simple laborer. He was also unhappy with his ignorance and, according to one version, with his inability to do such a simple thing as read. Perhaps, as has been suggested, he had been exposed to the popular public talks given at that time by the Sages, the descendants of the very group that he had despised, talks intended to attract common folk exactly like himself.

The picture of this young—or not quite so young—poor working man sitting down with his son and being instructed in the elements of reading, learning by rote the letters of the alphabet and then piecing them together to read the basic texts of Judaism, first Leviticus and then the rest of the Five Books of Moses, is both touching and unusual. It would be the equivalent today of an adult joining his child in his first grade class. Even if he already knew the Alef Bet, he still had to learn to read and understand biblical texts before going on to the unwritten and very complex Rabbinic traditions. This would have been an extremely difficult task.

### THE BEGINNING OF HIS ADVANCED STUDIES

At this early stage of his learning Akiva remained at home and had to continue to work in order to support his family. According to the early sources, however, at some point—perhaps when he was learning the biblical texts—he reduced his working time to a minimum. Akiva, then, did not immediately leave his home but continued life as before, with the added burden of intense study. He could not work regularly as before or he would have had no time to study: "He could not work a full day."[18] Instead he would gather straw (or in some versions wood), sell some of it, and use the rest to make a fire by which he could read and study. His neighbors complained about the smoke and urged him to sell them the straw and buy oil instead, which would be less annoying, but he would not because he also used the straw for heat and to make a bed.[19]

His first studies in a higher academy would not have required him to leave home at all. His first teachers were Rabbi Eliezer and Rabbi Joshua.[20] The great sage Rabbi Eliezer ben Hyrkanus had established an academy in Lod,[21] and it was there, where Akiva lived, that Akiva began his true introduction into Rabbinic studies.[22] Since Rabbi Eliezer left Yavneh together with Yohanan ben Zakkai only in the year 80,[23] we have a good idea of when it was that Akiva's studies in an academy might have begun. It is unlikely that Eliezer would have left Yavneh while Ben Zakkai was still its head.[24] Akiva's studies lasted thirteen years—"at the end of thirteen years he taught Torah to multitudes."[25]

Rabbi Eliezer was a close follower of Yohanan ben Zakkai. He studied with him in Jerusalem before the fall of that city and, together with Rabbi Joshua, smuggled him out of Jerusalem in a coffin so that Ben Zakkai could begin the work of re-establishing the center of religious life elsewhere—in Yavneh.[26] By the time Akiva began his studies, Eliezer had already established an academy in Lod with Rabbi Joshua, although Rabbi Joshua is also recorded as having a school at Pekiin.[27] The official court remained in Yavneh, where Ben Zakkai had established it, but other centers of study were scattered around the country. It was possible for a great sage such as Rabbi Eliezer to participate in the meetings of the Great *Beit Din* in Yavneh (now under Rabban Gamliel II) and still be the head of his own academy elsewhere,

After he had become proficient in the written Torah, Akiva began the study of Rabbinic traditions, the so-called oral Torah. *ARN*-A reports:

> Then he went and appeared before Rabbi Eliezer and Rabbi Joshua. "My masters," he said to them, "reveal the sense of Mishnah to me." When they told him one *halakhah* [law] he went off to be by himself. "This *alef*," he wondered, "why was it written? That *bet*, why was it written? This thing, why was it said?" He came back and asked them—and reduced them to silence.[28]

In the Jerusalem Talmud, however, it is said quite clearly that after thirteen years Rabbi Eliezer still did not know Akiva and that only then did Akiva speak to him and voice his opinions.[29] If that is the case, his initial inquiries concerning the Mishnah would have been only to Rabbi Joshua.

Mishnah as it is known today did not exist yet, rather the word referred to systematic collections of legal rulings arranged by subject rather than according to biblical verses, oral legal traditions handed down through the generations and formulated anew through the teachings of the Sages. The reference to letters here must be to biblical texts. From the very beginning Akiva was concerned with the connection between biblical texts and Rabbinic traditions. Akiva took a great interest in the teachings that eventually became the Mishnah. As a matter of fact, the Mishnah as we know it is ascribed to the work of Akiva as interpreted by his students.[30]

The story of Akiva's studies told in *ARN-A* concludes by detailing the wealth that Akiva eventually accumulated:

> Before he departed from the world he owned tables of silver and gold, and mounted his couch on ladders of gold. His wife used to go about in golden sandals and in a "City of Gold." "Master," his disciples said to him, "you have put us to shame by what you have done for her." He replied, "Many were the trials she endured for my sake, that I might study Torah."[31]

*ARN-B* contains a similar statement of his wealth and of the "City of Gold" that Akiva gave his wife, a golden tiara in the form of the walls of the city (which at that time no longer existed), also known as a Jerusalem of Gold. In this version it is his children rather than his disciples who complain, "People are making fun of us!" He replies, "I will not listen to you—she suffered with me over study of Torah."[32] His ownership of tables and ladders of gold and silver certainly sounds like a fable, but his wife's suffering and worthiness of a reward has the ring of reality.

These sources stand in complete contradiction to later legends about Akiva found in Babylonian sources.

The stories told in later Babylonian sources in answer to the question of Akiva's motivation tell a much different and more complicated story. As scholars have noted and discussed at length, these later legends tell us less about Akiva's life than they do about the lives and beliefs of those who related them,[33] nor do these sources always agree with one another. All of them tell of the circumstances of Akiva's marriage and of the role of his wife in changing his life or in permitting him to study.[34] As we have seen, in the sources originating in the Land of Israel nothing was written concerning the circumstances of his marriage nor does his wife play any part in his decision to begin to study. They did claim, however, that she helped finance his ability to study by selling her hair[35] and that she suffered in order to permit him to study.[36]

The Babylonian Talmud, which was edited hundreds of years later, sometime in the sixth century, recounts Akiva's beginnings in two different versions.[37] In both, his wife is not identified by name but is known only as "the daughter of Kalba Savua" (or Ben Kalba Savua), a man of legendary wealth whose charitable deeds at the time of the Great Revolt are recorded elsewhere.[38]

The more detailed version in the Babylonian Talmud, *Ketubot*, thought to be the older of the two stories,[39] notes that when Akiva worked as a shepherd for Kalba Savua,

> his daughter saw how modest and noble he was. She said to him, "If I would be betrothed to you, would you go and study at a *beit midrash*?" "Yes," he replied. She was then secretly betrothed to him and she sent him away. When Kalba Savua learned of this, he drove her from his house and forbade her to have any benefits from his property. [Akiva] departed and spent twelve years at the academy. When he returned home, he was accompanied by twelve thousand pairs of students.[40]

At that time he overheard his wife say that she wished he would study for another twelve years, and so he left and only returned twelve years later, this time bringing with him twenty-four thousand pairs of students. Akiva acknowledged publicly to his disciples that it was his wife who was responsible for all that he had accomplished, saying, "Mine and yours are hers," in other words, all our accomplishments and merits are due to her. Kalba Savua came to the great scholar, not knowing he was his daughter's secret husband, and asked that his vow not to support her be annulled, which Akiva did. He then gave Akiva "half his wealth."

A variation of this story in another tractate of the Babylonian Talmud, *Nedarim*, tells it somewhat differently:

> The daughter of Kalba Savua betrothed herself to Rabbi Akiva. When her father heard of it he vowed that she should not benefit from his property. In winter, she married him. They slept on straw, which he had to pick out of his hair. "If I could afford it," he said to her, "I would give you a Jerusalem of Gold!" Elijah appeared at their door disguised as a human being and cried, "Give me some straw. My wife is pregnant and has nothing to lie on." Akiva said to his wife, "You see, there is someone who does not even have straw!" She told him, "Go and become a scholar," so he did, studying twelve years under Rabbi Eliezer and Rabbi Joshua.[41]

The rest of the story repeats the idea that he went back again and returned only twelve years later with his twenty-four thousand pairs of students and praised his wife before them, after which he annulled Kalba Savua's vow and received wealth from him.

The main difference between this version and that in *Ketubot* is that here she became betrothed to him with no conditions, and only after she and Akiva had married and lived in poverty, with nothing but straw for a bed, did she council him, "Go and become a scholar." The *Nedarim* version also adds the miraculous appearance of Elijah and includes both the motif of the Jerusalem of Gold and the mention of straw beds.

Obviously both of these talmudic stories disagree with the earlier stories in *ARN*, in which Akiva began to learn only after he had a son, ascribing no role to Akiva's wife in causing him to study. In *ARN* the only mention of his wife is the general comment that she endured much so that he could study. There is no reference to her supposed father and his wealth, and nothing of Akiva's twenty-four year absence from home. On the contrary, according to that early story, as we have seen, he remained at home, earning a living by gathering each day a bundle of straw,[42] half of which he would sell and half of which he would use for heat and light.[43]

In attempting to determine the reliability of these later accounts, there are certain factual difficulties that must be noted, in addition to the folklore addition of the appearance of Elijah. One is that these sources all state that Akiva's wife was the daughter of Kalba Savua, whose legendary wealth and status were well-known. He was one of three wealthy men who were said to have supplied food to Jerusalem during the three years it was under siege at the time of the rebellion.[44] Among the many reasons to be suspicious of this story is the fact that Kalba Savua was a Jerusalemite, while Akiva lived in the lowlands.[45] It is also doubtful if Kalba Savua would even have been alive at this point. But most important is the fact that Akiva's father-in-law is clearly identified in an earlier source as a man named Joshua. This is mentioned casually in a reference in the Mishnah, edited about 200 CE, which seems completely reliable.[46] The Mishnah also identifies this same Joshua as the father of a rabbi, Yohanan ben Joshua, mentioned that once and nowhere else.[47] Since the Mishnah was edited several centuries before the Babylonian Talmud and originated in the Land of Israel, there is good reason to prefer its testimony.

It goes without saying that the figure of twenty-four thousand pairs of students is an impossibility. Another problem is the fact that Akiva is pictured in the Talmud as being away from home and totally cut off from contact with his wife for so many years, when in reality the main *beit midrash* in which he studied was in his very own home town of Lod. All of these problems make the reliability of the talmudic accounts questionable. The accounts in *ARN* may not be completely accurate either, but their very simplicity and general plausibility speak in their favor. The message that they attempt to convey is clear: it is possible to learn Torah and to become a sage even when one has little or no background and is neither wealthy nor from the aristocracy.

The Babylonian account is more concerned with Akiva's years away from home than with his problems with learning. These stories of his prolonged absence are found only in Babylonian sources. It has been suggested that they were invented and told in order to give weight and credence to the custom popular in Babylon at the time (but not in Judea) of students living away from home for years in order to study.[48]

The Babylonian versions also give great attention to Akiva's wife and the role she played in his becoming a sage, while the stories in *ARN* give her only slight mention. Dov Noy, the well-known expert of Jewish folklore, believed that *ARN* was edited after the Talmud and was based on it. He explained the absence of Akiva's wife in *ARN* as part of a deliberate attempt to downplay the role of women. However, if that were so, one would have expected those stories to have removed mention of her role completely, and not leave the very strong statement by Akiva that she suffered so that he could study Torah. It seems more probable that the creators of the talmudic legend were aware of that statement and simply expanded on it, enhancing the story by telling exactly what it was that she had done to warrant such a compliment—that she had insisted that he study; she had been willing to have him stay away for long periods in order to study and attain greatness.[49]

In any case, what remains credible of the beautiful, romantic legend of Akiva and his wife is that they lived in poverty, that she sacrificed to enable him to become a great scholar, and that he showed his love and appreciation of her, giving her public credit and presenting her with a precious diadem.

The sources then have provided us with three answers to the question, what were the beginnings of Rabbi Akiva?

1. The version in the Land of Israel (ARN-A and ARN-B), based on the simple statement in *Sifre Deuteronomy* and *Genesis Rabbah*, that as a married man and a father he came to the decision to study on his own, staying at home and earning a living with difficulty.

2. One story in the Babylonian Talmud (*Ketubot*) tells that the decision to study was a condition his future wife made in agreeing to marry him.

3. Another story in the Babylonian Talmud (*Nedarim*) has it that some time after his marriage, when they were living in poverty, his wife encouraged him to leave and study, which he did.

The version originating in Israel represents the earlier tradition and is the one closest in time and place to Akiva's life. It is also the simpler and more convincing, while the Babylonian versions contain factual errors and miraculous elements and exaggerations. Therefore, the versions of ARN are more likely to reflect reality and are to be preferred.

Both traditions, that of the Land of Israel and that of Babylonia, have the following in common:

· Akiva came to learning as a mature person.
· He was poor and had to struggle.
· The mention of straw beds.
· He was helped by his wife.
· He presented her with a gold ornament.
· He was successful and became a great teacher and leader.

## AKIVA'S WIFE

In none of the talmudic stories is Akiva's wife mentioned by name. She is known simply as *ishto* (his wife) or as the daughter of Kalba

Savua. In the Jerusalem Talmud and other sources from the Land of Israel she is equally anonymous. How is it, then, that she is so commonly referred to as Rachel? That name is mentioned only once. It appears in the printed texts of *ARN*-A. In relating that the poor have no excuse for not learning since Akiva too was poor, it is said that the poor will protest that he could do so "because his wife Rachel provided for them."[50] Even there the name is found in printed texts but not in manuscripts, as Schechter notes in his textual comments to that passage.[51] It is not found at all in *ARN*-B or in any other early Rabbinic texts. If her name was known, why does it not appear in all the sources rather than simply calling her "his wife"? It has also been shown that the name Rachel was not used during the entire period of the Second Temple and the Mishnah.[52]

The generally accepted conclusion is that the name of Akiva's wife was not known or recorded and that only much later did someone add the name Rachel in one place.[53] Perhaps the name was added to personalize the story and make it more touching. Why Rachel? Rachel is the name of the most beloved wife of the patriarch Jacob, and the stories of the fabled love of Akiva and his wife are reminiscent of those of Jacob and Rachel. It should also be noted that Akiva's name is a version of the name Jacob—Ya'akov. It has been suggested that the Aramaic phrase *rakhela batar rakhela azla*, "the ewe follows the ewe"—which is quoted in a statement about the fact that Akiva's daughter followed the example of her mother in allowing her husband to be away for a long period in order to study[54]—may have been understood as a hint that Akiva's wife's name was *Rahel* (ewe), which was then later incorporated into the stories.[55]

Exactly what role Akiva's wife played in his career is unclear, but all the sources place such an emphasis on his gratitude to her that it is impossible to deny her an important place. According to one story in the Jerusalem Talmud, his wife sold her braids to provide them with money while he was studying.[56] The Jerusalem of Gold diadem that he gave her became legendary.[57] It was even the source of jealousy of other Rabbinic wives.[58] It had become so well-known that whenever a "Jerusalem of Gold" was mentioned and needed to be identified, it was sufficient to recall that it was the gift that Akiva had given his wife. Since many of these instances are simply incidental, it is considered an old and reliable tradition.[59] But it is strange that we hear nothing more of his wife after that incident. Tales are told of her daughter and of the death of their sons, but his wife's demise is never mentioned. Even stranger is the fact that there is mention of Akiva taking another wife at the end of his life, the wife of Tineus Rufus, of all people, who is said to have converted![60] It is no wonder that this incident did not become part of the popular story of Akiva's life.

## AKIVA'S STUDENT YEARS

The *beit midrash* of Rabbi Eliezer that Akiva attended at Lod was set up as a circle, resembling an amphitheater. In the center was a stone upon which Rabbi Eliezer would sit. After his death, his colleague Rabbi Joshua kissed the stone and said, "This stone is like Mount Sinai and he who sat upon it was like the Ark of the Covenant."[61]

Studies were often informal. A good picture of the way in which students and teachers interacted can be found in the description of a session held by Rabbi Tarfon. He sat outdoors in the shade on a Sabbath afternoon. His students brought him a pitcher of cold water, and he said to them, "If one is thirsty and drinks water, what blessing does he recite?" "Let our master teach us," they said to him. He then told them the correct blessing, ". . . who creates creatures and their needs." They again asked him to teach them, and Rabbi Tarfon began to weave together biblical verses with the lesson that even when God is angry with the righteous, God has pity on them. How much more so when God is favorable to them! This somehow leads to a discussion of the merits of Judah, which led to his descendants being kings. Many answers are given as to exactly what these merits were, the final one being that when Israel stood at the sea and was threatened by Pharaoh's army, it was the tribe of Judah that plunged into the water. "Judah thus sanctified God's name at the sea." The lesson ends with water, tying it to the water that Rabbi Tarfon's students brought him and his question about the blessing recited over water.[62]

According to an account in the midrash *Song of Songs Rabbah*, Akiva was recognized by his fellow classmates as an extraordinary student. One time when he was late in arriving and was outside, a question was raised asking if a certain teaching was the accepted law. The other students said, "The law is outside." Another question was asked and they said, "Torah is outside." Yet another question was asked and they said, "Akiva is outside." They made room for him, and he came and sat at the feet of Rabbi Eliezer.[63]

Akiva's work as a student was described as being similar to a stonecutter who chipped away at tiny pebbles from a stone mountain. He was asked, "What are you doing?" and he replied, "I am uprooting the mountain and casting it into the Jordan." Others told him that it was impossible, but he continued until he was able to break away a big rock, loosen it, uproot it, and cast it into the river saying, "This was where you belong." "Thus did Rabbi Akiva with the teachings he derived from Rabbi Eliezer and Rabbi Joshua." His fellow student, Tarfon, later his colleague,[64] then said to him, "Things concealed from men you have brought to light."[65]

The relationship between Tarfon and Akiva was one of both rivalry and admiration. They often disagreed, usually with Akiva winning the argument. It must be remembered that these Rabbinic works were transmitted and edited by the disciples of Akiva, and we do not know how close they are to an actual record of the discussion and how much is a literary construct. There are, for example, two differing versions of a discussion concerning whether or not only priests who had no physical disfigurements were permitted to blow the trumpets that are described in chapter 10 in the book of Numbers. Akiva took the position that just as only perfect priests could offer sacrifices, so only perfect priests could blow the trumpets over the sacrifices. Tarfon angrily protested that he had been at the Temple and had seen a priest—his mother's brother—blowing the trumpet and he was a cripple! Akiva calmly replied that perhaps this was at an occasion not connected to sacrifices, and indeed Tarfon agreed that was the case. "Tarfon saw it and forgot, and Akiva explained it from his own understanding and gave the correct law. Happy are you, Abraham our father, from whose loins Akiva has sprung! One who separates himself from you separates from life itself!"[66] In both versions the conclusion is the same, but the format and the circumstances are different, probably because the editing was done by a different person.

"Thirteen years Rabbi Akiva studied. He went before Rabbi Eliezer and he did not know him." In his first discussion with Rabbi Eliezer, at the conclusion of thirteen years, described in the Jerusalem Talmud, Akiva disagreed with him and was able to prove that his (Akiva's) understanding of the law was correct. The discussion concerned a matter that was purely academic, since the Temple had been destroyed and sacrifices were no longer offered. The debate was over what could or could not be done to prepare for the slaughter of the Passover offering when Passover was on the Sabbath. Rabbi Eliezer took the position that in addition to the slaughtering itself, other more trivial matters were permitted as well. Rabbi Joshua took the opposite position but was unable to refute the arguments of Eliezer. What had been a controversy between two senior ordained Sages now changed its nature when Akiva spoke up and invoked the general rule that one was not permitted to do things on Shabbat that could be done before Shabbat and he was able to argue and prove his point using logical thinking.[67]

This discussion, the first of many between Akiva and Eliezer, took place at the *beit midrash* in Lod and marked the moment when Akiva the novice became recognized as a true Sage, if not yet ordained as such. Even Rabbi Eliezer, who had not acknowledged him previously, had no choice but to recognize him now, although he did so reluctantly, at one point even saying, "Akiva! You would override a verse from the Torah!"[68] In this discussion, Akiva did not use any new methodology; he used the inferences from minor to major that Eliezer himself had brought, but created examples that refuted his teacher's decision. It was a bold step on Akiva's part, since it was not considered usual or appropriate for a mere student to enter into a dispute with his teacher. Nevertheless, as other citations show, Akiva greatly valued Eliezer, considered him his teacher, and when Eliezer died, declared that "I have coins, but no money changer to sort them out!" meaning now there was no one who could answer Akiva's questions.[69]

Akiva's true master, however, was Rabbi Joshua. It was he who granted Akiva rabbinic ordination.[70] Ordination, the passing of authority from one master to his disciple, granted the new Sage the right to sit on court panels and to ordain others. The title that went with ordination, rabbi (master), had emerged some time in the first century CE. In the era of Hillel and Shammai, just before and after the first century CE, the title was not known. In the generation prior to the destruction in 70 CE it was already in use. At the time of Akiba's ordination it was granted individually by one Sage to his student. Thus "Rabban Yohanan ben Zakkai appointed [ordained] Rabbi Eliezer and Rabbi Joshua, and Rabbi Joshua [appointed] Rabbi Akiva, and Rabbi Akiva [appointed] Rabbi Meir and Rabbi Shimon."[71]

Students served their masters in the literal sense: helping them with all their physical needs and even preparing Shabbat meals for them. Akiva stated that he had done so for both Eliezer and Joshua. He was, however, much more intimate with Joshua, even following him into private places to see how he conducted himself so that he would know how to act. That too was considered Torah.[72] Joshua also instructed him in mystical matters, since he was known to have indulged in mystical speculation concerning the heavenly chariot and Akiva is said to have expounded on that before Joshua as well.[73]

In the Jerusalem Talmud Akiva relates a story of "how I began attending the scholars."[74] Seeing an unattended corpse on the way, he carried it four miles to a cemetery and buried it. He then related this to Rabbi Joshua and Rabbi Eliezer, who informed him that in doing so it was as if he was shedding blood, since he should have buried it immediately. Realizing that his ignorance condemned him even though he had good intentions, he vowed, "From that time I have never stopped attending to scholars." Some have understood this as another story of how he first came to study,[75] but the incident would seem to have happened when he was already studying with these Sages, not before he began to learn at all. It may reflect the time when he decided that he must attend them constantly, giving up any other occupation, and not assume that he was capable yet of making decisions on his own. Perhaps it was at that point that he absented himself more from his home in order to study rigorously with a variety of teachers.

Akiva's method of Torah commentary, which will be discussed in chapter 3, was influenced by that of the Sage Nahum of Gimzo. Nahum of Gimzo, with whom Akiva studied for some time, taught that there was nothing extraneous in the Torah. He even interpreted the word *et*, which has no translation and is simply a grammatical device to indicate a direct object, and learned laws and interpretations from it.[76] Nahum's most famous statement, from which his name is derived, was, "This too is for the best" (*gam zo l'tovah*), whatever happens is for the best,[77] a saying that Akiva adopted for himself as well.[78] Akiva later became a master of deriving from or connecting oral laws to words, letters, and even decorations in the Torah. As one legend has it, when explaining to Moses why there are decorations (crowns), on certain letters in the Torah, God said, "After many generations there will arise a man, Akiva ben Yosef by name, who will expound upon each decoration heaps and heaps of laws."[79]

Akiva also spent considerable time at Yavneh as a student. Rabban Gamliel II had become head of the Yavneh academy some time after Yohanan ben Zakkai, who, for reasons that are not clear, left there and moved to Bror Hayil. When Gamliel took over he became not only the head of the academy but also the highest political authority of the Jewish population, recognized as such by the Romans. At that time both Rabbi Eliezer and Rabbi Joshua returned to Yavneh as members of the Sanhedrin that Rabban Gamliel established, even though they continued to conduct their own academies elsewhere as well. Their pupil Akiva, who soon became their colleague, also went to study there under Rabban Gamliel, the greatest authority of the age.

In the *Sifre*, Rabbi Yohanan ben Nuri, who served as a proctor under Rabban Gamliel, testified that when he was a student "Rabbi Akiva was rebuked through me more than five times before Rabban Gamliel in Yavneh, when I would complain about him and Rabban Gamliel would rebuke him, yet I am certain that he [Akiva] loved me more each time."[80] It would be fascinating to know what Akiva did to warrant rebuke, but unfortunately there is no record.

When Akiva was ordained by Rabbi Joshua, after however many years it may have been, he quickly became a recognized authority and attracted many disciples. He also established his own school at B'nai Brak, not very far from Lod.[81] Perhaps that was when he came back to his home, trailed by his disciples, in order to pay tribute to his wife, acknowledge her role in his accomplishments, and present her with a visible symbol of her status, a Jerusalem of Gold tiara.[82] From then on Akiva became *Rabbi* Akiva, a leading scholar who played a key role not only in formulating Rabbinic law and lore, but in the running of the community as well.

# *Three*

## THE NEW SAGE AND
## PUBLIC FIGURE

Once Akiva completed his studies and received his ordination
from Rabbi Joshua, he embarked upon his career not only as a
rabbi and a participant in academic discourse, but also as a public
figure. The academy at Yavneh had now assumed the role of the
new Sanhedrin, the quasi-official authority of Jewish life, in more
than name. It was headed by the *nasi* (the leader or "prince" of the
nation), Rabban Gamliel II, and Gamliel chose Akiva to serve in
important capacities.

Rabban Yohanan ben Zakkai, Gamliel's predecessor, had been
concerned only with internal Jewish matters, attempting to reestab-
lish Jewish life and a center of learning after the destruction of the
Second Temple in Jerusalem in 70 CE. Gamliel II, a descendant of
the house of Hillel,[1] had a wider political vision: he saw himself and
the Yavneh synod as a semi-autonomous Jewish government.[2] He
went to the Roman authorities in Syria to petition them to appoint
him as its leader.[3] The Roman government acknowledged his status,
at least tacitly, and Gamliel was treated by Jews in the Diaspora
as the official representative of Jewry and the Jewish tradition. He
conducted himself as the head of a semi-autonomous ruling body
and as such appointed ordained rabbis to be his representatives, to
organize the community, to care for its needs, and to travel both

within the Land of Israel and in the Diaspora on official missions. Akiva was one of those appointed. Sometimes these missions were intended to raise funds to support the institutions of Jewry in the land,[4] other times they might have been political missions concerned with relations with the Roman Empire.[5]

Akiva was no longer a mere student. Although the sources do not give us enough information to be able to construct a complete story of his life at that time, we catch glimpses of him at various tasks and in different situations. Akiva had three public roles assigned to him by Rabban Gamliel: judge, member of a delegation to Rome, and manager of programs to help the needy. [6]

He would hardly have achieved such status were it not for the fact that his name and reputation had already spread among the Sages, even among those elders who had not known him personally as a student. Akiva, for example, was a member of a delegation of Sages who came to question the ancient and eminent Rabbi Dosa concerning a controversial ruling he was purported to have made. According to the Jerusalem Talmud, Rabbi Dosa greeted Akiva and called him "a mighty man of the Torah"[7] Another version of the meeting found in the later Babylonian Talmud is typically more expansive and laudatory. It enlarges upon the earlier account and quotes Dosa as saying, "You are Akiva ben Yosef—your name goes before you from one end of the world to another. Sit, my son, sit, and may your like multiply in Israel."[8] Even the modest and more likely phrase "a mighty man of Torah" would indicate that Akiva had achieved a reputation as an important scholar. This would explain why Akiva was appointed by Rabban Gamliel to the position of a judge in the Rabbinic court.[9] He served in that capacity throughout his life.

The most famous story concerning Akiva's role as a judge appears in *Avot de-Rabbi Natan* (*ARN*). It concerns the time when a man uncovered a woman's head in the marketplace, thus shaming her in public. She brought the case before Akiva, who decreed that the man should pay her 400 *zuz*. The culprit asked for an opportunity to prove his case and proceeded to place a broken jug of oil at her doorstep. She came out, found the oil, and in public uncovered her head and put the oil on her hair. On this basis he asked Akiva to reverse the ruling, but Akiva refused to do so because although one is permitted to abase or abuse oneself in public, "you who abused her are not—go pay her the 400 *zuz*."[10] Stories such as this portray Akiva as one who champions the cause of those who might otherwise be abused by people of greater status.

### TRAVELS TO ROME

In addition to appointing Akiva a judge, Rabban Gamliel also included him in the small and exclusive group of Sages who traveled with him on his visits to Rome. Akiva was by far the youngest and most recently ordained of the group; in all the sources his name always appears last in the list of participants. Accounts of these trips appear in such early sources as the tannaitic midrashim *Sifre Deuteronomy* and *Sifra* and in the somewhat later Jerusalem Talmud. As usual, one cannot rely on all the details of these stories, since they have undergone literary embellishment, but one can assume that they are based on actual journeys that Akiva made as part of Gamliel's entourage and contain some reliable information.

These trips were a continuation of an earlier one that Gamliel had undertaken to Rome together with Rabbi Eliezer ben Hyrkanus and Rabbi Joshua, a trip in which they made some initial contact with the Jewish community there.[11] Contacts with Rome itself surely could come through the indigenous Jewish community. This earlier trip had taken place before Akiva's ordination, probably toward the beginning of Gamliel's assumption of power.[12]

Rabbi Eliezer did not take part in the later trips to Rome, perhaps because of his advanced age or illness and the arduous nature of these sea voyages, but his pupil Akiva became a part of the delegation. The participants in these journeys were Rabban Gamliel himself; Rabbi Joshua, Akiva's teacher; Rabbi Eleazar ben Azariah, the aristocratic priest who was a descendant of Ezra; and

Rabbi Akiva, listed last, as was only appropriate for a younger and newer colleague.

Such sea voyages were obviously difficult and dangerous and would not have been undertaken by the leadership of the community, including its titular head, had there not been some pressing reason. Unfortunately those who composed and compiled Rabbinic literature had little interest in history or in recording "insignificant" events, which to us seem of great interest and importance. Therefore the purpose of these journeys can only be the subject of speculation. Were they intended to influence the Roman authorities, to mitigate certain decrees or ease burdens of taxation?

Some scholars and historians have posited that these journeys were undertaken to plead with the Roman government not to pass harsh decrees against the Jews. Others contend that they were made to spread the authority of Gamliel II and the new Sanhedrin over the Jewish community in the Diaspora or to cement relations between them. All that seems logical, but the sources remain silent on these issues. Since there are no texts that state those matters specifically, none of that can be proved.[13] The sources are more interested in recording the observances and practices of the Sages in regard to the commandments of the Torah and in their interaction with pagans than in informing us of political affairs. Unfortunately we have no Jewish chronicler of the times like Josephus to record the events of these crucial years. That these journeys reflect on Akiva's prominence and importance, however, is unquestionable.

It is logical to assume that while in Rome Akiva and the others gave sermons and lessons to the Jewish community. One such legendary tale is related in *Exodus Rabbah*, a late midrash from the Land of Israel, no earlier than the ninth or tenth century, although often based on earlier sources. The usual four—Gamliel, Joshua, Eleazar, and Akiva—preached before a crowd in Rome on the theme that God is unlike humans. Whatever God requires others to do, God does as well, whereas human rulers make laws and then do not obey them. A sectarian—a *min*[14]—proclaimed that their words were false since God does not observe the Sabbath but rather does all manner of work such as causing wind and rain. They defended their position saying that the world is the Lord's and therefore God can move things within God's own property.[15]

The Babylonian Talmud relates that once when they were in Rome these Sages were challenged by idolaters who wanted to know why the Jewish God—if such a one really existed—did not rid the world of all the idols. Their answer was that to do that would mean destroying the world, since the sun, the moon, and many other essential things were objects of idol worship. "Should God destroy His world because of fools?"[16] The same source records that a similar question was once asked of Akiva by an Israelite who wanted to know why it was that at times a cripple emerges cured from an idolatrous shrine. Akiva answered with a parable that made the point that afflictions have a set time when they are to be cured, and that time will be honored even if it happens to coincide with idolatrous worship.[17]

It is certainly possible that such encounters took place between Jews and idol worshipers and that Jews themselves had questions concerning idolatrous practices. In yet another story related in an eighth-century source Akiva met with a Roman official who wanted to hear wisdom from a Jewish master.[18] It is indeed likely that in their trips to Rome they took the opportunity to preach and teach, and they may well have met with non-Jews who were curious about their doctrines and with some who were antagonistic to it. Polemics between Jews and non-Jews were part and parcel of those times. Much less likely is the story told in ARN that during one of Akiva's trips to Rome he was slandered and was put in a room with two beautiful women, who attempted unsuccessfully to seduce him.[19] The story is part of a long discussion of sexual temptation that begins with a midrash concerning Joseph and Potiphar's wife in which she threatens to place him in prison if he doesn't surrender to her wiles, but he nevertheless resists. Similar stories about various Sages are then related, beginning with Rabbi Zadok, continuing with Rabbi

Akiva—also in prison—and concluding with Rabbi Eliezer ben Hyrkanus. Such tales, intended to demonstrate the righteousness of these men and their ability to resist temptation, are examples of the moralistic stories frequently told about the Sages, and they are highly suspect.[20]

The early tannaitic source *Sifre Deuteronomy* relates a beautifully crafted literary account of the four Sages' first trip to Rome. Arriving in Italy, they journeyed by foot toward the great metropolis of Rome, the place where they would be undertaking their task, the exact nature of which is not revealed. Three of them burst into tears when, while still at a great distance, they could clearly hear the sounds and tumult emanating from that great city. Akiva, however, began to laugh. Astonished, the others asked why he should laugh when they were weeping over the fact that while wicked Rome flourished, the Jerusalem Temple was desolate and lay in ruins. Akiva explained that that was exactly why he was laughing, for "if this is what God has given to those who anger Him, how much more will He give to those who fulfill His will!" They were pleased with this thought. "Akiva, you have comforted us."[21]

The motifs that appear in this early story are often repeated in tales of Akiva's life. He frequently took a position opposite that of his companions, a strange position that astounded them. When he explained his actions, they accepted his reasoning and that brought them comfort. At an early time, then, Akiva was already perceived as having had an independent streak, finding hope and comfort in his beliefs and bringing comfort to others. Presumably these were traits that he demonstrated in his actions and in his teachings, and they became templates for the stories told about him in the century following his death.

Several anecdotal stories are related concerning religious observances while on the seas in journeys to or from Rome. The purpose of all these tales is to relate information about proper observance of rituals under such circumstances. There is no reason to doubt that they represent authentic traditions concerning the practices of the various Sages. For example, the early tannaitic midrash *Sifra* relates the story of a journey undertaken by the four Sages on the festival of Sukkot. Only Rabban Gamliel had a *lulav*, the wand made of three types of plants that is carried and used on that holiday. Since the law required that each person have his own *lulav* on the first day of the holiday, Gamliel gave his as a gift to Joshua, who then gave it as a gift to Eleazar ben Azariah, who in turn gave it as a gift to Akiva.[22] The Jerusalem Talmud relates that Akiva built a sukkah at the front of the boat in order to fulfill all the commandments of the holiday. Unfortunately the wind blew it away, upon which Eleazar ben Azariah said (sarcastically), "Akiva, where is your sukkah?"[23]

Another story is told in the later Babylonian Talmud concerning this same group, listed in the same order, on a voyage returning from Brindisi, Italy, to the Holy Land, the purpose of which is never stated. What is related here is that Akiva and Joshua were stricter in their observance of Sabbath regulations on the high seas than were Rabban Gamliel and Eleazar ben Azariah. Akiva and Joshua refused to move more than four cubits, imposing a stricture upon themselves that was beyond the requirements of the law.[24] Akiva may have come from an unlearned and unobservant background, but his ritual observances now and until the end of his life were exacting and punctilious.

### CARING FOR THE NEEDY

Akiva traveled extensively throughout the entire area, as far as Babylonia on fund-raising missions, to support Gamliel's poverty programs. He became a well-known figure in the Jewish world including the Diaspora. We know he traveled widely because he is quoted as explaining what words were used for various objects in places he had visited in Arabia, Gallia, and Africa.[25] On these journeys he was also a teacher, a decider of Jewish Law, and a teller of legends and of midrashic interpretations.[26]

The Jerusalem Talmud relates that Akiva traveled to Antiochus, north of Damascus, together with his revered teachers Rabbi Eliezer and Rabbi Joshua, but without Rabban Gamliel, on behalf of a "fund for the Wise," in other words, raising money for the support of the Sages. In one instance they approached one generous contributor, Abba Yehudah, who was no longer as wealthy as he had been but was embarrassed to send them away empty-handed. He sold a field that remained to him and gave them the proceeds.[27]

Akiva was often described as busying himself "with the needs of the community," even when it might make it difficult for him to observe proper times of prayer. In the Tosefta, a very early and reliable tannaitic source, Rabbi Yehudah related that he was once traveling with Akiva and Eleazar ben Azariah, and when it was time to recite the morning *Shma*, he thought they were not going to say it because they were "busy with the needs of the community" and the correct time for the recitation was passing. They did recite it, however, even though it was somewhat later than the designated time.[28] Anecdotes of this sort were preserved as witnesses to proper observances of mitzvot and as such have a high measure of reliability. The picture they paint of Akiva is of one who was indeed "busy with the needs of the community" on many levels, in addition to his role as a judge and as the head of an academy of learning that produced many outstanding Rabbinic leaders.

As dedicated as he was to study of Torah, Akiva was far from being an ivory-tower scholar. Rather he combined the worlds of an activist and an intellectual. In his forty or so years as a scholar, starting in the last decade of the first century CE, he accomplished an unbelievable amount in many fields.

Akiva, who was charged by Gamliel with care for the needs of the poor, showed great concern for them. If the stories of the poverty of his youth are true, this would explain his feelings and his desire to help the needy. He is quoted as saying that even the poor in Israel were to be considered "free men who had lost their wealth, for they are the children of Abraham, Isaac, and Jacob."[29] This attitude is reflected in his legal decisions as well.

The Torah, which has many commandments that benefit the

poor and needy, ruled that farmers have to leave certain portions of their crops for the poor. Akiva's interpretations of these laws as recorded in the Mishnah, the earliest and most reliable tannaitic source (edited c. 200 CE), favored the poor rather than the landowner. In the case of a field sown with different crops, only Akiva ruled that there must be a *peah*, "the corners of the field" that the Torah allocates to the poor, for each crop's patch, not just in the corners of the field as a whole, as others had stated.[30] How large must a field be before one is required to leave the corners for the poor? Several important Sages, including Akiva's mentors Eliezer and Joshua, gave their various opinions. The smallest was "large enough for a sickle to cut two handfuls." That sounds small enough, but Akiva, the youngest of all those commenting, insisted that "even the tiniest field" is liable to *peah* and all other required matters.[31] *Olelet*, a defective grape cluster, also belongs to the poor. When the question was raised concerning a vineyard where all of the clusters are defective, Akiva's teacher, Rabbi Eliezer, ruled that in such a case they all belong to the owner. Akiva argued with him, taking the opposite position. In the discussion they each interpreted verses of the Torah to defend their position, with Akiva having the last word, which proved that all of them belonged to the poor.[32]

The Jerusalem Talmud adds that Akiva and only Akiva (according to Rabbi Yose) ruled that another law regulating what was to be left for the poor, the law of "forgotten things," applied to olive trees as well.[33] This would accord well with Akiva's other rulings on similar matters. On the other hand, regarding the tithe that must be given to the poor in the third and sixth year of each seven-year cycle,[34] Akiva required only half the amounts that the Mishnah specifies as a minimum. Rabbi Judah the Prince, the compiler of the Mishnah, agreed with Akiva.[35] Nevertheless the evidence indicates that in the majority of instances Akiva went out of his way to rule in ways that would be most helpful to the needy.

As one who was charged with providing for the poor, Akiva also would have had to deal with those who tried to take advantage of poverty programs, benefiting without being truly in need. This is reflected in his admonition recorded in ARN that it is forbidden to take even a small amount from charity if you do not need it and that if one pretends to be blind or otherwise afflicted in order to solicit funds, in the end "he will be speaking the truth."[36] Akiva here invoked the concept of *middah k'neged middah* (the punishment fits the crime). One who pretends to have an affliction in order to gain charitable funds will be punished by having that affliction actually occur.

### AKIVA'S ACADEMY

Sometime after his ordination, Akiva founded his own school at B'nai Brak,[37] but as was the case with other Sages and their schools, he was not tied to the institution and was often to be found elsewhere, involved with "the needs of the community."

Sages started academies of learning throughout the Land of Israel, from Yavneh and Lod in the center to communities in the northern Galilee. Ishmael taught in Kfar Aziz, Joshua ben Hananiah in Pekin, Joseph ben Halafta in Sepphoris, and Hananiah ben Teradion in Sikhnin.[38] Based on descriptions of unbelievably huge numbers of students enrolled in numerous academies, one can easily get the impression that Torah learning and the rulings of the Sages dominated the Jewish land. Archaeological evidence shows otherwise: the large numbers of disciples ascribed to Akiva and others can be nothing but a gross exaggeration, and many synagogues did not adhere to Rabbinic rules in such matters as artistic representation.

The true picture is that the masses of Jews more likely followed the Judaism of the Sages to greater or lesser degrees, each according to his or her inclination. It is true that following the Great Revolt there were no other major Jewish sects to compete with the new order that emanated from the Sanhedrin in Yavneh under the *nasi*, unless one considers the Christians to still be a Jewish sect, which may indeed have been the case. But that does not mean that the Sages dominated and had control of all Jewish life.[39] Nor should we believe that all male Jews attended these academies. The "students of the wise" were still the minority, the learned elite. Nevertheless in this post-Temple period, the latter part of the first century CE and the following few centuries, there seems to have been a significant movement in Judea of dedicated students, going from one master to another, some spending their lives devoted to the learning and the spread of Torah according to Rabbinic interpretation, others listening to lessons evenings or on days of no work whenever they could. Just as synagogues gained in importance following the destruction of the Temple, so too Torah study and academies of learning increased to fill that void. It is reminiscent of the Middle Ages in Christian Europe when monasteries dotted the countryside and large numbers of monks and priests dedicated their lives to the practice and teaching of Christianity.

It was in this milieu that Akiva flourished, playing a major role in Jewish affairs both domestic and foreign, teaching and preaching and contributing in a major way to the growth of Rabbinic Judaism and to the formulation of its basic works of Jewish Law and lore.

The number of Akiva's pupils was impressive, even if not nearly as large as sources state, which is anywhere from twelve thousand to forty-eight thousand.[40] The number of Akiva's students took on strange legendary proportions and served the purpose of emphasizing the importance of the master. One early midrash, for example, tells that Akiva raised up two sets of disciples. The first consisted of twelve thousand pairs, but they all died because they were too competitive with one another. He then taught a second group of only seven—Meir, Yehudah, Shimon, Eliezer ben Shamu, Yohanan HaSandlar, and Eliezer ben Yaakov.[41]

Also mentioned as students of Akiva are Eleazar ben Matya, Hananiah ben Hakhinai, Shimon ben Azzai, and Shimon the Yemenite.[42] The most famous were Shimon bar Yohai and Meir, who had also studied with Ishmael at one point but had then returned to Akiva and remained his disciple.[43] Early midrashim tell that Hananiah did not keep in touch with his family. Finally his wife sent him a message that it was time to come home and attend to finding a husband for his daughter, but he did not leave until Akiva, becoming aware of this, gave a general order that anyone with a daughter of eligible age should leave and attend to her needs.[44]

Akiva had a reputation for never wanting to cease learning or teaching. Accordingly his school was always in session except for the eve of Passover and of Yom Kippur.[45] If the tale found in the Haggadah is correct, Akiva himself remained in B'nai Brak on Passover as well. He conducted a famous seder there, together with Rabbi Joshua and Rabbi Eleazar that lasted all night and only concluded when the students reminded them that it was already time for the morning recitation of the *Sh'ma*.[46]

In his discussions with his students Akiva covered not only matters of law but also biblical interpretation and questions of morality and ethical behavior. One example was a discussion on the question "Why did Judah merit having the kingship come from his descendants?" Akiva gave several answers, one of which was, "Because he admitted his guilt in the matter of Tamar."[47] Akiva was not unique in this, since the sources record that other Sages had similar discussions with their pupils, even, as was discussed in chapter 2, on that same question. They often used the Socratic method of teaching, which emphasizes teacher-student dialogue: the Sage would ask a question, and then a discussion would begin on the answer given by the pupils or by the Sage.

Akiva maintained a close relationship with many of his students. There is an anecdote in the Babylonian Talmud that tells of Akiva visiting a student who was ill, when no one else had gone to see him. Akiva saw to it that his needs were tended to. When the student recovered and ascribed his recovery to Akiva's visit, Akiva taught, "One who does not visit the sick is like a shedder of blood!"[48] This may be simply an instance of ascribing a teaching to a venerated teacher, but it is indicative of Akiva's personality. But at times he could also be brusque with a student. An early tannaitic midrash, *Sifra*, relates that one of his disciples once made a rather foolish deduction by misunderstanding two verses. Akiva's remark to him was, "You have dived into deep water and brought up a shard in your hand," after which he showed him his error.[49] Such a tale has the ring of truth.

## AKIVA'S PERSONAL LIFE

Akiva's teaching and many other obligations left him little time at home, and we know little about his role as a husband. It is unfortunate that not much is written about Akiva's relationship with his wife after he became a major figure among the Sages, and only slightly more about his family. There is some information about a daughter, who remains nameless, and three sons, Joshua, a rabbi,[50] Shimon, and, Yose, who was also a rabbi.[51] Akiva's daughter is mentioned as supporting her husband in his studies, just as her mother had done[52] and as did the wife of his son Joshua.[53]

Joshua, probably named after his mother's father, had an intense discussion with his father concerning a Rabbinic teaching and even argued with him about the answers he had given.[54] When, while still a poor student, Joshua married, it was with the condition that his wife would support him so that he could learn Torah.[55] If the stories about Akiva's youth are to be believed, his son was simply following in his father's footsteps. Another story about Akiva's son, less realistic, found in a late source, recounts that the night he married he stayed up the entire night "reading in the Torah and studying *haggadot*." He asked his new wife to fetch a lamp, and she did so. And then he asked her to remain standing and hold the lamp all night, and she did so. When Akiva asked his son the next morning if she was a worthy wife, he replied that she was.[56]

There is also an early tannaitic tradition that at some point, perhaps when Joshua was leaving home to study elsewhere, Akiva charged his son with seven things.[57] The list, it must be admitted, is not profound: Don't study in a place where you will be interrupted. Don't live in a town that is poorly governed because its leaders are scholars. Don't enter your home or anyone's home suddenly. Arise early and have a good meal. Do not go barefoot. Be on good terms with a person whom fortune favors. Make your Sabbath like a weekday rather than depend on others. This last is the most well-known and probably the reason the list was preserved at all. Although the proper observance of the Sabbath requires one to have three good meals, rather than the two that was customary on other days, Akiva sanctioned not fulfilling that if it would mean soliciting charity from others to do so. Only one who has known want himself would think of this. The list is reminiscent of Shakespeare's famous speech that Polonius makes to his son Laertes in *Hamlet*, the words of a doting father to his son before he goes away from home.

Tragically, Akiva's son Shimon died at a young age.[58] Akiva, quite famous by then, was teaching at his academy at the time and was so determined never to take time away from Torah that he did not cancel his classes when he heard that the boy was gravely ill. Only when he received news of his death did he stop teaching and tell the students that now the mitzvah of care for the dead took precedence over the mitzvah of study of Torah. Overwhelmed by the vast numbers who came to the funeral, when it was over he sat on a bench and addressed them:

> Brethren of the house of Israel, hear me. Not because I am a scholar have you come, for there are other scholars here greater than I, and not because I am wealthy, for there are others wealthier than I. Men of the south know Rabbi Akiva, but how should Galileans know him? Men know Rabbi Akiva, but how should women and children know him? Yet I know that your reward will be great for you have troubled yourselves and come here in honor of the Torah and in order to perform a mitzvah. . . . Go home in peace.[59]

According to one report in the Jerusalem Talmud, Akiva's family was not poor. They were said to have furniture of gold and other luxuries.[60] If that is to be believed, his own lifestyle would have been a contradiction to his well-known teaching that "poverty becomes Israel as a red strap on the head of a white horse."[61] Tradition ascribes his wealth as deriving from his father-in-law, which is unlikely, and also from other similarly doubtful sources. The Babylonian Talmud, hard-pressed to understand the claim that Akiva was wealthy, listed several explanations, including money received from Kalba Savua, a gift from a wealthy admirer, or his finding logs full of gold coins washed up from a shipwreck.[62] Very likely this whole matter is nothing more than an exaggeration intended to show the reward that a pious person like Akiva can expect for all his hardships and loyalty to Torah. The story of the gold tiara, the Jerusalem of Gold, that he gave to his wife, which is probably true, may have been the inspiration for this further elaboration of an abundance of gold in his family.

The story mentioned above that his son Joshua, a scholar in his own right, married on condition that his wife support him so that he could learn seems to contradict the account of Akiva's wealth.[63] If Akiva was so wealthy, would he not have supported his son in his study of Torah? It has also been suggested that the story of Akiva's early poverty was merely an imitation of the story of his son's.[64] Just as early stories of his great poverty were an exaggeration, so too were tales of his great wealth.

Exactly how he made a living is unclear. Sages were not supposed to take a salary for teaching, and many are said to have had a craft or profession as well, dividing their time between work and teaching. This does not seem to be the case with Akiva; on the contrary, we read that as a Sage he never spent time in worldly occupations.[65] That needy Sages were supported by the *nasi* and by contributions from wealthy individuals and communities seems certain, and perhaps that was the case with Akiva. He had official duties to perform for the *nasi*, for which he must have been paid. Once he had attained the status of rabbi and revered Sage, poverty was not a problem for him and his wife, but that does not mean that they were suddenly to be counted among the wealthy. We may never know for certain to what extent his wealth has been exaggerated by the sources,[66] but it does seem extremely unlikely that his house was furnished in gold and that his wife was adorned in the fashion of the wealthy Roman matrons of the time.

### DEBATE AND DISPUTE IN ESTABLISHING JEWISH LAW

This period was a crucial time for setting Jewish Law, which was still in a state of flux. The Sages saw themselves as the only proper body for making such determinations. The laws as set down in the Torah were often unclear, lacking detailed directions, and they sometimes contradicted one another. Decisions had to be made, verses had to be interpreted, and ways of fulfilling the laws had to be decided. This was true even of laws that were no longer in effect because of the absence of the Temple. No detail was too small to be discussed, no law, be it ritual or civil law, could be ignored.

In addition to his other public roles, Akiva played a major role in this development of Jewish Law that was taking place in the discussions among the Sages at the academy in Yavneh. Once he received his ordination, Akiva did not hesitate to make decisions concerning legal matters and to argue with his teachers and his elders concerning the proper interpretation of biblical statutes and other traditions. When he was a student, Akiva had boldly debated with his teacher Rabbi Eliezer ben Hyrkanus, and he continued to disagree with him once he himself became a rabbi. *Sifre Deuteronomy* records a series of matters in which Akiva disagreed with Eliezer. In one of them Akiva permitted eating the paschal lamb for a longer period of time than did Eliezer.[67] Another dispute concerned the body of someone who had been slain and is found between two cities (Deut. 21:1). The Torah requires that it be determined which city was closer to the murdered person so that the elders of that city could perform a ritual of atonement for the bloodguilt incurred by the slaying, declaring that they had not shed the blood nor did they see it happen. The question in *Sifre* was, what if the head was found in a different place from the body? From which part do they measure? Eliezer and Akiva disagreed as to which part was the more important. Eliezer ruled that the head should be placed next to the body and the distances measured from there. Akiva said to move the body to where the head was found.[68]

*Sifre Deuteronomy* also records that they disagreed regarding laws pertaining to a captive woman whom a soldier wishes to marry. The verse says literally "and do her nails" (Deut. 21:12). Akiva and Eliezer disagreed on the meaning of that phrase. Eliezer said, "Cut them," reasoning that since regarding her hair it says to cut it off, here too that would be the case. Akiva said, "Grow them," because the idea is to disfigure them as her hair was disfigured. It would seem that Akiva was bent on making her so unattractive that the man would decide to reject her. Perhaps this was his way of stressing that lust should not be mistaken for love. They disagreed on other matters as well, such as the meaning of the captive woman mourning for "her mother and father." Eliezer maintained that it means exactly what it says, while Akiva insisted that it means mourning for "her idols," which she worships as her creators.[69] In this instance Akiva strayed far from the simple meaning of a text, something that often occurred in his biblical interpretations.

It is interesting to note that one of Akiva's most famous disciples, Shimon bar Yohai, differed with him on some biblical interpretations. "Rabbi Akiva had one explanation for the verse 'Could enough flocks and herds be slaughtered to suffice them? Or could all the fish of the sea be gathered for them to suffice them?' (Num. 11:22), and I have two different ones. I prefer my interpretation to that of my teacher." Akiva interpreted this as meaning, "Could anyone possibly gather that much meat and fish that would suffice for them?" while Bar Yohai took it to mean that they actually had sufficient flocks and fish with them but that would make no difference because this was just an excuse to stop following after God.[70] Bar Yohai indeed followed his teacher's example in freely contradicting him.

Akiva was often very bold in his arguments, even with Rabban Gamliel himself, regardless of Gamliel's position as *nasi* and the fact that Akiva owed his status and positions to him. An incident is related in the Tosefta concerning a time when Rabban Gamliel and other Sages, including Akiva, had dined together in Jericho. Which blessing should be said after their food was a matter of controversy in which Gamliel took one position and the other Sages took a different one. Gamliel's opinion was rejected by the majority. After the meal Akiva, without being asked, "jumped" in and pronounced a blessing other than the one that Gamliel had sanctioned. Gamliel said to him, "Akiva, why do you involve yourself in this controversy?" But Akiva replied, "Have you yourself not taught us that the law follows the majority?"[71] In a similar way Akiva confronted Gamliel when they were together in Rome concerning what was permitted or not on a festival day.[72] Gamliel forbade the reassembling of parts of a lamp that came apart on the eve of a festival, while the majority permitted it. These lamps were made of parts that could be assembled together and could also be taken apart. Gamliel held that putting it together constituted an act of building, which was forbidden on the festival. The majority disagreed with this designation. When this happened, Akiva, in the presence of Rabban Gamliel, put it together. When rebuked by Gamliel, Akiva again replied, "Have you yourself not taught us that the law follows the majority?"[73]

At another time Akiva acted on his own in regard to a question of taking tithes from food found in a town inhabited by Samaritans. Gamliel had ruled that their produce was to be considered as possibly having been tithed, whereas Akiva acted as if Samaritans were not recognized as Jews at all.[74] Gamliel accused him of acting against the rulings of his peers and asked, "Who gave you permission?" Akiva replied, "I did not decide the law—I only took the tithe from my own vegetables."[75] Akiva contended that he was not making a ruling on the issue itself, but only deciding that since there was no definite knowledge that tithes had been taken from the produce he had acquired, he preferred to take a tithe and be certain.

Of course Gamliel could give as well as he got. The Tosefta relates that when he heard Akiva teach that the words "Tear down their altars. . . . Do not do so to the LORD your God" (Deut. 12:3–4) means that "if one chips out one stone from the Hall of the Temple, from its altar, or from its courtyards, one violates a negative commandment," he responded tartly, "Could you possibly imagine that Israelites would tear down their own altars? Heaven forbid! Rather the verse means: do not do as the heathen do, for your evil deeds would then cause the Temple of your fathers to be destroyed."[76]

While it seems from all of these accounts that Akiva and Gamliel had a tense relationship, Akiva was no rebel against authority. According to a tannaitic teaching quoted in the Babylonian Talmud, Akiva disagreed with a ruling of Rabban Gamliel regarding baking on Passover, but he was respectful when inquiring of Gamliel on the issue, addressing him using the accepted formula, "Let our master teach us."[77] Nevertheless he disagreed.

His respect for authority was demonstrated in the famous incident in which Rabbi Joshua, Akiva's mentor, disagreed with Rabban Gamliel concerning when the new month began. This would affect which day was actually Yom Kippur, the most sacred day of the year. To demonstrate his authority, Gamliel decreed that Joshua appear before him on the day that, according to Joshua's calculations, was Yom Kippur, carrying his walking stick and a sack of coins. The Mishnah states that Akiva went to him and, seeing Joshua in great distress, counseled him to obey, even though for Joshua that day was Yom Kippur. Akiva's advice was that "whatever Rabban Gamliel decides is decided." His reasoning had nothing to do with Gamliel specifically, but with the authority of the position he held as head of the court. Akiva pointed out that the Torah says, "These are the holy days to the LORD, the sacred occasions, which you shall celebrate each in its appointed time" (Lev. 23:4), meaning that whatever time has been appointed by the court, that is the holy day. Joshua took his advice.[78]

Later when Gamliel's haughty authority and continued mistreatment of Joshua became unbearable, the Sages, with Akiva's support, removed Gamliel from office. When Rabbi Eleazar ben Azariah was then appointed *nasi*, Akiva was disappointed that he had not received that position and grieved, murmuring, "It's not that he is greater than I am in Torah, but that he is greater in family ties." Eleazar was a direct descendant of Ezra the Scribe; Akiva had no pedigree. The deposition did not last long, however. Gamliel humbled himself, went to Joshua to beg forgiveness for mistreating and humiliating him, and was returned to his position. When Eleazar had to be informed that his brief period in office was now over, it was Akiva who undertook that delicate task, diplomatically explaining that Eleazar was now the head of the Rabbinic court that decided individual cases, but not the head of the Sanhedrin, the academy that debated and decided issues of Jewish Law. The incident is recorded first in the older Jerusalem Talmud and elaborated in the Babylonian.[79]

A similar instance, related first in that same source, the Jerusalem Talmud, concerns the time when the great Rabbi Eliezer ben Hyrkanus was excommunicated. Eliezer, one of Ben Zakkai's greatest pupils, was a teacher of Akiva when he was the head of the academy in Lod, where Akiva first studied. As discussed above in the list of disputes between them, he and Akiva had a long and sometimes tempestuous history. Eliezer's illustrious career suffered a catastrophe in the famous case of the oven of Aknai. All the Sages declared it unclean, in other words impure, while Rabbi Eliezer declared it ritually pure. When all his arguments failed to persuade the others, he tried to prove that he was right by invoking the supernatural. He called upon a carob tree to be torn up, a stream of water to flow backward, walls to incline but not fall, and finally he invoked a voice from heaven to uphold his position—and behold a voice was heard proclaiming that the law was as Eliezer said! The others still refused to accept his ruling, protesting that "it [the Torah] is not in heaven!" Decisions on the meaning of rules derived from the Torah are in the hands of the Sages and decided by majority, not by miracles. Since Eliezer would not abide by the rule that one must follow the majority, a rule that Akiva had invoked in his arguments with Eliezer, the Sages took the extraordinary step of voting to excommunicate him.

This seems an extreme reaction to his actions. It has therefore been suggested that behind this move was the fact that Eliezer was suspected of—and indeed had even been arrested by the Romans—for having been involved in Christian beliefs. At that time, it was Akiva who spoke with him and showed him what he had done wrong: "Perhaps you were arrested because some heretical teaching was transmitted to you and you approved of it?" Eliezer then remembered that a Christian, Jacob of Kefar-Sekniah, had met him and engaged him in conversation about the meaning of the verse "You shall not bring the fee of a whore or the pay of a dog into the house of the LORD your God" (Deut. 23:19). Jacob explained that Jesus had said, "They came from a place of filth and should go to a place of filth," and that had pleased Eliezer.[80]

The question now was, who would inform Eliezer of this drastic decision that would isolate him from all others and remove his authority as a Sage? It was Akiva who volunteered, "lest someone unsuitable do it and thus destroy the world." Akiva put on black garments and went to Eliezer but sat far apart. When Eliezer asked what was happening, Akiva said, "My master, my master, your colleagues have excommunicated you," whereupon Eliezer tore his garments and wept.[81] For all the disputes between them, Akiva was still the most appropriate and compassionate person to convey the terrible news.

Akiva's sympathetic attitude toward his disgraced teacher is apparent in the visit that Akiva and others made when Rabbi Eliezer was on his deathbed, as recorded in *ARN*. Although the anecdote is undoubtedly embellished, the basic story is believable. Because of

Eliezer's excommunication, they sat far away from him. He spoke bitterly about the fact that his students had not visited him, and he predicted their deaths—with Akiva's to be the most bitter of all. Eliezer remarked that he had hundreds—perhaps thousands—of laws and traditions that no one had asked him about except Akiva. He then engaged in a discussion with them of things that were pure or impure, and he died uttering the word "pure." When that happened, Rabbi Eleazar ben Azariah proclaimed immediately that the ban was lifted, that he had died in a state of purity and would receive a proper funeral and burial. His pupil Akiva mourned him publicly, tearing his clothing, with blood running down his face, weeping, "Woe unto me, my master, woe unto me, my teacher—for your sake! The whole generation is fatherless!" Akiva gave the eulogy, beginning with the quote from 2 Kings 1:12, "My father, my father, the chariot of Israel and the horsemen thereof!" Akiva went on, "I have many coins but no money changer to sort them out."[82] The most reliable conveyer of traditions had passed from this world.

## OVERTURNING TRADITIONS

Akiva, who was bold enough to challenge his elders and his teachers, was also bold enough to contradict and even overturn laws that had been set by his own teachers if he disagreed with them. He did so even without resort to biblical verses. The early tannaitic midrash *Sifra* records that there was a law forbidding a woman from adorning herself during her time of impurity "until Rabbi Akiva came and taught that this would cause her husband to hate her and divorce her." Therefore he permitted her to make herself attractive and changed the law.[83] More than once the phrase "At first they used to say . . ." followed by "until Rabbi Akiva came and taught . . ." occurs.[84] For all his reverence for the laws that had been taught and passed down from generation to generation, when they were not anchored in anything but human reason, he found it possible to disagree and teach something new and sometimes even radical. The Tosefta records that Akiva changed another ancient law and made it more liberal: In former times they said that one should not sit on a bench belonging to gentiles on Shabbat, until Rabbi Akiva came and taught that one may sit on a bench belonging to gentiles on Shabbat.[85] The situation concerned benches used for selling merchandise. Sitting on it might be thought to imply that the person was doing business on Shabbat. Akiva evidently did not think that this was sufficient reason for forbidding the practice and changed the accepted law.

### AKIVA'S PRESTIGE

Akiva's fame and authority spread throughout the land. According to the Tosefta, when there was a matter of Jewish Law regarding agriculture to be decided in Meron, far in the north, not his usual territory, "they came and asked Rabbi Akiva" to decide.[86] There may not have been local Sages there capable of deciding halakhic matters, or they may have respected him more than other, less-revered Sages. Wherever Akiva traveled his opinion was sought on matters of Jewish Law. He is also said to have been in Zifron in the Galilee, although it is not clear if he was there on some visit or if he settled there over a longer period of time.[87]

What was the secret of Akiva's rise to positions of power and prestige among the Sages and his enormous popularity among the masses? Obviously much of that had to do with that indefinable quality known as personal charisma, but there were factors connected to his personality and intellect that could be pointed to as well, characteristics that stand out in the early stories told about him.

One factor often cited that could account for his high standing among the people was his modesty.[88] Another was his care and personal concern for others—people skills that made him the perfect person to send on sensitive missions. It was not accidental that he was chosen to inform Eliezer of his banishment and to tell Eleazar that he had lost his position as head of the academy. Another factor was his concern for those in need and his identification with the poor. For most of his career Akiva personified hope and gave comfort and encouragement. He always saw the positive side of things and brought comfort to those who listened to him. His message was one of the goodness of God and the expectation of better things to come.

At a time that was traumatic in the lives of Jews, he saw all humans as being created in God's image and the Israelites as God's special children. He had an extraordinary gift for creating stories and parables that would attract mass audiences, bringing ancient stories to life, delighting listeners, and using interesting and unconventional methods to stir interest in his lessons and sermons. Once, for example, "he noticed when he was sermonizing that his audience was dozing off. He sought to arouse their interest, saying, 'How is it that Esther ruled over 127 provinces? It was because Esther was the daughter of Sarah, who lived 127 years—it was Sarah's merit that caused this.'"[89] His reputation as a mesmerizing preacher was so widespread that it was considered worth noting that once on a trip to Ginzak in far-off Persia he preached on the subject of the generation of the flood "and did not make them cry"—until he found some story concerning the raven that made them weep.[90]

His standing among the Sages was assured because he was an intellectual giant, able to construct logical arguments to bolster his positions. He was considered to be the first Sage to be a master of all learning.[91] It was said of him that he was like a stone cutter who hacked away at an entire mountain, vowing to uproot it all, and succeeded, putting everything in its proper place. Therefore Rabbi Tarfon said of him, "Things concealed from others you bring to light."[92]

# *four*

## THE MYSTICAL
## INTERPRETER OF TORAH

The Torah, the Five Books of Moses, has stood at the center of Jewish life ever since the Judeans return from their Babylonian exile in the fifth century BCE. Under the supervision of Ezra the Scribe, the various written traditions that had existed until that time were given their final form and integrated into one document. At a great ceremony held in Jerusalem at the Water Gate in 444 BCE, this document was accepted as the official law of Judaism.[1] This ceremony was the equivalent of the ancient assembly at Sinai described in Exodus 19–20, when all the Israelites accepted God's covenant with the words "All that the LORD has spoken we will do!" (Exod. 19:8). And so this ceremony was a renewal of the covenant between God and Israel and an acceptance of the Torah as God's word. All of the people took an oath "to follow the Torah of God, given through Moses the servant of God, and to observe carefully all the commandments of the LORD our God, His rules and laws" (Neh. 10:30). The Torah was held in reverence. It was considered both the teaching of Moses and the instruction of the Lord. At the same time, the work of interpreting this book, of reconciling its various traditions, of applying its laws to the current conditions of life, became the task of scribes and teachers.

The various sects within Second Temple Judaism had their own ways of interpreting the Torah and their own authorities. They often disagreed with one another as to what it meant and how its laws were to be applied. Then, after the destruction of the Second Temple in 70 CE, these sects ceased to exist as organized groups, and the interpretation of Torah was left to the Sages, who developed their own ways of approaching the Torah and understanding it. Although no longer representing the Pharisaic party, which ceased to exist as a separate group, these Sages, who were now known as "rabbis" (masters and teachers of the Torah), basically followed the Pharisees' way of interpretation, ascribing oral traditions not recorded in the written Torah as also having their origins in the Sinai revelation. Thus "Torah" meant not only the written words in the Pentateuch, but also the teachings of the Sages from the time of Ezra up to the present. Those were traditions that groups such as the Sadducees had not accepted as sacred and that the Jewish-Christians also did not recognize. That is the meaning of the first section of Tractate *Avot* in the Mishnah, "Moses received Torah [instruction] from Sinai and delivered it to Joshua . . ."—Moses received oral instruction, which he in turn passed on to Joshua, who passed it to others, until the time of the Mishnah. Although many parts of the oral tradition were Rabbinic additions to the laws of the Torah and were subject to change, some unwritten laws were considered to be *halakhah l'Moshe mi-Sinai*, "Laws given to Moses from Sinai"—that is, directly by God at the time of the Sinai revelation—and therefore carrying the same degree of sanctity.[2] Some authorities went so far as to say that "whatever a distinguished disciple will rule in the presence of his teacher in the future was already communicated to Moses at Sinai"[3] in order to stress the divine nature of all oral teachings, even the newest.

The discussions that took place within the various academies after the Second Temple fell were often concerned with the very question of what were the appropriate ways of interpreting the sacred text. Furthermore, as important as the Torah had been before, its importance now increased greatly, since there was no longer the Temple to unite the people and to represent the Presence of the Almighty. Adherence to the teaching of Moses (*Torat Moshe*) became the uniting factor for Judaism. It was more important than ever to emphasize the significance of the Torah and of developing appropriate ways of interpreting it and preserving the oral traditions that had developed over the centuries.

The rise of Christianity was another factor necessitating the increased emphasis on the sacredness of the Torah. Pauline Christianity gained in influence, teaching that the Torah was "the Old Covenant," now superseded by "the New Covenant," that the Torah's laws were no longer binding and, in fact, were an impediment to true salvation.[4] For Judaism to survive, it was imperative for the Sages to emphasize the sacredness of the Torah and its eternal validity. This led to bitter rivalry between traditional Jews and Jews who accepted Jesus as the Messiah. The Sages ruled that the Christian books, the Gospels, were not to be saved from fire on Shabbat even if this meant that the name of God written in them would be destroyed. Akiva's compatriot Rabbi Tarfon went so far as to say that he would actually burn them together with God's name at any time that they should come into his possession and that he would enter a pagan temple to save his life, but not a place of Christian worship, "because while pagans are ignorant of the true God and deny Him, these people know the true God and yet deny Him!"[5] Rabbi Ishmael, Akiva's contemporary and rival, said that one should cut out the names of God and burn the rest, but Akiva said, "He should burn the entire thing, since it was not written in holiness."[6] Such was the volatile environment into which Akiva, the newly ordained Sage, was plunged. He attempted to meet the challenge by developing an approach to the written Torah that elevated it above and beyond all other books and that would also elevate the oral traditions to a place of equal importance.

Akiva's exaltation of the Torah found its ultimate poetic expression in his praise of it that can be found in an ancient tannaitic midrash; here Akiva compares words of Torah first to water and then to wine:[7]

> Words of Torah are like water—just as water endures forever, so words of Torah live forever. . . .
>
> Just as water cleanses the unclean, so words of Torah cleanse the unclean. . . .
>
> Just as water restores the soul, so words of Torah restore the soul. . . .
>
> Just as water is forever free for everyone, so words of Torah are forever free for everyone. . . .
>
> Just as water is priceless, so words of Torah are priceless. . . .
>
> Just as wine makes the heart rejoice, so the words of Torah make the heart rejoice. . . .
>
> Just as wine is better the longer it ages, so the words of Torah improve the longer they are within a person. . . .
>
> Just as wine keeps better in an earthen vessel than in silver or gold, so the words of Torah keep better in one who considers himself the lowliest of vessels.[8]

### AKIVA THE MYSTIC VERSUS ISHMAEL THE RATIONALIST

Akiva was not the only one who applied himself to the task of preserving and teaching the Torah and its interpretations. One other outstanding Sage who had a similar concern, although a different response, was Rabbi Ishmael ben Elisha.[9] These two men were later deemed to have been "the fathers of the world,"[10] an expression that means that they were the teachers upon whose words the world of Torah was built.

They could hardly have been more different in background, in temperament, and in their approach to Torah interpretation. Akiva was of humble background, while Ishmael was of prestigious priestly descent.[11] Ishmael was a disciple of Nehunia ben Hakana, who "expounded the whole Torah on the principle of generalization and specification," while Akiva had learned at the feet of Nahum of Gimzo, who "expounded the whole Torah on the principle of amplification and limitation"; he interpreted every *et* in the Torah, even though others thought that that word had no intrinsic meaning. Ishmael refused to accept that methodology.[12]

But the differences between them go further than this. As the highly regarded theologian Abraham Joshua Heschel explains in his masterful work *Heavenly Torah*, Ishmael's approach was rational, seeking the plain meaning of a text that used human language, whereas Akiva stressed the wondrous, the esoteric, the mystical meaning of a text that was wholly and totally divine.[13]

Both men were revered, and both methods were considered legitimate by the Sages. Both had a circle of devoted disciples, who created their own set of biblical interpretations, midrashim, to the four books of the Torah that contain laws: Exodus, Leviticus, Numbers, and Deuteronomy. The tolerance and mutual respect between them, for all of their sharp exchanges and criticisms, can be seen in how both circles quote the other in the Midrash.[14] Nevertheless Ishmael often chided Akiva for what he considered his incorrect reading of the text, one that in Ishmael's opinion opened possibilities of dangerous interpretations. Their relationship was one of cautious friendship, but also one of rivalry and an agreement to disagree.

Ishmael's way of interpreting the text was a continuation and an expansion of the seven rules of textual interpretation that had been developed a hundred years before by the great sage Hillel. Hillel taught that the verses of the Torah could be expounded according to (1) drawing an inference from minor to major, (2) analogy, (3) deriving a principle from one verse, (4) deriving a principle from two verses, (5) inference from general to particular, (6) inference from particular to general, (7) deduction from context.[15] Ishmael added others to these that were of a similar nature or more explicit, creating 13 rules for interpreting the Torah.[16] Perhaps the most important were rules 12 and 13: (12) an obscure text can be clarified by its context or by another verse; (13) when two verses contradict one another, a third can be used to reconcile them. All of Ishmael's rules use logic to solve the problem of understanding a difficult text that often contained contradictions.

Modern biblical scholarship explains that contradictions between verses stem from the fact that at least four different texts were redacted (edited) together to form the Torah, and these different texts sometimes contained different laws. But this view was certainly not acceptable or even contemplated in Rabbinic times, and since the Sages' task was to determine how the laws of the Torah were to be observed, contradictions had to be resolved and painful decisions made. Following rules of interpretation was the way to do so, and most of the Sages turned to Ishmael's rules, which were similar to grammatical rules used to interpret texts in the ancient Hellenistic world.[17] In that sense the Rabbinic commentators treated the Torah text in the same way that other important texts would have been treated at that time, using logic and inference to derive laws and to resolve contradictions.[18]

Akiva did not reject these rules; he often used them when determining the law.[19] For example, using Ishmael's thirteenth principle, concerning the reason for the deaths of Aaron's two sons, Akiva points out that two verses (Lev. 16:1 and 10:1) give different reasons for their death and then brings a third verse that decides the matter (Num. 26:61).[20] But for Akiva these rules of logic were useful but insufficient, because he was convinced that the Torah text was *not* equivalent to any other text and therefore had to be interpreted in a different way. Akiva believed that the Torah was unique in that it was, in the most literal sense, the revealed word of God in which every word, every letter, every mark, was there in order to convey a divine message, which could be understood by proper methodology, methodology that was within the power of the Sages to use. Ishmael, on the other hand, constantly reiterated that "the Torah speaks in human language."[21]

It should be stressed that the relationship between Akiva and

Ishmael was not the same as the legendary rivalry between Hillel and Shammai a hundred years earlier. Ishmael's criticisms of Akiva were of his interpretive methodology, not of his general approach to Jewish Law or practice. Ishmael himself is depicted as a concerned and caring individual, not harsh or strict in his rulings, as Shammai was reputed to be. Nor was Akiva always lenient, as Hillel was said to be.

We see Ishmael's character clearly in a story related in the Mishnah about a man who took a vow not to marry his niece. She was taken to Rabbi Ishmael's house, where she was "made beautiful." Ishmael then asked the uncle if this was the woman about whom he had taken the vow. He said, "No," whereupon Ishmael released him from his vow and they were married. Ishmael then wept and said, "The daughters of Israel are beautiful, but poverty has made them ugly." Evidently the young woman was in need of a groom (unmarried women then were not able to easily support themselves) but was not considered a good catch. Her uncle, who could marry her according to Jewish Law, was not attracted to her and bound himself by a vow so that he would not be forced into the marriage. Ishmael took pity on the girl and brought in those who could make her look attractive. When the uncle said that she was not the same person he had vowed not to marry (because she was now attractive), Ishmael could release him from the vow, and the marriage took place. The Mishnah concludes by saying that when Ishmael died the women wept for him, and he was eulogized with the words, based on 2 Samuel 1:24, "O daughters of Israel, weep for Rabbi Ishmael!"[22]

Since the School of Akiva was largely responsible for the redaction of the Mishnah and since the Talmud too reflects Akiva's views, we know less about Ishmael than about Akiva. In a sense we have a case here of the victor writing history and determining the tone of the story, thus it is all the more remarkable that this lovely tale about Ishmael was preserved there and that in general Ishmael is treated with respect.

If Ishmael represents the use of logic as the way to understand the text and arrive at the law, Akiva represents the use of more esoteric and mystical methods based on his concept of the nature of the Torah. This is understandable when we remember that Akiva was a student of mysticism. He entered into mystical studies and practice in a serious way, as evidenced in the famous story in the Tosefta, repeated in both the Jerusalem Talmud and the Babylonian Talmud, of "four who entered paradise [the *pardes*]."[23]

According to this account, four Sages "entered paradise [the *pardes*],"[24] in other words, they immersed themselves in the mystical traditions based on the story of the Creation from Genesis and the heavenly chariot as described in the biblical book Ezekiel: "Four entered paradise—Ben Azzai, Ben Zoma, *aher* [Elisha ben Abuya],[25] and Rabbi Akiva. One [Ben Azzai] looked and died. One [Ben Zoma] looked and was stricken. One [Elisha] looked and cut the shoots. One [Akiva] ascended in peace and descended in peace."[26]

Ben Azzai's death was ascribed to his mystical practices. Ben Zoma lost his mind. Elisha ben Abuya became an apostate. Only Akiva emerged unscathed,[27] which he explained as being "not because I am greater than my colleagues, but because 'your deeds will bring you close and your deeds will push you away.'"[28]

It is unclear if this story is intended to mean that all four engaged in this mystical exercise together at the same time or if each of them individually attempted to enter the *pardes*. Akiva was the most senior of the group, both in age and in knowledge, and the one with the most important standing in the community. The account in the Babylonian Talmud adds that Akiva instructed them what not to say when they arrived at "the stones of pure marble."[29] According to this, even if they did not attempt it together, Akiva was their guide in this mystical journey. The journey was considered a dangerous one, since doing or saying the wrong thing would indicate that one was not worthy and could therefore be punished or even killed.[30]

The chapter in the Tosefta containing this story begins with the laws concerning restrictions on mystical practices and speculation. The story is told as a cautionary tale, demonstrating the potential dangers involved in immersing oneself in Jewish mysticism. Rabbinic tradition considered the study of these mystical beliefs to be dangerous—literally—and attempted to restrict it to those of a certain age or of greater knowledge and ability who would be able to deal with it, such as Akiva.

On the other hand, these sources did not deny the truth and veracity of such mystical practices, and it is known that they were not uncommon, therefore the need for limitations and caution. The greatest figures of first-century Judaism are found engaging in mystical practices and expounding mystical doctrine. The same chapter in the Tosefta describing the journey into paradise clearly mentions that Rabbi Eleazar ben Arakh expounded on the heavenly chariot before Rabban Yohanan ben Zakkai, who praised him extravagantly for "knowing how to understand and expound upon the glory of his Father in heaven."[31] When this story is told in another source, miraculous events are said to have occurred as Rabbi Eleazar expounded on the mysteries of the heavenly chariot: "Fire descended from heaven and encompassed them and angels danced before them, as is done before the groom at the *huppah*. One angel emerged from the fire and proclaimed, 'Indeed the chariot is exactly as you have explained it, Eleazar ben Arakh,' after which all the trees of the forest opened their mouths in song!"[32] Furthermore Rabbi Joshua illuminates these matters before Ben Zakkai, Akiva before Joshua, and Hananiah ben Hakhinai before Akiva.[33]

There is a difference, however, between expounding upon the heavenly chariot and "entering paradise." The latter involves performing mystical exercises that enable one to actually experience the heavenly sphere, reaching the seventh heaven, seeing and hearing matters that are not of this world, indeed to literally enter into the heavenly enclosure—the *pardes*. The purpose is to be in the presence of the Holy One.

The terminology "ascended" and "descended" makes it vividly

clear that we are talking about an experience of ascending into the heavenly sphere, into paradise.[34] The verse that is used in the Tosefta to explain Akiva's experience, "the king has brought me to his chambers" (Song 1:4)—understanding "the king," as the Lord—makes this even clearer. Akiva was granted the opportunity of entering God's very presence.

Such mystical exercises are not a one-time thing but rather the culmination of intensive study and training. Doing this required practice and preparation. According to later mystical tracts, this entailed twelve days of ascetic practices, and something similar was undoubtedly required at Akiva's time as well.[35] These four must have undertaken this over a prolonged period of time, working together. Why these four are mentioned together and no others is a mystery in itself that remains unexplained. They are a strange grouping. Ben Azzai and Ben Zoma, students of Joshua ben Hananiah, were never ordained, although their teachings were honored. They were younger colleagues of Akiva. Ben Azzai, known as a pious and saintly man, was even reputed to have been the husband of Akiva's daughter,[36] although according to many early sources Ben Azzai was a confirmed bachelor who never married.[37] When Ben Azzai expounded on these mystical doctrines, the midrash states, "fire would burn around him." When this happened, others went and informed Akiva, who came and asked him, "'Are you dealing with the most inner parts of the chariot?' He replied, 'No, I am connecting the words of Torah to the Prophets and the words of the Prophets to the Writings, and the words of the Torah rejoice as they did at the time they were given at Sinai, for was not their giving at Sinai accompanied by fire?'"[38]

Of Ben Zoma it is said that Rabbi Joshua once met him and asked him from whence he was coming. Ben Zoma replied, "I have been gazing at the work of Creation and saw that there is only a droplet of space between the upper and the lower waters," upon which Joshua remarked to his students, "Ben Zoma is already outside."[39]

Elisha was a contemporary of Akiva, but a Sage of much less

importance, even though much revered by Rabbi Meir, Akiva's disciple, who considered Elisha one of his teachers. Elisha is also recorded as having seen the angel Metatron in heaven, recording the merits of Israel in a book.[40] Specific reasons for his apostasy are mentioned elsewhere, such as his having seen instances of those observing a commandment being killed and those breaking it not suffering any punishment.[41]

Although Elisha abandoned Judaism, some of his teachings were still recorded in *Pirke Avot*[42] and *Avot de-Rabbi Natan*.[43]

The mystic journey is described in later *Hekhalot* literature, where it is reiterated that this is extremely dangerous and can easily lead to death or madness.[44] In these later works the legendary figure of Akiva plays an important role. He is "the very prototype of the Merkabah visionary," the person who studies the mysteries of Ezekiel's vision and attempts to experience such a vision himself. He is described as one who hears the great hymns being sung "at the very throne of glory before which his soul was standing."[45] Such mysticism, as Gershom Scholem has shown, was neither foreign to nor opposed by normative Rabbinic Judaism of the time. Obviously not everyone practiced it, but those who did were not shunned. It was, however, dangerous and therefore caution was advised. The extent of its influence on the real Akiva cannot be known, but the many references he makes to God's appearance, to the heavens and the angelic beings, indicate that it was of major importance to him and that the account of his mystical journey is credible.

Akiva's delving into the most esoteric arts of mysticism at that time accords well with his concept of the Torah and its origins, as well as his general attitude toward midrashic interpretation. It is quite possible that his mystical practices and inclination stand at the core of his entire attitude toward the Torah and his methods of scriptural interpretation.

Later mystical literature ascribes these practices to both Rabbi Akiva and Rabbi Ishmael, but the early Rabbinic literature, while describing Akiva's mystic journey, makes no such mention of

Ishmael.[46] Everything recorded about Ishmael in early Rabbinic writing would indicate that he was a man of cool logic.[47] Akiva, on the other hand, was a man of vivid and fervent emotion and enthusiasm.[48] It was common practice to ascribe mystic teachings to earlier authorities in order to boost their credibility.

## AKIVA AND HEAVENLY TORAH

Underlying Akiva's method of interpreting the Torah text was his concept of the nature of the Torah itself, and in this too there was also a major difference between himself and Rabbi Ishmael.[49] It was Akiva who expanded the idea that the Torah was from heaven to mean that the entire Torah, word for word and letter for letter, existed in heaven before it was given on earth at Sinai. Whereas the phrase "Torah from heaven" may originally have meant that the Ten Commandments were spoken from heaven by God, to Akiva it meant that Moses literally ascended into heaven and brought the Torah down with him. As Heschel wrote, "This was the basis for expanding the concept of 'Torah from heaven' to embrace the entire Five Books of the Torah."[50] In a late midrash Akiva explains why Moses says, "Give ear, O heavens . . . let the earth hear" (Deut. 32:1), placing heaven before earth. It was because he was actually in heaven when being given the Torah, far from earth.[51] This concept was not universally accepted and does not appear in the works of the early rabbis prior to Akiva.[52]

A teaching of the Sages quoted in the Talmud states that the words "Because he has spurned the word of the LORD" (Num. 15:31) refer to one who says that the Torah is not from heaven, "even if he says that it is from heaven except for one verse uttered by Moses, not by God . . . or except a single point or deduction." This is a reflection of Akiva's doctrine, which had become the norm. The School of Ishmael, however, interprets this verse to refer to one who spurns the words spoken to Moses at Sinai in the Ten Commandments.[53] In a tannaitic midrash Akiva's disciples objected strongly when it was suggested that the verses following "So Moses . . . died there"

(Deut. 34:5) were therefore not written by Moses but "from here on Joshua wrote the rest." Said Rabbi Meir, "Is it possible that Moses gave the Torah while it was lacking even one letter? Rather, this teaches that Moses would write whatever the Holy One told him."[54]

Akiva, the mystic, had no difficulty imagining that Moses could have ascended to heaven to receive the Torah. Had not Akiva attempted to reach the seventh heaven[55]—and perhaps felt that he had done so—when engaging in the mysticism of the heavenly chariot, "entering paradise"? Akiva states clearly that the Torah Israel was given was the preexisting instrument with which the world was created.[56] It was not like any other written work; it existed before the world existed. Nor did God dictate it to Moses. Rather Moses received it complete and entire while he was literally in heaven. In the words of Heschel:

> One who locates the Torah in heaven must believe that it has an existence distinct and apart, transcendent; and the Torah we discourse over on earth is the same Torah that they discourse over in heaven. This point of view sees the Torah as infinite at its core. Its content—that is, that which is visible within the narrow confines of surface meaning—is like a mere drop in the sea. Rabbi Akiva believed that every detail and every stylistic form has a deep significance and a hidden intent.[57]

With this is mind, it is not difficult to understand Akiva's stance when there was a discussion at a gathering of the Sages in the upper chambers of the house of Nithza in Lod[58] on the question "Which is more important, study or practice?" Akiva's answer was "study." His compatriot Tarfon said "practice." The vote was a compromise, "Study is more important because it leads to practice."[59]

Akiva's mystical inclination can also be seen clearly in his explanations of the events at Sinai. As recorded in the *Mekhilta de-Rabbi Yishmael*, a tannaitic midrash from the School of Rabbi Ishmael, whereas Ishmael explains the difficult verse "All the people saw the thunder" (Exod. 20:15) as meaning simply, "They saw what could be seen and heard what could be heard," thus removing the mystery, Akiva says, "They saw *and* heard that which can be seen!"[60] Ishmael teaches that although Exodus 20:19 states, "I spoke to you from the very heavens," this is contradicted by other verses such as Exodus 19:20, "The LORD came down upon Mount Sinai," and concludes that actually it was only God's voice that was heard from heaven. Thus when Moses went up to God, it was not to heaven but to the top of Sinai. Akiva solves the problem of the contradiction between the verses by teaching that God "lowered the upper heavens of heaven down to the top of the mountain, and so God actually did speak to them from the heavens." The passage in the midrash concludes by quoting Rabbi Judah the Prince, who lived long after both of them and rejected mysticism, reasoning that this verse cannot be taken literally.[61] Yet that is exactly what Akiva did.

## AKIVA'S METHODOLOGY

What was Akiva's methodology in interpreting the Torah that was so influential—and why did Ishmael and others often oppose it? In a famous legend related by Rav, the third-century Babylonian *amora* (one of the rabbis who lived in the period following the completion of the Mishnah in 200 CE), Moses asks God why He is affixing crowns—ornamentations—to letters in the Torah. God replies that in the future Akiva ben Yosef will interpret each detail and be able to derive great heaps of laws from them.[62] Every letter, every crown, every word could be used to teach something. Torah language is not the same as human language.

Because Akiva believed that the Torah was a divine work, he thought that each mark in it, each word, each letter had divine meaning. Nothing in it was devoid of importance. One could learn manifold ideas and laws from things that in an ordinary human book would be mere phraseology. Akiva used this method in his interpretations of all scriptural texts, both in the realm of law (halakhah) and in the realm of narratives, poetry, and prophecy (aggadah).

Following his teacher Nahum of Gimzo, Akiva used the rules of extension, which meant that such words as "also," "only," and *et* (a Hebrew word that has no semantic meaning but is merely a grammatical indicator) could be used to include or exclude matters not found in the text.[63] Thus the word *et* requires an addition to whatever appears in the verse.

For example Deuteronomy 10:20, "You must revere the LORD your God," has the word *et* in it before the phrase "the LORD your God." Therefore, according to Akiva, this word is there to add something else. It teaches that in addition to revering the Lord, you also must also revere the Sages.[64] Another version has Akiva teaching that it means you must revere not only God but also God's Torah.[65] Thus the word *et* requires an addition to whatever appears in the verse. It could be used to expand and teach other meanings. This was not acceptable to Ishmael and earned Akiva criticism from many others as well. Interpreting the first verse of the Torah, for example, in which the words "heaven" and "earth" are preceded by the word *et*, Ishmael explained this as a grammatical indicator showing that the heaven and the earth are direct objects and not the subject. Otherwise one might have thought that the verse meant "In the beginning the gods—heaven and earth—created," thus implying, as paganism taught, that heaven and earth are divinities. Akiva, on the other hand, said that *et* is intended to add "the sun and the moon, stars and planets" and "trees, grasses, and the Garden of Eden."[66] Akiva also taught that "whenever the word 'saying' is found it requires an interpretation."[67] Akiva, who had learned this method from his teacher Nahum of Gimzo, then passed it on to his own students.[68]

Rabbinic literature is filled with examples of Akiva's interpretations of scriptural texts, legal and non-legal, that demonstrate his extreme methodology. Finding meaning in every detail, using words and letters as means of attaching his ideas and concepts to the text, he exercised an unprecedented freedom of interpretation, opening up the sacred text to almost unlimited horizons. Even if

Akiva's interpretations are not always inherent in the text, they are of value and of interest in and of themselves. These flights of fancy were often met with scorn by Ishmael, the rationalist, and by others as well who disagreed either with the method or with the interpretation itself.

Here are a few examples of Akiva's work—and of the comments of his opponents—first in the realm of halakhah and then in aggadah. Because the root meaning "to be cut off" appears twice in Numbers 15:31 concerning one who "spurned the word of the LORD," Akiva taught that he will be cut off "from this world and from the world to come." Ishmael responded that "being cut off" appears in the previous verse as well and asked Akiva, "Does this indicate that he will be cut off from three worlds?! Rather . . . the Torah is speaking in human language."[69] Similarly when "defiled" is written three times regarding a woman suspected of adultery (Num. 5:13–14), Akiva took it to mean that she is defiled for three things: her husband, her paramour, and eating the priestly portion. Ishmael responded that the verses simply teach that unless there is doubt, we never make her undergo the ordeal described in Numbers 5:16–31.[70] Ishmael, who favored literal and simple interpretations of Scripture, had little patience with Akiva's more esoteric explanations.

In the famous dispute between Akiva and Ishmael concerning the proper punishment for the daughter of a priest who commits adultery, Ishmael, who took the more lenient position, remarked, "Shall we impose the stricter punishment of death by fire because you interpret the superfluous *vav* [in Lev. 21:9]?" But Ishmael's argument was really not about interpreting that seemingly superfluous *vav*, because Ishmael also interpreted that letter, albeit differently.[71] His protest was against Akiva ordering death by fire, the most terrible punishment, when that superfluous letter does not unequivocally demand it.

Sometimes, then, objections to Akiva's interpretations were not about his methodology, but about his logic, that he played fast and loose without justification. Thus when he interpreted the words "*And every* sin offering" (Lev. 6:23) as meaning that the verse applied to every type of sacrifice, not only sin offerings, Rabbi Yose HaG'lili objected, "Even if you keep on repeating that all day, it still only refers to sin offerings." Yose then interpreted the phrase to mean that the law applies even if there is only one sin offering.[72] In this case there is no objection to the idea that a superfluous word can be used to convey a specific meaning; HaG'lili objected to the particular meaning that Akiva chose to give to it.

Eleazar ben Azariah objected to Akiva's interpretation that the repetition of the word "oil" in Leviticus 7:12 reduced the amount of oil required to half a log. Rather, he believed that the quantity of oil could not be determined by interpreting a verse of Scripture because it was an ancient law that had been passed on orally and carried complete authority—"Torah of Moses from Sinai."[73] Were Akiva to repeat his position on this matter all day long, Eleazar still would not accept his reading of the text. Akiva attempted to attach oral laws to biblical verses, whereas others like Eleazar believed that traditional laws had authority independent of the Torah texts.

Yet one must be careful not to come to the conclusion that Akiva used only esoteric ways of interpreting the Torah. There are many instances where the difference between him and others—including Rabbi Ishmael—is not in the methodology but simply in the application. A case in point is found in the *Mekhilta de-Rabbi Yishmael*.[74] Three Sages were walking together—Akiva, Ishmael, and Eleazar ben Azariah. They were discussing the question of the permissibility of saving a life on Shabbat. Each of them used the same methodology, namely the inference from minor to major: if in a certain matter that is minor it is permissible to desecrate the Sabbath, then certainly to save a life—which is of greater import—it would be permissible![75] There were times when Akiva and Ishmael may even have agreed on the specific law but proved it in different ways, Akiva by the repetition of a word and Ishmael by logical inference of the same phrase being found in two contexts.[76]

Tarfon, Akiva's older contemporary, also objected to some of

Akiva's legal teachings, preferring to learn the law from precedents he had seen rather than from Akiva's methods of interpretation. In the end, however, he had to admit that Akiva was correct: "Tarfon saw and forgot, Akiva interprets from his own logic and finds the correct law. Anyone who separates himself from you [Akiva] separates himself from his very life!"[77]

Similar objections were made to Akiva's interpretations of aggadah, non-legal texts. Sometimes the objection was to Akiva's mystical ideas that caused him to read meaning into words that were not necessary. A sharp and personal rebuke is found in an exchange concerning the interpretation of verses from Psalm 104, which refer to "springs" and "the inhabitants of the sky." Akiva interpreted this to mean pools where lepers immerse themselves while ministering angels—"inhabitants of the sky"—hover above them when they are healed. Ishmael said that it obviously means birds and interpreting it as angels is a distortion of the text. He advised Akiva, "You should give up these kinds of interpretations and instead study "Signs of Leprosy" and "Tents.""[78] Similarly, when Akiva interpreted "the bread of the mighty" (Ps. 78:25) as "bread that the angels eat," Ishmael retorted, "Akiva, you are mistaken; do the angels eat bread?"[79]

Rabbi Yose also protested against some of Akiva's interpretations, this time of Daniel 7:9 concerning thrones where "the ancient one sat." Akiva said that there was one throne for God and another for David[80] or that one was the throne of justice, the other of charity. Here too Eleazar ben Azariah is said to have told Akiva to stop interpreting aggadic texts and stick to such matters as the laws of leprosy and tents.[81]

Two similar rebukes are recorded in the name of Yehudah ben Betera, but in neither case was it Akiva's method that was attacked, but his lack of restraint. Akiva identified Zelophehad (Num. 26:33) as the anonymous man who violated the Sabbath (Num. 15:32) and stated that Aaron became leprous when Miriam did, although the verse does not say that (Num. 12:10). In both cases Ben Betera said, "Akiva! In either case you will have to give an account! If you are right, you have revealed him while the Torah wanted to shield him. If you are wrong, you have slandered a righteous person!"[82]

Ishmael preferred to let words mean what they literally appear to mean. On rare occasions Ishmael interpreted text figuratively. In three such instances we find in the Midrash that Ishmael expanded phrases to give them a broader meaning because he did not see that the plain text made rational sense. According to Ishmael, "walks upon his staff" (Exod. 21:19) means "in a state of health." "If the sun has risen on him" (Exod. 22:2) means the thief left him in peace. "They shall spread out the cloth" (Deut. 22:17), regarding showing bloodstains to prove virginity, means "They must make the matter as clear as cloth."[83]

Akiva often gave words mystical and esoteric meanings not apparent in the text.[84] This was the result of Akiva's general view that the Torah is divine, originating word for word and letter for letter from God's dictation, with a divine vocabulary, whereas for Ishmael the language of the Torah is human language, language that can be understood the way we understand any language.[85] This does not mean that Akiva never understood words in their plain sense. He often did. A clear example is Deuteronomy 20:8, which exempts a man from army duty if he is "afraid and disheartened." Rabbi Yose HaG'lili interpreted this as "he has a deformity," thus turning a psychological problem into a physical disability. Akiva, on the other hand said, "It means just what it says."[86]

Although Ishmael's teachings and his disagreements with Akiva were preserved even in the works produced by Akiva's students, and vice versa, since it was Akiva's disciples who formulated the major works of halakhic Judaism, it was Akiva's view that was most influential in the determination of how to view the Torah and how to interpret it.

## MEETING THE CHALLENGES OF THE AGE

In light of the enormous challenges that post-Temple Judaism faced, Akiva took it upon himself to prove that the Torah was the word of God, a divine book unlike any other written work, in no way the creation of human beings. In the absence of a Temple, of Jewish independence and Jewish government, living in the midst of the great and powerful Roman Empire and its civilization, and with a rising Christianity that reinterpreted the Torah as the basis for a new revelation and little else, the centrality of the Torah was the key to the survival of Judaism. In Akiva's view, nothing could more clearly differentiate Judaism from Christianity than that. Nothing could better serve to convince Jews of the importance and sacredness of the Torah, something worth one's very life.

Of course all the Sages held the Torah to be a book of divine revelation, but Akiva's radical view stood at one end of the spectrum, and Ishmael's more rational and logical view anchored the other. It could be said that whereas Ishmael appealed to the mind, Akiva appealed to the heart. It is fortunate for Judaism that emerging Rabbinic Judaism did not find it necessary to choose between the two. Thus even though the inclination toward Akiva's methods was clearly felt, the opposite ideas were not eliminated and continued to appear in ongoing deliberations and eventually in the written corpus of Rabbinic writings.

Nevertheless, Akiva's approach answered a need of that time more convincingly than Ishmael's. In contrast to Ishmael's rational interpretations of Torah, it was Akiva's more mystical approach that basically prevailed over time in the popular mind as being the authentic Jewish approach. The problems that this raises today for modern biblical scholarship, as well as for modern readers in general with more questioning minds, are obvious. Because of this it was important for Heschel, for example, to point out that regardless of the popular impression, many subsequent premodern Rabbinic interpreters did not accept Akiva's doctrine and that Akiva's theory had the unfortunate effect of closing the door on any attempt to bridge the gap between traditional theology and more modern approaches.[87]

Therefore it is worth pondering if Akiva's views concerning

the nature of the Torah are still valid today in view of the different concepts of the origin of the biblical text and of the nature of the Divine. It is certainly true that with but few exceptions in the Orthodox world, Akiva's concept of the nature of the Torah is not accepted in modern biblical studies among either Jewish or non-Jewish scholars. Greatly respected modern Jewish biblical scholars such as Moshe Greenberg, Yohanan Muffs, Jacob Milgrom, Shalom Paul, and Jeffrey Tigay, as well as scholars of Jewish thought such as Heschel himself and Louis Jacobs, all accept the fact that the Torah is a composite work based on documents from various religious circles within ancient Israel and subject to critical study. At the same time these commentators have found ways to reconcile this with a non-fundamentalist view of the Torah as a book of divine revelation. None of them, therefore, would accept Akiva's mystical view or his method of interpreting every word, every letter, and every crown. Ishmael's oft repeated statement that the Torah speaks in human language, on the other hand, would be acceptable and resonate deeply. This does not take away from the value or ingenuity of Akiva's interpretations and those of others who followed his methodology in the development of both Jewish Law and Jewish lore, but it does relegate them to the realm of creative midrashic exegesis rather than the simple meaning of the text.

On the positive side, Akiva's method allowed for a non-fundamentalist approach to the text, something that has differentiated Jewish understanding of the Torah from that of fundamentalist Christians and made it possible to appreciate the underlying truths of the Torah without having to slavishly defend the literal reading of texts that contradict scientific or historical knowledge. Similarly his actions opened the possibility of reinterpreting biblical laws in ways that made them appropriate for new situations and new understandings of moral demands. Although modern critical and historical understanding of Scripture undermines Akiva's assumptions that his interpretations are indeed implied in the text, it is still possible to appreciate his ideas and the insights that he provided.

It is necessary to consider not only Akiva's specific methodology and the theological concept that stands behind it, but also the emotional content and passionate fervor that characterized his approach to the biblical text. Combining Akiva's fervor with Ishmael's cool logic might be an appropriate approach for modern Jewish exegesis. Finding ways to relate current concerns and new ideas to the ancient text, which is what Akiva did, adds to the richness of biblical interpretation and serves to keep the ancient text ever new and capable of renewal.

# THE ORGANIZER OF TORAH

Akiva functioned on many levels. He was a public figure involved with the workings of the semi-autonomous administration under Rabban Gamliel II, traveling overseas and within the Land of Israel, dealing with the needy. He was also a preacher and teacher to the masses and a dispenser of justice. He was a master teacher in his own academy, inspiring others and creating a new generation of Sages. At the Yavneh academy, the Sanhedrin, he argued for his interpretation of the Torah and his ideas concerning Jewish Law and practice. But in addition he quietly took upon himself a nonpublic task of enormous importance: the preservation and organization of the unwritten traditions of Judaism.

When some seventy years after Akiva's death, Rabbi Judah the Prince, the most powerful and important leader of Judaism in the post-Temple period, assessed the importance of Akiva's work, he did not mention Akiva's belief that the Torah was given to Israel directly from God in heaven, his method of Torah interpretation, his mystical thought, or any of his teachings or public work. Rather it was Akiva's prodigious effort on his own initiative to collect, preserve, and organize all of the traditions of Judaism from the time of the giving of the Torah to his own day that he singled out:

He [Rabbi Judah the Prince] called Rabbi Akiva a well-stocked storehouse. To what may he be likened? To a laborer who took his basket and went forth. When he found wheat, he put some in the basket; when he found barley, he put that in; spelt, he put that in; lentils, he put them in. Upon returning home he sorted out the wheat by itself, the barley by itself, the beans by themselves, the lentils by themselves. This is how Rabbi Akiva acted, and he arranged the whole Torah in rings.[1]

Rabbi Judah the Prince was in a special position to be able to appreciate Akiva's work, since he was the one who took all the material that Akiva eventually produced, as further developed by his disciple Rabbi Meir, and created from it the authoritative Mishnah that brought the tannaitic period to a close. Rabbi Judah saw this as Akiva's main work and his major contribution to Rabbinic Judaism. The Babylonian Talmud says that Rabbi Judah was born on the very day that Akiva died.[2] This was a way of stressing the connection between the two, as if to say that Judah took up Akiva's mantle, and in a sense he did, since he brought Akiva's work, the Mishnah, to fruition. All further discussions were based on it, but no further major changes or additions were made. It is in that sense that Akiva was the main systematizer of the Mishnah.[3]

Akiva took it upon himself to amass a collection of all the ancient unwritten traditions, to sort them into appropriate categories, and to organize them in a way that would make it possible to remember and study them. One reason that this was so important was to ensure that Torah—in the larger sense of all religious teachings—would not be forgotten. As the tannaitic midrash *Sifre Deuteronomy* put it, "Had not Akiva stood up in his time, would not Torah have been forgotten from among Israel?"[4] This was said of no other early Sage.

Obviously there was concern that as this material accumulated—some of which was hundreds of years old, going back to the time of Ezra, and some, according to tradition, going back to Moses himself—it could so easily be lost. This was especially troublesome because in order to differentiate this material from the sacred Scripture, it was forbidden to reduce this material to writing in any official way. "Words that are written you may not say by heart. Words transmitted orally you are not permitted to recite from writing. . . . 'These' [words in the Torah] you may write, but you may not write *halakhot* [laws]."[5]

There was a collection of canonical works that were considered sacred, but nothing was to be added to them. In the late Second Temple period, texts continued to be written outside of the Pharisaic community. Groups such as the Dead Sea Sect created an entire new set of sacred writings, and now after the destruction of the Temple, the new Christian sect was creating its own set of sacred writings, which they came to call "the New Covenant" (*Brit ha-Hadashah*). The Sages continued the way of the Pharisees, accumulating the teachings of their leaders, which some called "oral Torah," in memory but not in writing. Their problem was finding a way to preserve these traditions, laws, and interpretations in some form that could be more easily retained in memory and passed on to future generations.

The usual way to do this was to remember those laws and ideas that were connected to biblical texts. This method was known as Midrash—searching or expounding upon the sacred texts. The problem with this was twofold. First, the laws of the written Torah are not organized in any systematic way, so connecting them to these texts does not make it easy to organize them. Furthermore the laws found in one book of the Torah will often contradict those in another. Another complication is that many laws and practices had accumulated that were not really connected to any specific text at all. Preserving them was a very arduous matter. Some Sages made collections of these laws for themselves for purposes of teaching, but nothing that was substantial or comprehensive. And of course as the years went by and each generation added its own material to what it received, it became very cumbersome and difficult to preserve these traditions without writing them down.

Another of Akiva's reasons for this monumental undertaking may have been because of his concern about the spread of Christian doctrines (see chapter 4). His older contemporary Paul, a Jew who accepted Jesus as the Messiah and a divine being, wished to take ownership of the Torah from Judaism, affirming its sacredness as the "Old Covenant" while proclaiming its supersession by "the New Covenant." Akiva refuted this claim, professing that the Torah was neither old nor was it superseded by new scripture, and certainly not the preface to the new Christian books. Rather it was the basis and part and parcel of all the unwritten laws and interpretations. As the Talmud later put it, "Whatever a disciple will teach before his master has already been revealed to Moses at Sinai."[6] To Akiva those extra-biblical developments were the result of interpretations of the Torah that were inherent in the text itself and had equal sanctity. From a functional point of view, the formats of midrashim (laws connected to biblical texts) and *mishnayot* (laws not related to Scripture) were to Judaism what the "New Covenant" was to Christianity. The difference was that they did not abolish the authority of Torah; if anything, they strengthened it.

By preserving these traditions and laws and anchoring them in the text of the Torah, it was possible to further distinguish Judaism and Christianity and to claim that an important and intrinsic part of the original covenant was totally unknown to Christianity. Torah was more than the Five Books of Moses, and only Judaism had all of this material. The Sages contended that there was more oral material than written Torah and that God's covenant was made with Israel "only for the sake of that which was given orally,"[7] thus excluding Christians, who did not possess that oral material.

Rabbinic Judaism developed at the same time that early Christianity was changing from a Jewish sect into a separate religion, claiming to be the true Israel. The development of both Midrash and the Mishnah provided a clear differentiation between the two faiths, emphasizing both the sacredness of the Torah and the existence of extra-biblical Jewish teachings.

For the same reason, Akiva was also concerned to see to it that translations of the Bible reflected the interpretations of the Sages, thus further "rabbinizing" or "Judaizing" the text. His disciple Aquila, a convert to Judaism, translated the Bible into Greek in a way that corrected many of the passages in the Septuagint (the ancient Greek translation that was in general use at the time), passages that might have led to Christian conclusions or that represented alternative readings to the masoretic (authoritative Hebrew) text. For Christians the Septuagint had become the standard text, even when it differed from the Hebrew text.[8] Aquila's new Greek translation of the entire Bible instead reflected Akiva's interpretations.[9] The Aramaic translation of the Torah, usually known as *Targum Onkelos*,[10] was also done in a way that accepted Akiva's teachings and those of his followers.

## COLLECTING THE TRADITIONS

According to the Jerusalem Talmud, "It is Rabbi Akiva who systemized the Midrash, Laws [Mishnah], and *aggadot* [non-legal material]. There are those who say that this was done by the men of the Great Assembly. What Rabbi Akiva did was to institute general and specific rules."[11] It is true that Akiva formulated general rules and then applied them to specific cases. We see this in the Mishnah, for example, concerning doing work on the Sabbath in order to be able to perform specific mitzvot that needed to be done on that day. Akiva formulated a general rule: "Anything that it is possible to do before the Sabbath does not push aside the Sabbath, but anything that cannot be done before the Sabbath and must be done to perform the mitzvah does push aside the Sabbath."[12] His main work, however, was systematizing all the non-written material into brief, logical codes.

The Tosefta describes how Akiva enlisted the help of others in collecting the traditions: "When Rabbi Akiva would systematize laws for his students, he would say, 'If anyone has heard some reasonable argument against his fellow student, let him come forth and tell it.'"[13] If there was some variant teaching, he wanted to hear it and judge it; he was eager to gather whatever traditions others had heard and use them in editing his collection of laws. In response to Akiva's request we hear of several students—including at least one who was a follower of Rabbi Ishmael—quoting laws of the Schools of Hillel and Shammai. As Rabbi Judah the Prince said, Akiva collected all the material he could and arranged it "in rings," in appropriate formats.

Initially Akiva accumulated the material and preserved it in two collections—Midrash and Mishnah. According to Rabbi Yohanan, a third-century *amora* from the Land of Israel, both formats were used by Akiva, "Our Mishnah comes directly from Rabbi Meir, the Tosefta from Rabbi Nehemiah, the *Sifra* from Rabbi Judah, and the *Sifre* from Rabbi Shimon, and they all are according to the view of Rabbi Akiva."[14] The *Sifra* and the *Sifre* are collections of Midrash. Akiva felt that both forms, Midrash and Mishnah, were important. Mishnah collected the laws according to topic regardless of biblical texts. Midrash, from the root meaning "to search out, to inquire," consisted of a careful explanation of the biblical texts following the order of the Torah itself and was probably the older of the two forms. Attaching everything to the biblical text provided a convenient if problematic framework. Midrashic works were eventually compiled for each of the four Torah books that contain laws: Exodus, Leviticus, Numbers, and Deuteronomy. Following the order of the Torah, these works preserve interpretations both of legal sections and aggadah (narratives), thereby connecting laws and interpretations to biblical verses.[15]

Akiva was not the only Sage concerned with organizing this post-biblical material. Rabbi Ishmael, his contemporary, friend, and frequent rival, also undertook this task, but unlike Akiva, he confined himself to compiling just Midrash. Two sets of midrashic works connected to those four books of the Torah were eventually compiled, one of the School of Rabbi Ishmael and one of the School of Rabbi Akiva. Both Akiva and Ishmael created midrashic collections, the final compilations of which took place well over a hundred years after the deaths of both Sages. Although there are differences of terminology between the two schools, they quote and borrow from one another. The collections of Ishmael, which are more extensive, emphasize his own rules of exposition, while Akiva's reflect his more extreme methods of interpretation (see chapter 4). Both are worthy contributions to Jewish interpretation and understanding of Scripture.

## ORGANIZING THE MISHNAH

The change in emphasis from laws connected to biblical passages to those that carry their own justification and explanation came about in the post-Temple period when there was a need to edit the laws in a way that could more easily be transmitted and preserved. Akiva and his followers championed that method, and the Mishnah that Rabbi Judah the Prince eventually redacted was based on their work. As important as compiling Midrash was, Akiva's work in creating the form and content of the Mishnah was even more crucial. In the end, it was Mishnah that became the official foundation for Jewish Law, for only some of the collections of Midrash were preserved, and they did not carry the same weight in legal decisions as did the Mishnah. Once Rabbi Judah the Prince officially promulgated the Mishnah, it became the authoritative collection of Jewish Law upon which all further discussions were based.

Akiva had developed a system of interpretation of the Torah that was more comprehensive than any before, since it offered greater opportunities for deriving or attaching laws to the biblical text, yet paradoxically Akiva's greatest contribution to the development of Jewish Law was in the realm of the Mishnah, the great codex of Jewish law that, for the first time, attempted to separate received law from connections to and dependence on the biblical text, instead organizing it according to categories of law without the need for references to biblical sources.

Ishmael, on the other hand, is not credited with the creation of the Mishnah and, on the contrary, seems to have been opposed to this form of transmission of law. As talmudic scholar David Weiss Halivni writes, "Rabbi Ishmael may have insisted on adhering to the older mode of learning, that of Midrash, and frowned upon the innovative mode of Mishnah." The Mishnah is mentioned only in sources deriving from the School of Akiva, never from those of Ishmael.[16] It was Akiva who championed this form and who first created a complete version. Presumably it was Akiva who selected the six major categories, or orders (sedarim, sing. seder), in the Mishnah: Agriculture, Holy Days, Women, Damages (Civil Law), Holy Things, Purities. These, in turn, were subdivided into individual tractates dealing with specific matters.

The Mishnah organized the law into logical categories, not according to the chronology of biblical texts, and is confined almost exclusively to legal matters. Although aggadic matters (non-legal, such as stories and aphorisms) appear in the Mishnah from time to time, there is only one section exclusively devoted to non-legal matters, the section known as *Avot, Fathers* (also known as *Pirke Avot, Ethics of the Fathers*). It may have once served as a preface and introduction to the entire work.

Although the Mishnah, at least in the version we have today, consists largely of laws without reference to their origin in the Torah, it is not correct to assume that law and Bible text were always separated. In *Mishnah Sotah* 5:1, for example, Akiva rules that the water of the *Sotah* (woman suspected of adultery) tests not only the woman but also her lover and, if guilty, makes her forbidden to her husband and her lover. He then states that the biblical proof of this is in the repetition of the words "enter" in Numbers 5:22 and 5:27 and "defiled herself" in 5:27 and 5:29. In the very first chapter of the entire Mishnah, the verse from Deuteronomy 6:7, "when you stay at home and when you are away, when you lie down and when you get up," is quoted by both the School of Hillel and the School of Shammai to prove their differing ideas concerning when and how one is to recite the *Shma*.[17] And there are many other such examples.

The real difference between Mishnah and Midrash is not the absence of biblical texts, but that in the Mishnah they are not required and the order of the laws is determined by topic, not biblical chronology.

To collect all the legal material, sift and sort it, and then organize it properly was Akiva's task. But Rabbi Akiva did not create the Mishnah by himself out of thin air. Brief collections of such laws had existed long before Akiva and were passed on orally from generation to generation. Certainly since the time of Hillel and Shammai, first century BCE, and probably even before, the Sages taught them to their students, who memorized them. The earliest Sages are recorded in chapter 1 of Avot: the men of the Great Assembly, Shimon the Just, Antigonus of Soko, Yose ben Yoezer, Yose ben Yohanan, Joshua ben Perahyah, Nittai the Arbeli, Judah ben Tabbai, Shimon ben Shetah, Shemiah, and Avtalyon—and finally the great legendary Hillel and Shammai, who each founded an entire school of scholars whose purpose was to develop and establish Jewish Law.

Although students sometimes made informal notes, the material had to be formulated verbally exactly as it was told to them and then learned by heart. This required that it be repeated over and over. Written notes by Sages and students recording their own teachers' words were not official and were unreliable;[18] they were never used in public teaching. Individuals gifted with excellent memories were given material and served as the reciters in the academy. They were chosen not for their intellect but for the ability to memorize and transmit traditions without making corrections or changes. They were known as Tannaim (sing. *tanna*), "reciters." "The *tanna* recites and he understands not what he says."[19] "Tannaim" was the name later used to describe all the early Sages until the time of Rabbi Judah the Prince, who prepared an official, authorized version of the Mishnah around 200 CE. Even then his work was not committed to writing but preserved only by oral transmission.[20]

Akiva was intent on creating a complete collection of all of them.

Different pupils had different traditions, and there was no one complete set of teachings accepted by all. These formulae were in need of revision, reorganization, and order, and Akiva took all the material and edited it, correcting it and giving it structure. He collected all the traditions that he could and then placed them in logical sequence that could be memorized and repeated as the basis for discussion or brought up for reference whenever needed. It is remarkable that he could do this at a time when putting these permanently in writing was not permitted. Of course he was able to consult the informal notes that his pupils and others had collected, and perhaps he even made notes himself, although that is by no means certain. The official text existed only in the head of the *tanna*, whose task it was to present the material on call. When he completed a section, Akiva taught it to a *tanna*, who then taught it to another *tanna*, and so on.[21]

Akiva's pupils continued his work after his death, and eventually it fell to Rabbi Judah the Prince to take the various versions that had been created by his time and make one final version of all the laws, which was officially recited and accepted by all. Material he did not include was remembered and preserved as outside teachings, much of which was collected in the Tosefta (addition), which was organized in sections parallel to those of the Mishnah.

Rabbi Judah's Mishnah was based on Akiva's work as transmitted by his pupil Rabbi Meir, but it was not identical to Akiva's, since Judah made the final decisions about what was included and what was not.[22] Unfortunately there is no way to know exactly what Akiva's Mishnah did or did not contain. That information existed only in the minds and memory of those who knew it and who have long since perished. In view of Akiva's interest in anchoring traditional laws to biblical texts, perhaps his Mishnah contained more biblical verses than are there now. The eventual completion, editing, and publication of the Mishnah by Rabbi Judah the Prince, some seventy years after Akiva's death, was the culmination of a process that Akiva had undertaken. With that, the period of the Mishnah and its teachers came to an end.

That mishnaic method—establishing laws that need not have explanations or justification—did not continue after the compilation of the Mishnah itself. On the contrary, the discussions in the academies following the completion of the Mishnah were an attempt to reconnect the Mishnah with the biblical sources of the law and explain them. They became a new collection known as the Gemara, and the Mishnah and Gemara together became the Talmud.

In the words of David Weiss Halivni, "Esteem does not correlate with adherence. Rabbinic literature esteems R. Akiba and his school far more than it does R. Ishmael and his school, yet the mode of learning it finally adopted is closer to the school of R. Ishmael than it is to the school of R. Akiba."[23] It may be true that the method advocated by Rabbi Ishmael, law anchored in the Bible and taught together with the scriptural text, prevailed in talmudic discussion, but it was the Mishnah, based on the work of the School of Akiva, that provided the foundation and the framework for these further discussions. It is impossible to even imagine the later stage of Rabbinic Judaism without the Mishnah. All further attempts at Jewish codification were based one way or another on the framework that it provided.

Both Akiva and Ishmael developed an extensive literature of Torah interpretation that has remained important and influential to this day, yet in the end, it was Akiva's approach and method that became the dominant teaching. According to the Mishnah, "when Akiva died the glory of the Torah died," a saying that is then expanded in the Talmud to read that when he died "the arms of the Torah ceased and the fountains of wisdom were stopped up."[24]

## CONNECTING ORAL TRADITIONS TO BIBLICAL VERSES

Even though the Mishnah, Akiva's supreme creation, does not connect most of its laws with biblical verses, the attempt to find a connection between oral laws and verses in the Torah text was another major part of Akiva's work and became one of his most important contributions to the foundation of Rabbinic Judaism.

As Rabbi Joshua said when hearing Akiva prove that a law that previously had been simply a traditional teaching was anchored in a biblical verse, "Who will remove the dust from your eyes, Rabban Yohanan ben Zakkai . . . your pupil, Rabbi Akiva, has found a text in the Torah proving it!"[25]

According to the *Sifra*, the tannaitic midrash to Leviticus, Akiva denied that there are two Torahs, a written Torah and an oral Torah, as many Sages, including Rabban Gamliel himself, had taught. "Agnitus, the [Roman] general, asked Rabban Gamliel, 'How many Torahs were given to Israel?' to which Rabban Gamliel replied, 'Two, one oral and one written.'"[26] When the word *torot* (the plural of *Torah*) in the verse "These are the laws, rules, and *torot* that the LORD instructed" (Lev. 26:46) was interpreted as meaning "Two Torahs were given to Israel, one written and one oral," Akiva demurred: "Did Israel have two Torahs? Did not Israel have many Torahs?" He then pointed to the many times Scripture uses the phrase "and this is the Torah of . . ." (*Torah* meaning "instruction"). Akiva then interpreted the end of the verse, "that the LORD gave between Himself and the Israelite people through Moses on Mount Sinai," by explaining, "Moses became the messenger between Israel and their Father in heaven. This teaches that the Torah, its laws, its fine points, and its explanations were given at Sinai by Moses."[27]

According to Akiva, all the laws, written or unwritten, were part of the same divine revelation. All "Torah" is one corpus. Akiva objected to the concept of a separate oral Torah because it implies that what is written and what is conveyed orally are two different things. He feared that oral traditions without a biblical basis would be dismissed as unauthentic, lacking a divine origin. He believed that while the Torah contains many different "instructions," *torot*, the written Torah and the oral traditions, "its fine points and explanations," were all given at the same time and are all part of God's covenant with Israel. They cannot be separated, and one part is not less holy than the other.

As Louis Finkelstein, the great scholar of Rabbinic Judaism and biographer of Akiva, wrote, "Rabbi Akiva had taught that virtually the whole of the Oral Tradition could be derived by proper exegesis of the Written Pentateuch. Hence there was no need for a separate Oral Tradition."[28] And as taught in *Avot*: Moses received Torah from God at Sinai and then passed it on to the elders.[29] This passage deliberately does not say "*the* Torah," but "Torah," in order to include both the written Torah and all other unwritten teachings. Both are equally divine in origin.

Whereas Rabbi Ishmael taught that "generalities were spoken at Sinai, details at the Tent of Meeting," Akiva insisted that both "were spoken at Sinai, repeated at the Tent of Meeting and again in the steppes of Moab."[30] While Akiva sought to find a source for the laws that were followed but not found in the written Torah, the Jerusalem Talmud says that Ishmael was quite ready to admit that there are times when the Torah says one thing, but the received unwritten law says another. He was not concerned about finding any justification for these laws in the written text. "In three matters the halakhah [received law] circumvents the Torah, and in one instance it circumvents midrash [Rabbinic rules of interpretation]." He then describes them; one example here will suffice: regarding a divorce Deuteronomy 24:1 states, "and he writes her a book [*sefer*] of divorcement," while the law says, "any type of detached document."[31]

Akiva felt it was his task to prove that all the Torah was one and that whatever was not written in the Torah was implicit in it. Thus anyone who claimed to accept the Torah and who did not acknowledge the divinity of the so-called oral traditions was rejecting the true teaching of God. This was also an important way for Akiva to differentiate Judaism from Christianity: he held that a religion that did not contain these oral traditions was not an authentic representative of the divine revelation.

## JUSTIFYING ORAL TRADITIONS

A collection of Akiva's teachings in which he justifies ancient oral traditions by making a connection to a biblical text is found in the

Mishnah. This occurred on a day that became so notorious that it is referred to simply as "*that* day." It was the day when Rabban Gamliel II was removed from his position as head of the academy and Rabbi Eleazar ben Azariah was appointed in his place. Gamliel's rule had been autocratic and at times cruel. His deposition encouraged many of the Sages to proclaim ideas important to them in the new, more open atmosphere that now prevailed.[32] On that day Rabbi Akiva conveyed three different rulings on widely different subjects.[33] In all of them he followed the same methodology, connecting an oral teaching with a written text. A fourth ruling, also following Akiva's methodology, is recorded in the name of Joshua ben Hyrkanus.[34]

A recent study of these widely dissimilar teachings has convincingly shown that they are grouped together because they all illustrate not only Akiva's powers of interpretation but also his basic concern: finding a scriptural basis for an oral law that was unquestioned but not proved to originate in Bible text.[35] It is in fact unusual that the Mishnah, which is based on the separation of law from Scripture, should contain these discussions at all. Perhaps this demonstrates that Akiva saw no contradiction in his concern to create a code of received law according to topics, the Mishnah, and his desire to prove that all these laws were rooted in the written Torah.

In each of these teachings Akiva asserted his method of basing all traditions, both legal (halakhah) and non-legal (aggadah) on biblical texts. Two of each kind are found in this collection in the Mishnah.

The first two deal with matters of law. Akiva used the grammatical form of a verb in Leviticus 11:33 to prove that one impure vessel makes another vessel impure. Although this had long been accepted as the law, it was based only on oral tradition, and there was fear that it would not be followed. Since the verse does not say *tamei*, "is unclean," but *yitma*, Akiva read it as *yitame*, "makes unclean." In this way he provided a scriptural basis for the law. Since the words in the Torah have no vowels, it was not unusual for the Sages to change the usual reading in order to derive their desired meaning from it.

Akiva next dealt with the problem that arose because two verses, Numbers 35:4 and 35:5, give different figures concerning the geographic limits of cities of refuge. He stated that they do not contradict one another but that each one refers to a different matter, one to open space for cattle, the other to the Sabbath limit. The Sabbath limit, the distance one was allowed to walk on the Sabbath, was two thousand cubits. This was accepted as the law, although never stated specifically in the Torah. Here Akiva grounded it in a particular verse in the Torah. Not every Sage was interested in finding such connections. We see this clearly in what follows, for a later Sage, Rabbi Eliezer ben Yose HaG'lili, simply stated that the two thousand cubits in the verse refers to the inclusion of fields and vineyards. He was not concerned to find a verse that would specify the Sabbath law as was Rabbi Akiva.[36]

The last two matters were aggadic, non-legal. Exodus 15:1 contains the word "saying," which seems superfluous: "Then Moses and the Israelites sang this song to the LORD. They said, saying. . . ." Akiva applied his general rule that whenever the word "saying" is found, it must be interpreted as teaching something specific; therefore this word teaches that when Moses sang his Song at the Sea, the Israelites repeated each verse after him, "as when reciting the *Hallel*."[37] However Rabbi Nehemiah then said, "They recited it as we recite the *Sh'ma*, not as we recite the *Hallel*." The contrast between Akiva and Nehemiah is not merely on how the Song at the Sea had been recited, but on the very use of the extra word in the verse to teach us something. Nehemiah did not refer to the verse at all and made no attempt to learn from it, whereas for Akiva each word was important and could teach us important matters.[38]

The fourth mishnah concerns the question of Job's motivation for serving God. Rabbi Joshua ben Hyrkanus asserted, on the basis of Job 13:15, "Though he slay me, yet will I trust in Him," and Job 27:5, "Until I die I will maintain my integrity," that it was not fear but love that motivated Job. Upon hearing this, Joshua again said, "Who will remove the dust from your eyes, Rabban Yohanan ben

Zakkai, for all your days you expounded that Job served God only from fear, as it is said, 'a blameless and upright man who fears God and shuns evil' (Job 1:8), and now Joshua, the pupil of your pupil [Akiva] has proved that he acted from love!"[39] Joshua's words to the long-deceased Ben Zakkai would be strange if Ben Zakkai had been pleased with the fact that Job served only from fear. It is understandable, however, if we assume that Ben Zakkai stated what he did simply because the verse in Job says that specifically and there is none that mentions his love of God. Ben Hyrkanus, however, following in the footsteps of Akiva, who connected love of God with the willingness to die for God, proved love of God from verses that state that Job remained faithful to God "though he slay me" and "until I die." Like Akiva, he found a way to connect his idea with the text of the Bible.

It is, of course, impossible to know if this compilation of teachings is an accurate reflection of what happened "on that day" or if it is a literary construct intended to demonstrate Akiva's methodology and its acceptance as the correct way to interpret laws and narratives, which is the implication of Joshua's laudatory comments. Certainly the fourth mishnah is different enough to make one assume that it was placed here mainly because it included the saying concerning Ben Zakkai that was so similar to that in the first mishnah.[40] These examples of Akiva's methods and the praise and approval given by his teacher Rabbi Joshua are further expressions of the high regard the other Sages had for Akiva's powers of midrashic interpretation and his ability to connect traditional law with biblical verses.

Akiva indeed preserved Torah—traditional teachings—when they were in danger of being forgotten in two ways: attaching oral traditions to the written text and creating the Mishnah, a comprehensive and logical arrangement of Jewish Law.

# *Six*

## AKIVA AND THE SONG OF SONGS

The theme of love—both loving God and loving humankind—plays a central role in Akiva's teaching. It is for this reason that the biblical book Song of Songs had a particular place of importance in his thinking. No other book, with the exception of the Torah itself, was as precious and holy to him.

Akiva's expression of his deep love of Song of Songs is found in the Mishnah as a part of a larger discussion concerning which scrolls are to be considered sacred and which are not.[1] It is recorded that "on that day," the day when Rabbi Eliezer ben Azariah replaced Rabban Gamliel as head of the academy (see chapter 5), one of the matters discussed and voted on was whether or not certain well-known books were to be considered part of *kitvei hakodesh*, Holy Scripture. Prior to that time, the end of the first century CE, only the contents of the first two sections of the Hebrew Bible, the Torah and the Prophets, had been formulated.[2]

The Mishnah states that two books were discussed, officially voted on, and accepted: Ecclesiastes (Kohelet) and Song of Songs. Until then, these books had been considered controversial. Ecclesiastes contains ideas about God and piety that appear to be in conflict with normative biblical views and frequently contains inherent contradictions as well,[3] while Song of Songs can easily be read as an erotic poem, and indeed was. The dispute concerning Ecclesiastes had already divided the Schools of Hillel and Shammai. Hillel considered it sacred and Shammai rejected it.[4] During that same period of time Ecclesiastes was found in the library of Scripture of Qumran, indicating that for some Jewish groups it was considered canonical. For the Sages, it was still a matter of debate.[5] The dispute about Ecclesiastes, according to Rabbi Shimon ben Menasya, was that while Song of Songs was written *b'ruah hakodesh*, "under the Holy Spirit"—that is, with divine inspiration—Ecclesiastes was written *b'hokhmato shel Shlomo*, solely through the wisdom of Solomon.[6] Human wisdom was not sufficient. Divine inspiration was required.

In the discussion in the Mishnah, Rabbi Yose rejected Ecclesiastes outright, but when he dared to suggest that there was a controversy concerning Song of Songs, Rabbi Akiva objected vehemently: "Heaven forbid! No one in Israel ever suggested that Song of Songs was not canonical. For the entire world is not as precious as the day upon which the Song of Songs was given to Israel, for all of the writings are holy and Song of Songs is the Holy of Holies! If there was a controversy, it was only concerning Ecclesiastes."[7]

One could not imagine a more extreme view than that concerning the nature of Song of Songs. Akiva's view that no one ever objected to Song of Sings was his own. The Mishnah itself indicates that there was a difference of opinion concerning both books but that "they debated and decided" that both were sacred Scripture, thus putting an end to the controversy forever.[8] With that decision the biblical canon was complete.[9] It is quite likely that one of the reasons for the official vote concerning the canonization of Scripture was the need to strengthen Judaism against claims made by Christians and others concerning the holiness of their books. In order to make an official statement about what was in and what was out of the Bible, such decisions were necessary.[10]

And so by the end of the first century CE the Hebrew canon was complete and Song of Songs was a part of it—not only a part, but according to Akiva "the Holy of Holies." His reason was simple:

Song of Songs was the ultimate expression of love between God and Israel, an expression that was found nowhere else in such explicit form.

The truth is that long before then the Song of Songs had already been interpreted by some Sages as an allegory depicting the relationship of God and Israel.[11] *Avot de-Rabbi Natan* (ARN) fancifully dated this interpretation back to biblical times, claiming that three books, Proverbs, Song of Songs, and Ecclesiastes, had been suppressed because they were thought to be mere human parables "until the men of Hezekiah [the pious eighth-century-BCE king of Judah] came and interpreted them."[12] This was based on an interpretation of Proverbs 25:1, "These too are proverbs of Solomon, which the men of King Hezekiah of Judah copied," as meaning not "copied" but "interpreted." In actual fact, we know that Rabban Yohanan ben Zakkai himself, soon after the destruction of the Temple in 70 CE, had interpreted verses of Song of Songs as referring to the people of Israel and not merely to some man and woman in love.[13] In a midrash ascribed to the School of Rabbi Ishmael, many of the Song of Songs verses are interpreted as describing either the giving of the Torah at Sinai or the crossing of the Sea at the time of the Exodus.[14] However it is also true that in non-scholarly circles many ordinary people looked upon that book as a collection of love songs. According to the Tosefta, a supplement to the Mishnah, Akiva himself lashed out at those who sang verses from Song of Songs at banquets and treated it as nothing more than a simple song: "They will have no portion in the world to come."[15]

Akiva's statement that it was the Holy of Holies served to confirm the transformation of the Song of Songs in Jewish tradition from a profane work into a divine love song in the strongest possible terms. More than this, Akiva believed that the Song of Songs not merely described the Sinai theophany but also "was given" on the same day that the Torah was given at Sinai, so that the status of its holiness was no less than that of the Torah itself. His use of the term "was given" is significant, in that elsewhere that expression is used in Jewish tradition only about the Torah itself. All other books of Scripture were considered simply written by human beings under divine inspiration.

The Babylonian Talmud ascribes books to various people: Samuel wrote Judges and Ruth, David wrote the Psalms, Jeremiah wrote Kings and Lamentations. Some books are said to have been edited by others: Hezekiah and his group "wrote" Isaiah, Proverbs, Song of Songs, and Ecclesiastes; and the Men of the Great Assembly, the proverbial group assembled by Ezra, "wrote" (meaning edited) Ezekiel, the Minor Prophets, Daniel, and Esther. A later midrash, *Song of Songs Rabbah*, edited in the Land of Israel sometime between the fifth and eighth centuries, specifies that Song of Songs, Proverbs, and Ecclesiastes were written by Solomon.[16] Akiva would have disputed that, since he considered Song of Songs to be divinely given at the same time as the Torah. And so Akiva contended that like the Torah, which was written not by Moses but by God and came directly from heaven, so the Song of Songs was uttered by God Himself at Sinai.[17] For Akiva, who steeped himself in mystical practices and speculation (see chapter 4), Song of Songs too was a mystical work, on a level with the study of the heavenly chariot and the secret speculation about Creation.[18]

Although other Sages were also convinced of the uniqueness of this biblical book, they did not think of it quite as Akiva did. As mentioned above, in the midrash *Song of Songs Rabbah* there are many Sages who make it clear that in their view the book was written by King Solomon. The Midrash takes the position that "wherever it states 'King Solomon' it means King Solomon, and wherever it states simply 'King' it means the Holy One Blessed be He," or that "'King Solomon' refers to the King to whom shalom [peace] belongs [i.e., God]. 'King' refers to the community of Israel."[19]

Akiva's "fixation on Song of Songs," as Judah Goldin, the great scholar of Rabbinic Midrash, put it, was particularly strong.[20] He did not create the interpretation of Song of Songs as the story of the relationship of God and Israel, but he carried it to new heights of importance. Akiva, the man who stressed that one of the most important teachings of Judaism was that one must love God with all of one's mind, heart, and very life (see chapter 7) was naturally drawn to the one book in Scripture that devoted itself to the depiction of the human relationship of love between man and woman and could be used to describe the relationship of Israel and God in those same terms.

## LOVE OF GOD AND HUMAN LOVE

As historian and scholar Gerson Cohen pointed out so eloquently, terms describing the relationship of God and Israel that relate to human love, marriage, fidelity and infidelity, adultery, and divorce are already found in the Torah itself and, later, in the Prophets.[21] The demand in the Ten Commandments for absolute fidelity to God and God alone is at the root of this concept, and "those who love Me" are mentioned there specifically (Exod. 20:6). Exodus 34:14–15 uses terminology of lusting and jealousy as descriptive of the relationship of God and Israel. Love of God is a major theme of the book of Deuteronomy, especially in the verses that became part of the doxology recited twice daily, "And you shall love the LORD your God with all your heart and with all your soul and with all your might" (Deut. 6:5). Hosea and Jeremiah extended these metaphors significantly; as Heschel wrote, Hosea "came to spell out the astonishing fact of God's love for man. God is not only the Lord who demands justice; He is also a God who is in love with His people."[22] Yet there was no single book devoted entirely to such love. The Song of Songs answered that need and fulfilled that purpose.

Since the love of God was the inspiration behind much of Akiva's thinking and actions, it was only natural that the Song of Songs, the supreme song of love, should have meant so much to him. The two motivating factors that lead humankind to serve God—love and fear (the latter sometimes interpreted as reverence or awe)—have always been at the core of Israelite religion. It may be argued that both are needed. As *Sifre Deuteronomy* remarks in a section that is ascribed to the School of Ishmael, "Only in regard to God do we find love combined with fear and fear combined with love."[23] But that very same section makes it clear that although there may be times when fear is needed in order to move one to obey God's demands, love is a far stronger motivation: "He who performs out of love receives a doubled and redoubled reward."

All the Sages quoted there in *Sifre Deuteronomy* agree that the phrase in Deuteronomy about the love for God "with all your soul" means "with your very life"—or "until the last drop of life is wrung out of you." In the Talmud, Rabbi Akiva interprets "your soul" as "even if He takes your soul."[24] His disciple Rabbi Meir similarly taught that "with all your soul" refers to Isaac, "who bound himself on the altar."[25] Rabbi Akiva explained that the term for "with all your might" (*b'khol me'odekha*) is related to the word *middah*, "measure": one must love God "with whatever measure God metes out to you, whether for good or punishment."[26] This is a frequent theme in Akiva's teachings, and he described how many biblical heroes, most notably Job, accepted both the good and the bad from God, blessing God no matter what.[27]

The various stories of Akiva's final moments all describe him as referring to these verses from Deuteronomy: "I always wondered if when the time came, I would be able to fulfill the verse 'with all your soul.'"[28] The concept of love of God requiring one to be willing to die for the sake of God may not have originated with Akiva, but it was he who stressed it. Late in his life, at a time when Jews were being persecuted by the Romans for observing religious commandments, Akiva interpreted a passage in the Song of Songs to mean that Jews must be willing to die for the love of God. He took the verse "Therefore do maidens [*alamot*] love you" (Song 1:3) and read the word *alamot* as *ad mavet*, "unto death": "Therefore they love you unto death"—being willing to die for God.[29] When Rabbi Nathan came to Babylonia from Israel at the time of the Hadrianic persecutions, he interpreted "Those who love Me and keep My commandments" (Exod. 20:6) as "These are the Israelites who dwell in the Land of Israel and give up their lives for the commandments."[30]

It may seem strange that Akiva, the well-known comforter and optimist, should have put such stress on sacrifice and suffering, but acceptance of whatever God chooses to mete out to you implies that suffering too comes from God, and whatever the reason, as with Job, it must be accepted with love. That is the dark side of love, in contrast to the Song of Songs, which expresses the great joy that the love of God can bring.

Commentators like Judah Goldin have suggested that the love of God is built on the experience of human love. He wrote, "The notion of loving God could not have arisen if there had not been an experience of human love, and the experience of human love (in other words, a very strong emotional force) can point the way to an understanding of a preoccupation with a love which no longer has in mind what we call sexual love: and it is still love!"[31] It is therefore not accidental that of all the Sages, it was Akiva whose marriage was described as one built on romantic love. Although, as we have read in chapter 2, the story of his marriage has been greatly expanded by legend, the fact remains that there is no other Sage about whom such a romantic love story has been told. Whatever the exact facts may be, and they are hard to come by, the sources depict his relationship with his wife quite the opposite of an arranged marriage. His feeling for her must have been one of great love and gratitude, as shown by the way he publicly acknowledged his debt to her and by the gift of a precious diadem, a Jerusalem of Gold, and is more likely to be based on fact than fantasy

Akiva's concept of marital love was clear: "A man and a woman [*ish, ishah*], when they are worthy, the Presence of God dwells between them. If not, fire consumes them"[32]—playing on the fact that in those two words, *ish* contains a *yud* and *ishah* a *heh*, which together form the name of God, while without those two letters all that remains in both words is *eish* (fire).

It is Goldin who has suggested that Akiva's experience of human love influenced his legal decisions concerning women and marriage.[33] According to Akiva, "One who marries a woman who is unfit for him transgresses five negative commandments: *You shall not take vengeance* (Lev. 19:18), *nor bear a grudge* (Lev. 19:18), *You shall not hate your kinsman in your heart* (Lev. 19:17), *Love your fellow as yourself* (Lev. 19:18), *Let your brother live with you* (Lev. 25:36). If he hates her, he desires her death and neglects the commandment to be fruitful and multiply."[34] Note that Akiva ignores the masculine here, reinterpreting them as gender neutral in order to stress the seriousness of taking an unloved wife. He will hate her, want to mistreat her, ignore the command to love her, and even wish that she would no longer be alive.

According to both *Sifre Deuteronomy* and the Mishnah, Akiva ruled that one may divorce his wife "even if he finds another woman more comely than she is." He bases this on the fact that the verses concerning divorce begin with "if she does not find favor in his eyes" (Deut. 24:1).[35] On this matter Akiva's view is even more lenient than that of the School of Hillel regarding divorce. Goldin's explanation for the ease with which Akiva would permit a man to divorce his wife is that "in a marriage, . . . the relationship must be based on love."[36] This also explains Akiva's bold stand overruling the ancient accepted law that a woman may do nothing to make herself attractive when she is having her period and forbidden then to have relations with her husband. Said Akiva, "If so, you make her repulsive to her husband, with the result that he will divorce her!"[37]

If Goldin is correct, this could also explain the difference between Ishmael and Akiva regarding the law of *Sotah*, the bitter waters a woman must drink if her husband suspects her of adultery when there is no actual proof. Whereas Ishmael said that the Torah only grants the husband permission to demand this, Akiva said that it requires him to do so.[38] If marriage must be based on love, any suspicion in the mind of the husband will only corrupt and ultimately ruin that marriage. Therefore the suspicion *must* be tested and, if unfounded, be uprooted. The fact that this ordeal, like the ease of divorce, may be unfair and devastating to the wife seems not to be a consideration. It should not be forgotten that at that time, for all the care and consideration that was given by the Sages to the rights of women in marriage, marriage and divorce were still matters that were male centered and where the initiative in both came from the man.

Talmud scholar Judith Hauptman has pointed out that in matters concerning a woman's impurity, Akiva consciously took a lenient position.[39] An incident is related in the Mishnah in which a woman came to him because she had seen a spot of blood and assumed that she was therefore prohibited to the husband. Akiva suggested to her the possibility that it was not menstrual blood but came from a bruise that, although healed, had opened up again. When she agreed that that might be so, he declared her clean. His students seemed astounded at this ruling, and he said to them, "Why is this matter difficult for you to understand? The Sages did not say these things to be stringent but to be lenient, as it says, 'And a woman from whom blood flows forth' (Lev. 15:19)—this means a flow of blood and not a bloodstain.'"[40]

Akiva deliberately found a word in the verse that sustained his ruling and could exclude many occurrences of blood from the definition of what is prohibited. What was his purpose in doing so? Was it to keep the days of a woman's impurity to the minimum possible? If so, was that to broaden the times of sexual activity, which would make the marriage strong? Was it for the benefit of the woman, or was it for the increased pleasure of the man?

Akiva had a similar ruling regarding immersion for male emissions known as *zavim*. These rules were based on verses in Leviticus 15 that make a distinction between semen that was discharged and pus or other discharges from the male organ. The rules for discharges that were signs of infection or illness were much stricter than those for semen, requiring a seven-day period of cleanliness, immersion, and a sacrifice. In Akiva's time these rules were no longer practiced because of the absence of the Temple. Akiva's ruling was that if the discharge came following any eating or drinking, it was not to be considered impure, making it unlikely that any emission would ever be considered polluting. His pupils protested that the result would be that there would be no more instances of the category of *zavim* (emissions). His reply was, "You are not responsible for declaring males to be unclean."

Akiva's motivation was unclear and is never stated, but what he did relieved men of what could have been many difficult periods of ritual impurity. Since the text of the Torah does not specify how the distinction is to be made or what causes it, Akiva allowed himself the leniency of assuming that if there was anything at all that could have caused a natural emission, that should be the assumption.[41]

In the case where a woman and a man who is a *kohen* (priest) are engaged and a year has passed and they have not yet married, the groom is required to care for her needs. She may eat from his food. The Mishnah states that Rabbi Tarfon, Akiva's companion, ruled that he may give her food entirely from the *terumah*, food that is set aside for priests, while Akiva said, "Half from *terumah* and half from non-sacred food."[42] The reason was that during her period, she could not eat from *terumah* and would therefore have nothing. In this case Akiva clearly seemed more concerned with the woman's welfare than was Tarfon.

Another mishnah describes a case brought before Akiva of a man who had made a vow that required him to divorce his wife and give her the money from her *ketubah* (wedding contract). The amount was four hundred *dinar*. The man complained that he had inherited only eight hundred *dinar* from his father, of which four hundred went to his brother. If he had to give four hundred to his wife, he would be left with nothing! Would not two hundred suffice? "You must give her the entire amount of her *ketubah* even if you have to sell your hair!" was Akiva's reply.[43] This last remark was particularly pointed because it was usually women who when impoverished sold their hair, as Akiva's wife was reported to have done.

On the other hand, Akiva's view that love must be the basis of the relationship between men and women did not mean that he was always concerned with giving women greater rights or status within Judaism. There were many instances when, on the contrary, Ishmael took a more positive position toward women than did Akiva.[44] For example, concerning the burning of the Red Heifer, the Torah reads, "A man who is clean shall gather up the ashes of the cow" (Num. 19:9). Since it says "who is clean," Ishmael ruled that anyone who is clean—"including women"—may do so. Akiva ruled that since it specifies "a man," women are excluded.[45] In midrashim attributed to the School of Akiva the tendency is to exclude women, while in those of the School of Ishmael they are frequently included.[46]

In some of these instances the biblical text is itself quite explicit in its exclusion, but in others there could be room for interpretation. Akiva's son, Rabbi Yose ben Akiva, for example, said that the verse "And you shall teach them to your children" (Deut. 11:19), in which "your children" is in the masculine, means "Your sons, not your daughters," which would then exclude women from being educated.[47] Did this reflect his father's view? Concerning the wearing of fringes, in *Sifre Numbers* "Speak to the sons of [*b'nai*] Israel . . . and they shall make for themselves fringes" (Num. 15:38) is interpreted as meaning that women *are* included—understanding *b'nai* to mean "children" rather than specifically "sons." Akiva's staunch disciple, Shimon bar Yohai, however, said, "Women are exempt from fringes because it is a time-bound commandment."[48] Regarding the question of the testimony of witnesses needed to permit a woman to be married, Akiva's opinion was that the testimony of a woman, a male or a female slave, or relatives was not acceptable.[49] It was of Ishmael, not of Akiva, that it was said that when he (Ishmael) died the women wept for him and he was eulogized with the words, based on 2 Samuel 1:24, "O daughters of Israel, weep for Rabbi Ishmael!"[50] (See also the discussion in chapter 4.)

Love was at the very core of Akiva's religious values: the love of human beings for God, God's love of humanity, and the love of men and women for each other. Akiva may not have learned that from the Song of Songs, but it was that belief that resulted in his exaltation of this book above all other books. It is largely a result of Akiva's teachings and of his emphasis that the Song of Songs describes the relationship between Israel and God that Rabbinic Judaism places an overwhelmingly strong emphasis on love in its description of our relationship with God, on God's love for Israel and for all humanity, exalting God's mercy over God's justice. And at the center of all his teachings is that we must love one another. It was after all Akiva who taught that the verse "Love your fellow as yourself" (Lev. 19:18) is "a fundamental principle of the Torah."[51]

# Seven

## ASPECTS OF AKIVA'S THEOLOGY

The Sages of Israel did not write systematic theology, and Akiva was no exception. But that does not mean that they had no personal beliefs about God, humanity, and the world. As Max Kadushin, eminent scholar of Rabbinic thinking, showed, they based themselves on value concepts that underlie their sayings, stories, interpretations, and legal opinions rather than on systematic theology.[1] The verbal expressions of their beliefs and concepts are articulated in their sayings, pronouncements, and midrashic parables and interpretations scattered throughout the various collections of Rabbinic writings. They give us at least a glimpse into the matters that concerned them, even if they do not enable us to construct a complete theology. Of course their reliability is also dependent on the problematic nature of Rabbinic sources that we have mentioned previously.

Some important aspects of Akiva's theological concepts, such as his ideas concerning the divine origin of the Torah and of biblical book Song of Songs, have already been discussed and can be found in previous chapters of this book. These were truly revolutionary concepts for their time, placing the Torah on a new level of holiness and allowing for greater flexibility of interpretation, adaptation, and change in religious practice than ever before. Song of Songs was also elevated in its sacredness when Akiva interpreted its depiction of human love into a metaphor of the relation of God and Israel. We shall now address other aspects in greater detail.

## AKIVA'S CREED IN *AVOT*

The one tractate of the Mishnah in which theological maxims of the Sages are collected is *Avot* (also known as *Pirke Avot, Ethics of the Fathers*). This collection of brief but sometimes veiled sayings is supplemented by *Avot de-Rabbi Natan* (ARN), which comments on some of these phrases and adds others from the same tannaitic period. Akiva is quoted in *Avot* extensively in a series of connected sayings that express his core beliefs. As noted earlier, there is always the caveat that we can never be completely certain that the attributions to Akiva are accurate, especially since some of the same or similar adages are found in ARN and other works in the names of other Sages.[2] Nevertheless in view of the fact that the Mishnah was carefully constructed and published by Rabbi Judah the Prince from the collection of Rabbinic teachings collated by Akiva and passed on by his students, it is not unreasonable to assume that the attributions there are accurate.

The central saying of Akiva in *Avot* is characterized by its three-fold structure, a form common in this work. The first part concerns the great love shown to humans by God: "Beloved is man, for he was created in the Image; greater still was the love in that it was made known to him that he was created in the Image of God, as it is written, 'For in His image did God make man' (Gen. 9:6)."

The second part proclaims that "beloved is Israel" and describes the great love shown by God to Israel in that "they are called God's children" and that this was made known to them in the verse "You are children of the LORD your God" (Deut. 14:1).

The third part teaches that this love for Israel was also demonstrated by the fact that "they [Israel] were given the precious instrument with which the world was created," the Torah, and that this was made known to them in the verse "For I have given you good instruction, My Torah—do not forsake it!" (Prov. 4:2).[3]

In presenting his sayings in such a manner, Akiva made very clear his basic beliefs concerning the relationship of God to all humanity and to the people Israel in particular, as well as his concept of the unparalleled value of the Torah, all of which is based on love. In these three doctrinaire statements Akiva, who had stressed the importance of love in many different ways, including his interpretation of Song of Songs as the love song of God and Israel (see chapter 6), affirmed God's love of all humankind, the sacredness of human life, and the special relationship that God has to Israel. He again stressed the unique importance of the Torah, which is not simply a scroll, but the preexisting instrument with which the entire world was created.[4] These themes are to be found throughout Akiva's teachings and legal decisions.

## THE CENTRALITY OF LOVE

Love played a major role in Akiva's thought. He stressed not only the love of God and God's love of human beings and of Israel, as in this statement in *Avot*, but also the love of one human being for another. It was Akiva who crowned the verse "Love your fellow as yourself; I am the LORD" (Lev. 19:18) as "a fundamental principle of the Torah." His younger colleague Ben Azzai demurred and suggested that Genesis 5:1, "This is the record of Adam's line.—When God created man, He made him in the likeness of God," was an even greater fundamental principle.[5]

What was the basis of their disagreement? It is often claimed that by stressing that humans are made in the divine image, Ben Azzai was including everyone, whereas "your fellow" could be interpreted as meaning only Israelites. It has also been pointed out that "as yourself" could mean that if you do not respect or love yourself, you would not have to love anyone else. As Ben Azzai said, "That one should not say, 'Since I have been disgraced, let others be disgraced.'"[6] But there may be more to it than that. After all, Akiva himself had taught that humans are precious because they were created in God's likeness,[7] as discussed above, yet here he deliberately chose to give more importance to the verse from Leviticus, designating it a "fundamental principle." Perhaps he preferred this verse over Genesis 5:1 because it emphasizes love by specifically using that word. It does not merely teach the importance of all human beings but tells us how we should act toward one another. And so it is a much more powerful teaching and has proved to be so through the ages.

It is doubtful if either Akiva or those who taught his words thought of "fellow" here as referring to anything other than all human beings.[8] After all, Akiva was following in the footsteps of Hillel the Elder, who generations before had taught that all of the Torah could be summarized in the words "What is hateful to you, do not do to your fellow," an Aramaic interpretation of the verse "Love your fellow."[9] For Akiva too that verse was a summation of the entire Torah. Hillel had further emphasized the importance of love in his statement also in *Avot* calling for the Sages to follow the way of Aaron, which was "Love peace and pursue it, love all humans and bring them to the Torah," again stressing the importance of love.[10] The teachings of Hillel seem to have had a major impact on Akiva.[11]

Paradoxically, according to Akiva the major underlying principle of the Torah, a book written in heaven by God in language that is different from human language,[12] is our relationship not to God but with humans: "Love your fellow as yourself" (Lev. 19:18).[13]

### LOVE OF HUMANITY

The Hebrew text of the first part of Akiva's saying in *Avot* uses the word *haviv* to denote "beloved" or "precious," a cognate of the more common *ahuv*. It is found in the Bible, for example in Deuteronomy 33:3, where God is called *hovev amim* (Lover of the people), and is commonly used in Rabbinic writings to indicate being held in great closeness and high esteem. As a prooftext, Akiva cited, "For in His image did God make man" (Gen. 9:6), the same verse Akiva used to teach that shedding human blood is a diminution of the divine image.[14] Furthermore, as the scholar of comparative religions David Flusser put it, "It appears Rabbi Akiva understands Genesis 9:6 as though it means 'Shedding the blood of man is akin to shedding the blood of God, for in His own image God made humankind.'"[15] On this matter Akiva made no distinction between Jews and others.

Because humans are all created in the image of the Divine, the taking of any human life is, in Akiva's view, a most serious matter, to the extent that if he had his way, no one would ever have been condemned to death by the Sanhedrin. As careful as judges may be, there is always the chance of an error or of false witnesses, in which case a human life—so sacred—would have been taken and the image of God diminished. While other Sages spoke negatively of a Sanhedrin that rules to execute one person in seven years or even in seventy years, Akiva and his fellow Sage Tarfon said, "Had we been in the Sanhedrin, no one would ever have been executed."[16] By their careful examination of the witnesses and their strict applications of the various laws, they would have made it impossible to convict anyone of a capital offense. Considering the frequency in which the death penalty is invoked in the Torah and in Rabbinic law, this was a bold statement and demonstrated the intensity of Akiva's (and Tarfon's) belief in the sanctity of human life. Rabban Shimon ben Gamliel II opposed Akiva's view, asserting that it would only encourage murderers.[17] To this day the arguments concerning capital punishment have been framed in these terms.

This teaching was proclaimed at a time when no Jewish court such as the Sanhedrin actually had the power to impose a death penalty, not only because of Roman rule but also because the Sages themselves ruled, "The death penalty may be imposed by the Great Court which is in Jerusalem, but not by the court at Yavneh."[18] This did not prevent the Sages, both Akiva's generation and the later Amoraim, from discussing the death penalty in great detail in the Mishnah and the Talmud. It may have been theoretical at the time, but should independence return, as they all hoped, it would become actuality. They took the matter seriously, and therefore we should look upon their rulings and teachings in a serious manner. Akiva was not just voicing some pious wish. His abhorrence of the death penalty was emphasized by his ruling that if and when the Sanhedrin executed someone, all its members would be required to fast the entire day.[19]

False witnesses who could lead to an execution were obviously an abomination. Akiva believed that the seemingly superfluous words "three witnesses" in the phrase "two witnesses or three witnesses" (Deut. 17:6), delineating how many witnesses were needed in order to execute someone, indicated that even though the third false witness's testimony was irrelevant, since two would be sufficient to convict, the third one would be punished as severely as the first two.[20] Human beings were beloved of God, created in God's image. The taking of a life was the most serious matter possible and was to be avoided at all costs. It was Akiva who stated that in a situation in which two people are wandering in the desert and one had enough water to enable him to survive, the owner should drink it and live. Another Sage, Ben Patura, advised that they should share it even though they would both die.[21] Although Akiva based his ruling on an interpretation of the verse "Let your brother live with you" (Lev. 25:36)—"with you" implying that "your life comes first"—perhaps here too Akiva was influenced by the fact that he saw human life as sacred, so that sacrificing two lives when one could be saved was wrong.

Akiva's favorable attitude toward all human beings is further reflected in the saying attributed to him in the Tosefta that if one finds favor in the sight of human beings, one finds favor in the sight of God, but if one does not find favor in the sight of humans, then God is not delighted with that person either.[22] This idea is repeated in Akiva's interpretation of the requirement to observe all the commandments, "for you will be doing what is good and right in the sight of the LORD your God" (Deut. 12:28). Akiva, as usual, found a different meaning for each word: "that which is good" in the sight of heaven "and right" in the sight of human beings. Ishmael said that both words refer to the sight of heaven, which is a more literal understanding of the verse. For Akiva, however, the good opinion of humankind's judgment was important as well, not to be disdained, and he quoted Proverbs 3:4 to prove it, "And you will find favor and approbation in the eyes of God and man."[23]

## THE LEGAL STATUS OF THE NON-JEW

Although Akiva stressed the special relationship of God and Israel, he also insisted on proper treatment of non-Jews. He taught that "the robbery of a heathen is forbidden" and gave as prooftext Leviticus 25:47–55, which states that if an Israelite in dire straits sold himself to a non-Jew as an indentured servant, he must be redeemed with money and cannot simply up and leave his service, since that would cheat the non-Jew out of his money. "He shall have the right of redemption even after he has given himself over. One of his kinsmen shall redeem him . . . . He shall compute with his purchaser the total from the year he gave himself over until the jubilee year. . . . He shall pay back for his redemption in proportion to his purchase price." This indicates clearly that the non-Jewish purchaser must be appropriately compensated [24]

Akiva went even further and taught that stealing from a non-Jew or defrauding him was worse than stealing from a Jew because it also desecrated the Name of God—*hillul ha-Shem*, causing non-Jews to have a negative opinion concerning Israel's God and Israel's Torah. Rabbi Ishmael advised that when judging a case between a Jew and a non-Jew, if one can justify the Jew by Jewish Law, one should do so, and on the contrary, if one can justify the Jew by using the laws of the heathens, one should do that, but if neither one can justify the Jew, one should use subterfuges to do so. Akiva ruled that it is forbidden to use such subterfuges, since they cause desecration of God. According to Akiva, defrauding a non-Jew was forbidden by Jewish Law.[25]

Akiva's insistence on treating the non-Jew fairly, however, did not extend to tolerance of paganism. Akiva had no illusions about such practices, the common religion of non-Jews at that time, which he scorned. In a discussion of Deuteronomy 12:31, "for they perform for their gods every abhorrent act," Akiva added, "I myself saw a heathen who tied up his father and left him before his dog, whereupon the animal devoured him,"[26] a gross exaggeration of known practices in the Roman world. Just as Akiva was dedicated to the exclusive existence and worship of the One God, so too was he concerned to see the eradication of the worship of idols. Paganism was still the dominant religion of the Roman Empire. Thus in his interpretation of the laws requiring the destruction of trees, pillars, and images found in Deuteronomy 12:1–3, Akiva's position was that "You shall surely destroy" (12:2), with the Hebrew root "destroy" repeated, means both to cut these down and to uproot them. The additional phrase "obliterating their name from that site" (12:3) means "you must change their name as well."[27] Similarly Akiva explained that the abhorrent act Sarah saw Ishmael doing when, as the verse states, he was "playing" (Gen. 21:9) and which resulted in Ishmael being sent away, was that he was worshiping idols.[28]

Akiva was not willing to admit that pagan religious leaders could perform wonders of any sort. There is a description in Deuteronomy 13:2–3 of the situation in which signs and wonders predicted by a "prophet among you" who tells you to worship another god actually come true. Yose HaG'lili taught that this refers to a pagan prophet, indicating that "Scripture permits heathens to have power over the sun and moon, stars and planets." Akiva protested. It cannot refer to pagans, but to prophets of Israel. "Heaven forbid . . . Scripture speaks here only of true prophets who lapsed and became false prophets."[29] Akiva also counseled Jews not to live among non-Jews "so that you will not come to worship idols."[30] Paganism had its attractions, and it was best to avoid temptation.

## GOD'S LOVE OF ISRAEL

As discussed in chapter 6, Akiva interpreted the lovers in the biblical book Song of Songs as God and the people of Israel. But in the second part of his teaching in *Avot* he saw the relationship of God to Israel as that of a parent to a child. Here he used another symbol: God as the loving parent, Israel as the beloved child. Akiva has been credited with coining the phrase *Avinu Malkeinu* (our Father, our Sovereign) when praying for rain.[31] As a parent feels a unique closeness to a child, so God's relationship to Israel is also unique. While Akiva held high the value of all human life, he was nevertheless Israel centered, seeing a special place in God's plan for the people Israel, God's beloved firstborn child. For that reason, Akiva believed that although they were now suffering under foreign rule, there was a great future in store for Israel and that the glory of Jerusalem and the Temple would be restored.

Akiva had faith in the imminent restoration of the Temple and saw in the desolate ruins of the Temple a reason to believe that it would be rebuilt in his own day. When others saw in the Temple ruins a reason for mourning, he saw them as a sign of imminent rebuilding.[32] In the dispute with Rabbi Tarfon concerning the correct liturgy for the Passover seder, it was Akiva who insisted that the blessing before the meal itself include a lengthy prayer for the restoration of the Temple in his own time: "So too, Lord our God, bring us to other festivals and seasons in peace, rejoicing in the restoration of Your city and joyful in Your service."[33] It is not a hope or dream for the future. We will rejoice, be redeemed, and bring thanks in the restored Temple.

Akiva trusted that Israel, God's beloved son, now suffering under foreign rule, deprived of self-government and independence, had a great future in store and that the glory of Jerusalem and the Temple would be restored. Akiva was probably referring to this when he said, "Even as the day is now overcast and now bright again, so shall darkness be made bright."[34] No wonder then that when a leader came along who seemed capable of restoring national glory, Akiva was willing to consider him to be the Messiah, a most unfortunate lapse of judgment. His hope proved to be a dream for the far-off future and not for the immediate present.

Akiva considered the Land of Israel as God's special land and gift to God's treasured people. Concerning the Land he taught, "Do not quit the Holy Land, lest you worship idols . . . he who leaves the Land of Israel and goes to another land is accounted by Scripture as if he worshiped idols."[35] Akiva considered being buried anywhere in the Holy Land "is as though he is buried under the altar."[36] When his disciple Shimon bar Yohai said that God found no nation worthy of the Torah other than Israel and no land worthy of Israel other than the Land of Israel,[37] he was no doubt following the teachings of his mentor.

### HUMAN LIFE AND GOD'S JUDGMENT

Akiva's threefold creed in *Avot* is followed by his general concept of human life, free will, and God's judgment. "Everything is seen [*tzafui*] and permission is given. The world is judged favorably, and all is according to the preponderance of deeds."[38]

The word *tzafui* is frequently translated as "foreseen" or "anticipated," in which case this saying would be concerned with the question of God's knowledge of the future, implying that everything we do is determined in advance. However that need not be the case, since *tzafui* can simply mean "seen" or "viewed." If so, Akiva was indicating that all of our deeds are seen by God, that God is aware of all we do. Nevertheless God does not interfere but gives us permission to act however we will, thus affirming the doctrine of free will. And so then we are responsible for our deeds and should be judged accordingly.

However, when judging the world, God, being merciful, does so favorably and not strictly. Even if there are more sins than virtues, God looks to the good. The last phrase, "all is according to the preponderance of deeds," would seem to contradict the idea of being judged favorably and would appear to mean that whichever is preponderant, virtue or sin, determines the judgment. *Mahzor Vitri*, a medieval text, has a different reading: "all is *not* according to the preponderance of deeds"; in other words, even if there are more sins than good actions, God uses mercy and does not destroy the world. This would accord well with another of Akiva's teachings, "In this world if there are 999 angels that testify to a person's guilt and only one who declares him innocent, the Holy One will rule according to his merit!"[39] Here again we see Akiva's tendency to bring comfort and to encourage people rather than to castigate them and emphasize their failings—"The world is judged favorably."

When it came to human courts, however, Akiva was insistent that judgments be given according to what the law requires, and in opposition to Tarfon, who favored the weak in certain cases, Akiva maintained that in a lawsuit the court should award the monetary settlement not to the person most in need but to the one who by law should have it. His general principle was "there is no place for mercy when determining the law."[40] Charity is one thing, justice another.

Concerning God's judgment of human beings, Akiva believed in the efficacy of atonement and was opposed to ideas, such as those taught by Christianity, that man was sinful by nature and could not be cleansed except through the sacrificial death of Jesus. In the following teaching Akiva played upon the Hebrew root *k-v-h*, which can mean either *tikvah* (hope) or *mikveh* (a ritual bath): "Happy are you, O Israel! Before whom are you purified and who purifies you? Your Father in heaven, as it is said, 'I will sprinkle clean water upon you and you shall be clean' (Ezek. 36:25), and it says, 'The LORD is Israel's *mikveih*' (Jer. 17:13). Just as the *mikveh* [ritual bath] cleanses the impure, so the Holy One cleanses Israel."[41] Jeremiah may have meant "hope," but Akiva reads it as "a ritual bath." The Holy One—and no one else—is the bath that cleanses us of sin. There is no doubt that Akiva chose these two verses because they specify that it is God—our Father—and God alone who purifies and cleanses sin. His message is twofold: forgiveness is possible, and it is attained through the Lord alone. There is no other way and no need for any other.

In *Avot* Akiva continued the theme of God's judgment with a parable introduced with the following saying: "Everything is given on loan against a pledge, and a net is spread out over all living."[42] The idea of a net is also found in the famous parable of the fox and the fish ascribed to Akiva.[43] There the net represents danger to the fish that may be caught in it, a usage found in Habakkuk 1:15, "He has fished them all up with a line, pulled them up in his trawl, and gathered them in his net." Its use here is unclear, but it may indicate that all will in the end be required to account for whatever they have done.[44]

The parable follows:

> The store is open and the storekeeper gives everything on credit.
> The ledger is open and the hand records.
> Everyone who wishes to borrow may do so.
> The collectors make the rounds daily and collect from the individual, with or without one's consent, and they have accurate accountings.
> The verdict is just, and all is ready for the feast.[45]

The parable itself is easy to understand. The idea of an open book in which everything is written is a familiar image reminiscent of the High Holy Days, when the books of life and death are open in which all our deeds are written and we are judged accordingly. Here it becomes the store's account ledger that represents human life. Nothing in this world really belongs to us, though we have permission to use it. Everything is merely on loan, and we are called to account for whatever we use and whatever we do. The accounting, the verdict, is just. If earlier Akiva indicated that God judges the world favorably, here, in the life of the individual, he stresses that justice is always done. This does not exclude the possibility of mercy, but it does preclude an individual from charging that his/her fate was unjust and undeserved. As Akiva taught elsewhere, fools and the wicked say, "There is no justice and no judge," but in truth there is justice and there is a Judge.[46] As we shall see later, Akiva believed in the doctrine of *tziduk ha-din* (the justification of God's judgment), that whatever happens, God's justice cannot be questioned. The feast may represent the reward that awaits the righteous in the world to come. Placing it at the end of the parable enabled Akiva to once again emphasize hope rather than punishment.

God's love and mercy as well as God's concern that we act lovingly toward others can also be seen in Akiva's interpretation of the phrase *nakeh lo y'nakeh* (literally "He will remit, He will not remit") in Exodus 34:7, one of the attributes of God. In Hebrew parlance the meaning of this double phrase is simply "He will not completely remit [one of sin]." Akiva, however, took each part as a separate phrase and said, "He *will* remit" sins between humans and God, but "He will *not* remit" sins between one human being and another.[47] God can forgive sins against God, but not sins against other human beings. This interpretation eventually found its way into the liturgy. Whenever Exodus 34:6–7 is quoted as the "thirteen attributes of God," stressing God's love and mercy, verse 7 is always cut off after the word *nakeh* so that the verse is made to mean "He *will* remit sins," the exact opposite of the true intention.

These major statements of Akiva indicate that he believed in a world in which all human life is of supreme value and in which Israel has been selected to be especially close to God, something that is seen in the fact that the Torah, God's supreme and unique creation, has been given into Israel's charge. Human beings have free will and are accountable for all that they do. They are judged in accordance with their deeds, but the world is judged in a favorable way because God is a God of mercy who has special love and affection for human beings created in God's image. In *ARN-A* Akiva stated, "Which is the greater measure, the measure of reward or the measure of punishment? Surely the measure of reward!" There is no doubt, however, that punishment awaits those who transgress. And there is even punishment for one "who attaches himself to transgressors [in other words, becomes part of such a group, spending time with them], although he does not do as they do," but there is also reward for one "who attaches himself to those who carry out the commandments, although he does not do as they do."[48]

## THE NATURE OF JUDAISM

Since he never openly referred to it, it is impossible to know if Akiva was aware that there were Christians who asserted that Judaism is a harsh religion and its God a God of wrath, in contrast with Christianity, which is presented as a religion of love. In Akiva's own time, the second century, some, such as Marcion, an influential leader of an important movement in Christianity, carried this to an extreme, even positing two gods, the Jewish God of wrath and the Christian God of love and mercy. Although this teaching was declared heretical, the contrast that it fostered remained in general Christian thinking and became a part of the stereotypical way in which much of the Western world thinks of Judaism even to this day. It is the Jew—represented by Shylock—who demands his pound of flesh. It is the "Old Testament" God who is the God of fire and brimstone. It was all too easy to forget that when Jesus, in the Christian Bible, teaches the importance of loving one's fellow human being, he is only quoting Leviticus 19:18 and not presenting some new doctrine. Was Akiva knowingly attempting to show that this Christian view was false? His teachings certainly can be seen as a refutation of that claim, or at least as an affirmation that Judaism is not a harsh religion and the Jewish God is not a cruel judge. Whatever the case, it is certainly true that Akiva went further than any of the Sages of his time in stressing God's love and mercy.

At the same time this was not a love that forgave evil or looked the other way. There were times when Akiva could seem harsh and unforgiving. There is a lengthy discussion in the Mishnah concerning who will have a place in the world to come and who will be excluded. Rabbi Akiva excluded the ten lost tribes and the generation of the wilderness, those who rebelled against God and wandered with Moses for forty years. Rabbi Eliezer disagreed with him and asserted that they will have a place. The dispute is based on verses in the Bible that according to Akiva's interpretation indicate clearly that he is correct. Concerning the generation of the wilderness, for example, Numbers 14:35 states, "In this very wilderness they shall be consumed and there they shall die." Akiva interpreted this as "'they shall be consumed' in this world and 'they shall die' in the world to come."[49] As usual he found a specific meaning in each phrase. Rabbi Eliezer, however, cited a verse in Psalms that indicates that they will return: "Bring in My devotees, who made a covenant with Me over sacrifice!" (50:5). The question is, why was Akiva, the comforter, so harsh in these instances? Rabbi Yohanan seemed astonished by it and remarked, "Rabbi Akiva abandoned his love!" Akiva was known for his love for Israel and for his belief in the efficacy of atonement, and so one would have expected him to use his powers of interpretation in their favor and not against the generation of the wilderness.

There were, it seems, limits to his love, at least when it came to those who in the past had committed terrible sins and had not shown signs of atonement. More typical of Akiva was his disagreement with Rabban Gamliel's teaching that the children of the wicked of Israel who died before maturity would have no portion in the world to come. Akiva, citing Psalm 116:6, "The LORD protects the simple," insisted that this refers to the young, to children, and furthermore brought as proof Daniel 4:20, "Hew down the tree and destroy it, but leave the stump with its roots in the ground."[50]

### THE MEANING OF SUFFERING

Suffering and chastisement played an especially important role in Akiva's worldview and in his teachings. The subject is dealt with in the famous midrash in *Sifre Deuteronomy* interpreting the *Shma* where the discussion states that we must love God "even if He takes your soul." To Akiva this meant that one must willingly accept whatever measure God metes out, be it "of good or of punishment."[51] He supported this with examples from the Bible, including statements made by Job. Akiva, for example, totally reversed the simple meaning of Job's statement to his wife, "You speak as one of the impious women speaks" (Job 2:10), which is usually read as a rebuke to her suggestion that Job should blaspheme God and die. Akiva, however, took it as meaning that Job says that she *should* do what the impious women did—referring to the women of the generation of the Flood: instead of complaining, they readily accepted the punishment God brought upon them! We too, says Job (according to Akiva), should accept without complaint whatever happens to us, for bad as well as for good. Akiva continued with general comments on chastisement and suffering. His advice was that "one should rejoice more in chastisement than in prosperity." Akiva's conclusion therefore was that suffering—chastisement—is preferable to prosperity because it brings about the forgiveness of sin.

This point is illustrated by the story of the visit that the Sages, including Rabbi Akiva, made to Rabbi Eliezer when he was ill. All of the others attempted to comfort Eliezer by pointing out his greatness and lauding his importance. He was not comforted. Akiva, as usual, did the unexpected by saying, "Master, precious are chastisements." Eliezer perked up and wanted to hear more. Akiva then demonstrated that suffering was the only thing that caused the notorious King Menasseh to repent and return to God, resulting in his subsequent return from exile (2 Chronicles 33). "Hence, precious are chastisements."

According to Akiva, the suffering of the righteous in this world is justified, since no person is free of sin. Furthermore chastisements pave the way for unalloyed rejoicing and reward in the next world. The suffering that the righteous undergo in this world is God's way of punishing them for whatever few sins they had committed so that they will have only joy in the world to come. The pleasure that the wicked have in this world is exactly the opposite—it is all the reward that is coming to them, while punishment alone awaits them in the world to come.[52]

In another recounting of a visit to the suffering Rabbi Eliezer, while the others wept to see him suffering, Akiva laughed, causing them to wonder at him—a literary motif that occurs in so many stories about Akiva. Why did he laugh? Because having previously seen that all was well and prosperous with Eliezer, he was afraid that Eliezer had received all his rewards in this world and that none would be left for him in the world to come. He realized that that was not the case since Eliezer was now suffering the pain of illness, a clear sign that great rewards awaited him in the world to come. When Eliezer asked Akiva if he (Eliezer) had neglected anything he should have done, Akiva quoted Ecclesiastes 7:20 that there is no righteous man who does not sin.[53]

Akiva's formulation "Precious are chastisements" was adopted by many of his pupils, who elaborated on the theme. Shimon bar Yohai, for example, stated that three wonderful gifts were given to Israel—Torah, the Land of Israel, and the world to come—and all of them were achieved only through chastisements.[54]

Whereas Rabbi Ishmael believed that God punished the wicked in this world for each sin but was less exacting with the righteous, Akiva believed God was equally strict with all. Yet for all that, to Akiva, God was *rahamana*, "the Merciful One."[55] It is because of this outlook that Akiva ruled that even when reciting the Blessing after Meals in a house of mourning, one must include the fourth blessing, "[God] is good and does good for us." The Sages, on the other hand, said that in a house of mourning one should substitute for that the words "Blessed is the true Judge," something recited when receiving bad news. Akiva certainly believed that God was the true Judge, but he wished to stress the goodness and mercy of God even at such an unhappy time.[56] One must bless God for the bad as for the good.

When two Sages, Rabbi Shimon and Rabbi Ishmael (not the famous Rabbi Ishmael who was often Akiva's opponent) were executed in circumstances that are not explained, Akiva said to his students, "Be prepared for suffering, for were anything good to be coming for this generation, Rabbi Shimon and Rabbi Ishmael would have been the first to receive it." These two men were taken from us, he continued, because God knew that this generation would have to endure great suffering. He quoted several verses, among them Isaiah 57:1, "The righteous man perishes, and no one considers; pious men are taken away, and no one gives thought that because of evil, the righteous was taken away. [Yet he shall come to peace (57:2).]" Akiva seemed to be saying that they died early to prevent their having to endure the greater suffering that was yet to come. Thus death in this case was a kindness granted to the pious.[57]

There is a well-known story in which Akiva was traveling and could not find a place to lodge, and he had no choice but to sleep outside. During the night his rooster and his donkey were eaten by animals, and the flame on his oil lamp was extinguished. Each time he said, "The All Merciful does what is best," and indeed it proved to be so because during the night some bandits came and carried away all the inhabitants of the lodging where he would have stayed. Had they heard the noise of his animals or seen a light from his lamp, they would have attacked Akiva as well. Again he repeated, "Did I not say, 'The All Merciful does what is best?!'"[58] It may have been good for him, but what about the inhabitants of the town? What would they have said? Akiva ignored that question. Indeed this tale, found only in the Babylonian Talmud and not in any tannaitic sources, has all the markings of a moralistic folktale, related for the purpose of illustrating the saying "The All Merciful does what is best." It may not have originated with Akiva but perhaps was only told about him much later in order to illustrate that saying, which was integral to his thinking. In truth, Akiva's view was not quite that simplistic. It is not that he thought nothing bad ever happened. He acknowledged that bad things do happen, that misfortune occurs, but he insisted that even when they do, God's name must be blessed.

As a strict monotheist, Akiva could not believe that suffering, evil, or "the bad" came from a source other than God, but neither could he accept that it was unjustified. Therefore, as he said, one must be like Job and accept the bad together with the good. This is more sophisticated than the simple phrase "The All Merciful does what is best," the Aramaic version of "This too is for the best," would imply.

In general, Akiva's view of suffering was that it was part of God's plan and was justified. Since all humankind sins, the suffering of the righteous is a just punishment for whatever wrongs they have done, perhaps even less than they deserve. In the words of Akiva's pupil Rabbi Meir, "For the sufferings I [God] brought upon you are not at all commensurate with the things you have done."[59]

Not for a moment does Akiva question God's righteousness. Therefore one must bless God when suffering just as one blesses God for good things. As Akiva said, "'Do not do with Me' (Exod. 20:20)[60] means, 'Do not treat Me as the pagans treat their gods. When good comes to them they honor their gods, but when bad things happen they curse them. . . . But you are different. When I bring good things upon you, you give thanks, and when I bring suffering, you give thanks.' Furthermore one should rejoice even more in adversity than in prosperity . . . because it is suffering that brings forgiveness."[61]

At the same time, Akiva's belief that love of God requires one to love God even when that means giving up one's life—as with the patriarch Isaac—seems to imply that death itself is not necessarily a punishment for sin. After all, everyone must die. The death of the righteous through martyrdom, however, is another matter. To die for God would be the ultimate test of loving God. At the moment of supreme sacrifice and the ultimate suffering, one is not to question God's justice but, through all the suffering, to continue to proclaim the words of the *Shma*, the proclamation of unquestioning love for the Creator. As the sources constantly stress, Akiva attempted to fulfill this at the moment of his own death.[62]

It would be tempting to think that this belief concerning dying for God came to Akiva late in his life when Jews were suffering because of their loyalty to God and to observance of the Torah, but there is no indication that the basic interpretation of the *Sh'ma* on which this rests is a late formulation. It may be, however, that this thought began simply as the idea that when one is dying, as everyone must, one should continue to love God, but later was expanded to include the idea that one must also be willing to give up life, to be martyred, for the sake of God, *kiddush ha-Shem* (the sanctification of God's Name). Believing this was particularly important during the later period of Akiva's time, when it was important to strengthen and give comfort to the Jewish people, who saw the terrible things that were happening and knew what the consequences of their own actions might be. The killing of the righteous was unjustly committed by the Romans, but it was nevertheless the ultimate test of the depth of one's love of God.

### THE CONCEPT OF GOD

Just as Akiva, like other early Sages, had no systematic theology, so there is no clear definition of God to be found in sayings attributed to him. Since he was by nature a mystic, one may assume that Akiva's concept of God was a mystic one, closer to kabbalistic theories than to philosophical musings. His God was very personal, suffering and loving, merciful and just, expressing emotions. We do not know if Akiva accepted the idea of God having a body, a notion that was certainly prevalent in ancient Israel and in mystical circles. He often stressed the idea that humans were created in "the image of God," which may have suggested that God did have a physical form similar to that of humans. Akiva believed that God certainly had physical manifestations and that one could experience being in God's presence if one knew the proper mystical ways, but it is unclear if this meant actually seeing God, something that various midrashim ascribe to figures in the Bible. According to Rabbi Eliezer ben Hyrcanus, Akiva's teacher, at the crossing of the Sea God was seen by all the people from the highest to the lowest.[63] However in the *Sifra* Akiva denied that this could be done. He interpreted Exodus 33:20, "Man may not see Me and live"—taking the Hebrew *vahai* (and live) to mean *hayot hakodesh* (the celestial animals that carry the throne of God)—as "Even the celestial animals cannot see God."[64] There is no indication that by this interpretation Akiva meant to teach that God is without physical properties.

To Akiva, God was not an abstract principle or idea, but a real, active being filled with love of and concern for human beings.

## THE SUFFERING AND REDEMPTION OF GOD

The Torah and the prophetic books all depict God as having human-like emotions: love, hate, jealousy, anger, sorrow, and regret. Akiva made no attempt to explain or reinterpret that. When asked about the origin of earthquakes, for example, he replied plainly that when God sees the heathens prospering and flourishing, "God becomes angry and begins to roar," causing the earth to tremble.[65] On the other hand, neither in the Bible nor in Akiva's thought is God a human being, even a human being writ large. The Lord is not subject to physical needs, to birth or death. But neither is God the philosopher's diety or the unmoved mover.

Akiva took the daring step of extending his discussion of suffering, referred to above, to include God as well. God "as it were" (*kivyakhol*, Akiva's word) also experiences suffering and even exile and redemption, a bold and daring concept that originated with Rabbi Akiva and was passed on through his disciples. Akiva often used the word *kivyakhol* when describing God in terms that might be seen as detracting from God's omnipotence or otherwise inappropriate, as in this case. He was aware that his ideas were radical and that only because they appear in the biblical text was he justified in uttering them. It must be pointed out, however, that they are only present in that text according to Akiva's interpretation and certainly not in the simple meaning. In prophetic writings God suffers, as Heschel frequently pointed out.[66] Akiva went one step further and described God as enslaved, exiled, and redeemed together with Israel. Indeed, according to Akiva, God is so involved with humans that God joins in their suffering.

We find this is a dispute recorded in the tannaitic midrash *Mekhilta de-Rabbi Yishmael* in a discussion between Rabbi Eliezer and Rabbi Akiva regarding the meaning of certain difficult words in 2 Samuel 7:23, "Your people, whom You redeemed for Yourself from Egypt, a nation and its God."[67] Eliezer understood "its God" to be a reference to an idol that the Israelites had with them when they left Egypt. He referred to "the idol of Micah" mentioned in Judges 17. Akiva, on the other hand, insisted that the phrase refers not to an idol but to the true God, the God of Israel: "Were it not written in Scripture it would be impossible to utter it. As it were, Israel said to God, 'You have redeemed Yourself.'"[68] The same dispute is found in the Jerusalem Talmud, where Akiva is even more vehement that the word "God" in that verse does not refer to an idol, as Rabbi Eliezer contended, but to the true God. "Heaven forbid," Akiva said, "that you would make the Divine profane!"[69] The same interpretation of the phrase "its God" is quoted in a later midrash in the name of Akiva's disciple Rabbi Meir: "The redemption [from Egypt] was both Mine and yours! As it were, I [God] was redeemed together with you, as it is said, 'whom You redeemed for Yourself from Egypt, a nation and its God.' This month [of Nisan] was then set aside for Me and for you."[70] Akiva, citing the same verse, carried this idea almost to the point of absurdity: "Was God concerned with [redeeming] us? God was concerned with Himself! God was redeeming Himself—not us."[71] In his statement Akiva was asking, what kind of a God is it who requires redemption? Is it not a God who is intertwined with humanity, who in a sense depends on human beings—not as pagan gods do for food, drink, and magic sustenance—but in order to accomplish that which God wants to accomplish in this world?

Having established that God was in exile in Egypt together with the people of Israel, Akiva then expanded on it: "So too you find that wherever Israel went into exile, as it were, God's Presence was exiled with them. They were exiled to Egypt, God's Presence was exiled with them." Akiva then brought verses to show that this was the case also in Babylonia, Elam, and Edom (Rome) and concluded, "And when they will return in the future, as it were, God's Presence returns with them."[72] Returning to his favorite scroll, Akiva then interpreted Song of Song 4:8, "With me from Lebanon, my bride," as God's statement to Israel in exile: "You and I, as it were, were exiled from Lebanon [Lebanon being understood as a reference to the Temple][73]—you and I will go up to Lebanon."[74] When Israel was deprived of the Temple, God was also exiled from it and will return to it only when Israel does.

This daring concept appears in another midrash that teaches that "whenever Israel is enslaved, God's Presence, as it were, is enslaved with them." According to this midrash, while Israel was enslaved, God's image was seen in the heavens accompanied by the tools of slavery. When the Israelites attained their freedom, God appeared without those implements because God now was free. This is derived from the verse that first states, "And they saw the God of Israel and under His feet there was the likeness of bricks,"[75] and then uses the phrase "like the very sky for purity" (Exod. 24:10). The midrash interprets this as describing two different times. When the Israelites were slaves, God was seen with bricks; when the Israelites were free, under God's feet was only the pure sky.[76] Although this midrash is not specifically ascribed to Akiva, the context and the wording echo his particular ideas concerning God's slavery and redemption.[77]

The biblical basis for this idea of a suffering God is Isaiah 63:9, "In all their troubles, He was troubled." In Heschel's phrase, "Israel's suffering is God's grief."[78] Christianity took this dramatically further by asserting that God assumed human form in order to suffer and even die, the purpose of which was to bring about the redemption of humankind for the sin of Adam. None of this is present in Akiva's teachings. Akiva too depicted a suffering God, but never a God who dies. Akiva's teaching, which was adopted by his students and later by many Jewish theologians as well, went as far as Judaism could go: that God—always with the caveat "as it were"—joined in the suffering of individuals and of Israel, was enslaved with them, exiled with them, and eventually found redemption along with them. In this way Akiva created a very powerful symbol of a suffering God, a God who is neither on the side of those who cause human suffering nor indifferent to it, but a God who identifies totally with those who suffer. Perhaps this was Akiva's rebuttal to Christian teaching. Yes—God suffered—but God never became human, never died and came back to life. God suffered *with* Israel. Akiva's disciple Rabbi Meir, however, went even further, saying that "God travailed and suffered for you."[79]

The "exile" of Israel in Akiva's time, an oppressed people living in its own land but under occupation by the hostile and despised Roman authority, with so many Jews living in the Roman exile, meant that God too was in need of redemption. Akiva was convinced that this exile would come to a speedy end, that God too would return to "Lebanon"—the rebuilt Temple in Jerusalem—and dwell there once again. But sadly, that was not to be. Instead a martyr's death awaited him, and more suffering and an even greater defeat awaited the Jews of Judea.

## THEODICY

Akiva never seemed to have questioned God's actions or God's silence. He never dealt directly with the problem of theodicy. He never complained to God, as did the prophets[80] and the Psalmist.[81] Akiva insisted that no matter what happens, God is to be blessed. The book of Job presents two different Jobs: the patient Job who accepts whatever happens and refuses to curse or question God, and the Job who argues with God, insisting on his innocence, maintaining that he does not deserve what is happening to him. Akiva identified only with the patient Job. He had no questions. Even when he was facing imminent death, he uttered not a word of complaint. This could easily be interpreted as simple unquestioning faith. Perhaps it is that, but it could also be understood as Akiva's method of differentiating his monotheism from paganism.

Pagans see their gods as capable of evil and complain about them. "When good comes to them they honor their gods, but when bad things happen they curse them."[82] In Judaism there is no divine power in the world other than the Lord—the God of Israel. It was inconceivable to Akiva that this God would cause evil. That suffering, the bad, exists is obvious, but Akiva never questioned it. He assumed that it is always justified and must be accepted. The God of Israel is all goodness and mercy, and therefore whatever happens must not be questioned. Perhaps one can say of Akiva what was said of Job the patient: "For all that, Job did not sin nor did he cast reproach on God" (Job 1:22).

This was not the only response to humankind's pain and suffering by the Rabbinic Sages, but it was Akiva's way.[83] And even today Akiva's way is implicit in the traditional Jewish practice of quoting Job when a death has occurred, "The LORD has given, and the LORD has taken away; blessed be the name of the LORD" (Job 1:21). It is also implicit in the prayer said at the time of burial known as *tziduk ha-din*, the justification of God's verdict, in which the assertion is made that God is perfect in all God does and who can question God's actions?

## LITURGY

In the post-Temple era, when Akiva was one of the most important teachers and authorities, Jewish liturgy was still in its infancy. The basic outline of the daily prayer, the *Amidah*, was in place, although the exact text was not fixed. That was done under the auspices of Rabban Gamliel II in Yavneh around the year 90 CE,[84] and there is no specific indication that Akiva was involved. It may have taken place before he was ordained. The daily recitation of biblical passages known as the *Sh'ma* had been created when the Temple still existed, but some details of its recitation were still in dispute. The *Hallel*, an ancient Temple prayer consisting of a series of psalms of praise referring to Israel's salvation from Egyptian slavery, was now recited on important holy days. Nevertheless differences in specific ways of its recitation existed.

Many practices were not yet codified, and differences of opinion were rife. When to shake the *lulav*, how it was made up, exactly what do to at the Passover meal, how many people read the Torah on different occasions, among other things, were still in flux. It is difficult to know exactly how much influence Akiva had on liturgical practices, since so many sections of the Mishnah are not cited with a specific Sage's name. Since, as has been noted, the core of the Mishnah was the work of Rabbi Meir following Akiva,[85] statements therein with no authority's name attached may have been Akiva's ideas or practices he championed. For example, in the Mishnah there is a discussion of the meaning of the words "with all your might" in the recitation of the *Sh'ma*. The interpretation that Rabbi Akiva gave to that phrase in *Sifre Deuteronomy*[86]—that it means with whatever measure God gives you, good and bad—is cited anonymously.[87] Were it not for the text in the *Sifre* we would never know that that section of the Mishnah was the teaching of Akiva. There must be many other such instances where we are not aware of his influence.

Later authorities frequently assumed that certain anonymous laws were originally Akiva's opinions. For example, the days on which the Megillah, the book of Esther, may be read in different places depending on when Purim falls in the week, is understood by the Babylonian Talmud to be the opinion of Rabbi Akiva,[88] an opinion, incidentally, that was not accepted in Babylonia.[89]

Akiva's views were not always adopted and are sometimes ignored in the Mishnah, even though the Mishnah was compiled by his followers. There is a misconception that because the School of Akiva—that is, his disciples—was responsible for the creation of the Mishnah, his views always prevailed. That is not the case. Akiva ruled that the *Havdalah* prayer (the separation between the holy and the profane) added to the *Amidah* at the conclusion of the

Sabbath or festival should be a separate blessing, but his view was not accepted and instead it was inserted into another paragraph.[90] Another small but striking example is how many people are called up to the Torah on different days: Rabbi Ishmael ruled that there should be five on holidays, six on Yom Kippur, and seven on Shabbat. Rabbi Akiva agreed on five for holidays but ruled that there should be seven on Yom Kippur and six on Shabbat. Ishmael did not permit adding to the number; Akiva did. The argument is recorded in the early tannaitic work the Tosefta.[91] In the Mishnah itself, there is no mention of a disagreement, but Ishmael's figures are the ones given, not Akiva's, and they have been adopted in Jewish practice.[92] No reason is offered for their differing opinions, though some have been suggested, such as how long one would be expected to stay in the synagogue on those days.[93] Was Akiva being considerate of the congregation and the length of time they would have to spend at the service each week? Or was this a theological statement on his part, that in the ladder of holiness Yom Kippur is higher than Shabbat and that the number of readers should reflect this fact? What was actually done in synagogues? Evidently each could choose, and we would assume that by the time of the editing of the Mishnah, Ishmael's practice had been adopted by most.

Akiva's consideration for the comfort of the congregation is also mentioned elsewhere. It is said that when he prayed with a congregation, he did so quickly and briefly, so as not to delay all the others, but when he prayed by himself, he would begin in one place and end somewhere else, because of his repeated bowing and prostrating.[94]

Similarly in the matter of the composition of the four species required for Sukkot, the Torah does not specify how many of each there are to be: "On the first day you shall take the product of the *hadar* tree, branches of palm trees, boughs of leafy trees, and willows of the brook" (Lev. 23:40). "The product of the *hadar* tree," which was defined as the *etrog*, a kind of citrus fruit, seems to imply one fruit, and on that Akiva and Ishmael agreed. They also agreed on one palm branch. However Ishmael ruled that three myrtle branches were needed and two willow branches. Others agreed with him, and that view has prevailed. Akiva, however, said, "Just as there is one *etrog* and one *lulav* [palm], so one myrtle and one willow."[95] The Mishnah gives no explanation for their divergent views, although the Talmud indicates that Ishmael based his opinion on a simple reading of the biblical text.[96] Why did Akiva think one of each would suffice? Did he simply feel—as he seemed to say—that since only one is specified for two of the four species, all should be the same? It is unclear. Certainly Ishmael's ruling seems closer to the simple meaning of the text. In any case, in this instance again Akiva was overruled.

Regarding the times when the *lulav* is to be waved during the recitation of the *Hallel* prayer, Akiva remarked that he watched his teachers, Gamliel and Joshua, and they waved it only at Psalm 118:25, "O LORD deliver us! O LORD let us prosper!" and not at the other times that either the Schools of Hillel and Shammai required.[97] Akiva's way has not become the accepted custom. Instead we follow that of the School of Hillel.

There were also times when Akiva's own pupils disagreed with him, as he himself had sometimes disagreed with his teachers. Shimon bar Yohai, for example, said that there were four scriptural expositions of Akiva's with which he disagreed, one concerning the meaning of the phrase "the fast of the tenth month" in Zechariah 8:19. Akiva said it referred to the tenth of Tevet, when the king of Babylon laid siege to Jerusalem, according to Ezekiel 24:1–2. Shimon contended that it referred to the fifth of that month, when "a fugitive came to me from Jerusalem and reported, 'The city has fallen'" (Ezek. 33:21).[98] In this case Akiva's view prevailed.

Concerning the recitation of the daily *Amidah*, while Rabban Gamliel ruled that each individual should recite an entire *Amidah* three times daily, Rabbi Joshua felt that a shortened version was sufficient. Akiva took a practical stance: if one knew the prayer well, one should recite it fully; if not, a short version would do.[99]

The basic Rosh Hashanah liturgy had been formulated by then, in particular the inclusion of three special sections in the *Amidah*: "God's Sovereignty," "Remembrance," and *Shofarot*.[100] However there was a difference of opinion between Yohanan ben Nuri and Akiva concerning the sounding of the shofar. Both agreed that it should be sounded at three different times, but Ben Nuri did not connect the first sounding with the recitation of the *Malkhuyot* (God's Sovereignty) section, while Akiva did, reasoning, "If we do not sound the shofar then, why say that section at all?"[101] In the Galilee they followed Ben Nuri; in Judea they followed Akiva.[102] Later Akiva's practice was universally adopted.

The most important liturgical feature of Yom Kippur is the *Vidui*, the individual's confession of sins. At this early time the various forms of confession that are now an integral part of the service, the brief confession *Ashamnu* and the long alphabetical list *Al Het*, had not yet been formulated or finalized. The question was asked in the Tosefta, "How does one confess?" Yehudah ben Betera answered, "One must specify all of one's sins," but Akiva disagreed and said that there was no need to go into details. A general confession that one had sinned was sufficient.[103] Akiva explained his position by citing Psalm 32:1, "Happy is he whose transgression is forgiven, whose sin is covered over."[104] Akiva tended to lay greater stress on God's forgiveness than on the weight of human sin. Thus the passage in the Jerusalem Talmud concludes with Akiva's reminder that God is the *mikveh*—the ritual pool of cleansing for Israel. Later developments in liturgy did not follow his teaching and established lengthy and detailed lists of sins to be recited.[105]

Akiva was concerned for the welfare of minor children on the fast day of Yom Kippur. They are permitted to eat until they reach a year or two before maturity, when they are obligated to observe the commandments (usually twelve for girls and thirteen for boys).[106] To make certain that they would be fed, Akiva would send those in attendance out of the *beit midrash* on Yom Kippur specifically to feed the children.[107] He is also said to have introduced games on Passover night to keep children awake and alert.[108]

As mentioned earlier, in the Babylonian Talmud Akiva is credited with originating the formula "Our Father, Our Sovereign," *Avinu Malkeinu*, which plays an important part in the liturgy of the High Holy Days and fast days. The story is told that at a time of drought, when a fast was being held to petition God for rain, the great Rabbi Eliezer prayed with no result, but when Akiva prayed and said, "Our Father, our Sovereign, we have no Sovereign but You. Have mercy upon us, our Father, our Sovereign, for Your own sake," the rains came.[109] Another earlier version in the Jerusalem Talmud simply says that Akiva's prayer was answered, without specifying what he said, and has Akiva explaining modestly that it was not because he was better than Eliezer. Rather it could be compared to a sovereign who had two daughters, one who was nervy (*hatzufa*) and one who was worthy. The sovereign always admitted the nervy one quickly so she that she should also leave quickly, but required the worthy one to continue to ask permission because he enjoyed hearing her.[110]

Perhaps the most significant liturgical decision made by Rabbi Akiva concerned the concluding blessing of the Passover seder recited before the meal. According to the Mishnah, Akiva's contemporary, Rabbi Tarfon, suggested saying simply, "Blessed are You, O Lord our God, Ruler of the universe, who redeemed us and redeemed our ancestors from Egypt." Akiva insisted on a much longer version:

> Blessed are You, O Lord our God, Ruler of the universe, who redeemed us and redeemed our ancestors from Egypt and brought us to this evening when we eat matzah and *maror* [bitter herbs].
>
> So too, Lord our God, bring us to other festivals and seasons in peace, rejoicing in the restoration of Your city and joyful in Your service. Then we shall partake of the sacrifices and the paschal lamb whose blood will be sprinkled on the walls of Your altar for Your acceptance, and we shall give thanks unto You, singing a new song of redemption and salvation.
>
> Blessed are You, O Lord, who redeemed Israel."[111]

This lengthy and detailed recital reflects Akiva's fervent hope and belief that the restoration of the Temple would take place in his own lifetime. For him the Passover seder was a splendid opportunity for everyone to reiterate that belief. Tarfon was content with mentioning a redemption that had taken place a thousand years before, with the feeling that we too—those alive now—were part of that redemption. Akiva insisted on emphasizing what would happen in the future, hopefully the near future—namely another redemption bringing freedom and renewal. Akiva was not the only one to harbor such a belief, but he was a major force in bringing that idea to the fore. In this case it was Akiva's version that became the accepted practice.

Akiva may never have written systematic theology or attempted to answer all the questions that could be asked about God, but he did have a consistent view of the value and meaning of human life and God's connection to humankind and a concept of the One God who is loving, merciful, immanent, concerned, and approachable.

# Eight

## AKIVA—RESISTANCE, IMPRISONMENT, AND DEATH

Hadrian (Publius Aelius Hadrian, 76 CE–138 CE) is one of the most reviled figures in Jewish history. His name has been joined with Amalek, Nebuchadnezzar, Haman, Antiochus, and Titus as a despicable enemy of Jews and Judaism in ancient times. Yet when he came to power as Roman emperor in 117 CE, the inhabitants of Judea might have been forgiven for thinking him a friend, in the company of Cyrus of Persia, who restored the Jews to their land after the Babylonian exile. In 118 CE Hadrian had put to death the hated governor of Judea, Quietus, who had savagely fought against the Jews in Mesopotamia during the uprising in 115 CE and under whose rule the Jews had suffered persecution. Hadrian was an enlightened Hellenist, an expert in Greek literature and art, as well as a renowned architect who had designed the largest temple in all of Rome, dedicated to Venus and the goddess Roma.[1] But if Jews thought that this cultivated man would be more favorable to their cause than the warlike emperors who had preceded him, they were sadly mistaken.

There is no reason, however, to think that Hadrian particularly hated the Jews, but neither was there a reason for him to be particularly favorable to them, in view of the many rebellions that the Jews had fomented against Rome. There was the Great Revolt in 66–73 CE, and the period prior to Hadrian's rule had not been peaceful either. Ever since the quelling of the revolt there had been unrest and armed uprisings against Rome in the Jewish Diaspora and in Judea as well. The most serious had been during the time of Trajan in 115–117 CE,[2] when the Moorish general Lucius Quietus was sent to Mesopotamia and then to Judea to quell the uprisings, in what became known in Jewish tradition as the "Kitos War." He had remained as procurator until he was removed and executed by Hadrian. The land had known little quiet, but Akiva, always the optimist, had high hopes for the future, even contemplating the restoration of the Temple, something that pious Jews had prayed for three times daily since the time of its destruction nearly fifty years before.[3] When Hadrian went through Judea for the last time on his way to Egypt in 129 CE everything seemed peaceful and calm.[4]

### REBUILDING THE TEMPLE

The Romans had no plans to permit the rebuilding of the Jerusalem Temple. This was unusual, since everywhere else local populations were permitted to rebuild shrines that had been destroyed in warfare. The Romans may have felt that a rebuilt Temple, representing a ritual and a belief so foreign to other religions of the time, would become a center for rebellion. For reasons of internal Roman politics, the destruction of the Temple was glorified long after the event. As British scholar Martin Goodman, an expert in both Roman and Jewish history, has written, "The explanation lay in the need of the emperor to manipulate his public image in order to ensure support for his regime."[5]

It is not entirely clear why, but it was not long after his ascension before word spread that Hadrian was considering the possibility of rebuilding the Temple on its ancient site in destroyed Jerusalem, not as a place of idolatry, but as a center of Jewish worship. It is likely that Hadrian, the architect and builder, was simply interested in rebuilding Jerusalem for his own glory. It was less likely that he ever intended to rebuild the Jewish Temple, but in Jewish eyes such a thing was not impossible. Had not Cyrus the Persian permitted the Jews to return from their exile in Babylon and rebuild the destroyed Temple some seventy years after its destruction, fulfilling the prophecies of Jeremiah? No wonder the later prophet of the Babylonian exile, generally known as Second Isaiah, had hailed Cyrus as the redeemer of Israel (Isa. 44:28). This hope was expressed in the Sibylline Oracles, Jewish pseudonymous writings of uncertain origins, where Hadrian is called "a most excellent man and he will consider everything."[6]

In the fifty years following the fall of Jerusalem the lamentation for the destruction of the Temple had never stopped, nor was the hope for its rebuilding ever put aside. The extreme mourning that some had taken upon themselves, refraining from all merriment, abstaining from meat and wine, had been discouraged by Sages such as the moderate Joshua ben Hananiah, but the people continued to remember and to mourn in less extravagant ways by leaving a patch unfinished in the house, leaving out a course in a banquet, or wearing one less piece of jewelry.[7] The Sages did everything they could to keep alive the memory of the Temple and the hope for its rebuilding.

Akiva, now in his seventies and at the height of his fame, had long been one of those who led the mourning for Jerusalem. A young man when it was destroyed, Akiva may or may not have ever actually seen the Temple in its glory, but it remained constantly in his thoughts. He taught that the ninth of Av, the day of the destruction, must be strictly observed as a fast day and that no one, even the most humble laborer, should work on that day. "He who works on the ninth of Av will never see a sign of blessing." he declared. "He who does not mourn the Temple will not live to see it rebuilt!"[8] As has been noted earlier, when the words to be recited at the Passover seder were being formulated, it was Akiva who insisted that the benediction recited before eating the meal, the benediction of "Redemption," not only should refer to the Exodus from Egypt, but must also include a prayer for the redemption and restoration yet to come.[9] Perhaps that time had arrived.

Sometime prior to Hadrian's coming to power, Akiva, together with Rabban Gamliel II, Rabbi Eleazar ben Azariah, and Rabbi Joshua, visited the desolate ruins of the Temple.[10] Approaching them above from Mount Scopus, they could look down upon the ruins, and when they saw them they tore their garments as a sign of mourning. They then descended to the Temple Mount itself and, as they approached the Western Wall, the crumbling remnant of the Holy of Holies that was still standing, they saw a fox leaving the sacred site, and they began to weep. Akiva, however, did not weep; rather he laughed. When his startled companions asked him to explain his bizarre behavior, he said that what they had witnessed was nothing less than the fulfillment of the prophesy in the book of Jeremiah, "Zion shall be plowed as a field, and Jerusalem shall become heaps of ruins, and the Temple Mount a shrine in the woods" (26:18). But, Akiva reminded them, there was also another prophecy, that of Zechariah, "There shall yet be old men and women in the squares of Jerusalem" (8:4). "Before the first prophecy came true, I was afraid that the second would not be realized. Now that the first has come true, I am certain that the second will come to pass." "Akiva, you have comforted us," said his companions, "Akiva, you have comforted us."[11] These words of Akiva would have resonated loudly at this time.

For Akiva the sacredness of the Temple was of extreme importance. He taught that one must always show respect to the site of the Temple, no matter where one happened to be.[12] According to the Tosefta, he also strived to learn everything he could about how the rites of the Temple had been performed, since this would be important when the Temple was restored.[13] For example, he transmitted and preserved the knowledge of which psalm had been recited each day in the Temple and may have been responsible for transferring that practice to the daily synagogue service.[14]

If the rumors of Hadrian's intentions to rebuild the Temple were true, comfort would indeed soon be forthcoming. Unfortunately, the years went by and Jerusalem remained desolate, and any hope that Hadrian would permit its rebuilding disappeared. A midrash records that after announcing the plan to rebuild the Temple, the Romans, under pressure from the Samaritans, decided to move the site of the Temple or somehow change the building plans so that they would be different from that required by Jewish Law, which of course the Jews would oppose.[15] In any case, according to that midrash, the Jews did oppose that plan and were on the verge of violence to prevent the new Temple from being built when the venerable Sage Joshua ben Hananiah stepped up and quashed the hotheads. Joshua, a teacher of Akiva, was a disciple of Rabban Yohanan ben Zakkai and had lived through the Great Revolt that had failed so miserably. He had helped smuggle Ben Zakkai out of Jerusalem in a coffin and had undoubtedly adopted Ben Zakkai's teachings of moderation and his warnings about rising up against the Romans. The midrash depicts Joshua as continuing the tradition, cautioning against making the same mistake twice. "It is enough that we were able to enter into discussion with this nation in peace and emerge in peace!" There is no historical record attesting to this gathering with Joshua, and it is most unlikely that it ever took place.[16]

Even if this gathering took place as described, it was only a temporary respite. In the long run, the temptation to bring about the end of Roman rule was too great, and some of the Sages, including Rabbi Akiva, seem to have adopted a militant stance, favoring the rebellion. Although there is no evidence that the Bar Kokhva Rebellion was instigated or led by the Sages, they certainly did nothing to prevent it.[17] When the critical moment came, there was no one with the status of Ben Zakkai or even of Joshua ben Hananiah to stop the flames.

### AELIA CAPITOLINA

As the hope of rebuilding the Temple evaporated, bitterness increased and agitation for action against Rome grew. It was a time of unrest and constant tension. The Romans, not known for any aversion to cruelty nor great respect for human life, executed prominent Sages as well as ordinary citizens when they violated Roman decrees or were suspected of treason against the state. A Rabbi Shimon and a certain Rabbi Ishmael (not to be identified with the great Rabbi Ishmael ben Elisha, Akiva's opponent[18]) were seized by the Romans and sentenced to death. The exact nature of their crime is not known, but they were to be executed like common criminals.[19] When Akiva heard the bitter news, he went into mourning, donning sackcloth and ashes. "O Israel," he said, "if good had been destined for this generation, the first to receive it would have been these two. But now that it has been revealed to God that dire punishment is destined, they have been taken from the world!"[20] Even Akiva, the perpetual optimist, began to feel that there was not much hope for the future. This feeling of despair is reflected in his remark "One who fasts so that the *Shekhinah* [Divine Spirit] will rest upon him should have his desire fulfilled, but—alas—our sins have driven [the *Shekhinah*] away from us, as it is written, 'But your iniquities have been a barrier between you and your God' (Isa. 59:2)."[21]

By now the situation was growing so bad and feelings were so intense that some despaired of the future of the people. Rabbi Ishmael ben Elisha, often Akiva's opponent in theological discussions, once said, "From the day that a government has come to power that issues cruel decrees against us and forbids us the observance of the Torah and mitzvot and does not allow us the week of the son [circumcision], by rights we should vow not to marry and have children and the seed of Abraham our father would come to an end by itself. But let Israelites go their way and err in ignorance."[22]

Whatever his original idea concerning Jerusalem may have been, Hadrian, an ardent Hellenist, decided to turn the ancient site into a Greco-Roman city and build a pagan temple there.[23] It is most likely what he had in mind all along. There is no reason to think that his feelings toward Judaism were any different from those of the rulers who preceded him. Ever since the destruction in 70 CE Judaism had been vilified. Jews throughout the world had been required to pay an annual tax of two drachmas each year to the rebuilding of the temple of Jupiter in Rome. This tax was in place of the annual contribution Jews had made previously to the Temple in Jerusalem. Only one emperor, Nerva, in 97 had briefly abolished it. By 98, when Nerva died and Trajan became the ruler, the tax was reinstated. Rome looked down on Jews and Judaism, and Jews throughout the empire hated Rome.

The year was 130 CE. Hadrian had visited all the provinces of Rome, instituting major changes in governance. In 129 he came to Asia Minor and, on his way to Egypt, stopped in Judea, even issuing a coin commemorating his visit. Cassius Dio, the Roman historian, wrote that Hadrian planned to rebuild Jerusalem, but it would not be a glorious center of Jewish life; it was to be a pagan city—Aelia Capitolina ("Aelia" after Aelius Hadrian, "Capitolina" after the god Jupiter Capitolinus)—a center of idolatrous worship, capped by a magnificent temple and dedicated to Zeus-Jupiter.[24] In accord with his love of Hellenism, he would build a Roman colony in the Hellenistic style where Jerusalem had been, and it would be populated exclusively by non-Jews.

Scholars are divided over whether Hadrian planned to build his pagan temple on the very site of the Temple or not. Some have said that he deliberately did not want to do so. The most recent archaeological evidence, however, points in the opposite direction.[25] Shlomit Wexler-Bedolah, who has been involved in excavations near the Western Wall Plaza, stated, "If there were Second Temple buildings still standing after the destruction, the Romans destroyed everything that remained."[26] The construction of this city, given a new name of Aelia Capitolina, which in itself indicated that Jerusalem was to be eradicated forever, began several years before the outbreak of the revolt.

If the pagan temple was indeed to be erected on the site of the Second Temple, that would certainly have been cause enough to justify a full-fledged war against Rome. Not that much was needed to arouse such feelings. The very fact that since the end of the Great

Revolt Rome had stood in the way of any Jewish independence, of any formal Jewish government, of any revival of a Jewish monarchy, and of any resumption of the all-important Temple rites would certainly have been sufficient. Jews were not the only ones to chafe under Roman rule and to desire independence. There had been other revolts in Britain and Gaul and a spectacular one by the Germanic Batavian tribe in 69–70, which had initial success but then was defeated, as was the Jewish revolt at that same time.[27] Of course none had succeeded.

It has been suggested that one of the causes of the Bar Kokhva Rebellion was that the Roman law against castration and bodily disfigurement, which included a ban on circumcision, was applied by Hadrian to Jews in Judea. Although this enactment was not originally intended specifically as an impediment to Judaism, it may indeed have become that. As a midrash put it, a Jew being executed when asked, "Why are you going to be crucified?" would answer, "Because I circumcised my son."[28] On the other hand, it is not at all certain that this law was actually applied before the revolt. The Israeli historian Aharon Oppenheimer, for example, believes that it was enforced only after the revolt, in which case the true immediate cause of the revolt was the building of Aelia Capitolina.

Just as the ban against circumcision may not have been originally directed against Judaism, so too the decision to build this city may have simply been an extension of normal Roman practice, another attempt "to strengthen the Hellenistic foundations of Hadrian's empire."[29] Goodman argues persuasively, however, that Hadrian's idea was that doing this would put an end to Jewish hopes once and for all of rebuilding the Temple and that this would prevent any further Jewish uprisings.[30] In actuality it had the exact opposite effect, bringing on, as Dio said, "a war of no slight importance."[31]

Historians have argued over whether the city was built before the Bar Kokhva Rebellion or as a punishment after it was over. However recent evidence based on coins that have been found on the site indicates that Dio was correct and construction was under way before the revolt.[32] This act was seen by Jews as a declaration of war on Judaism, an attempt to delegitimize Judaism, which had once been considered a legitimate religion by Roman law, and to change the character of the country by making Judaism's once greatest city into a pagan shrine. The fact that the Bar Kokhva coins contained the phrase "For the freedom of Jerusalem" indicates that this was indeed their goal. As far as can be discerned, however, no specific attempt was made to recapture the site of Jerusalem or to rebuild the Temple. If there was such, it failed. There is no evidence that the rebels ever reached that place. Hadrian was building Aelia Capitolina. Bar Kokhva and the Jews countered with the hope for the freedom of Israel and the liberation of Jerusalem.

## BAR KOKHVA

Akiva was now an old man, not nearing 120 as legend has it but somewhere in his eighties. He had already been bereft of one, possibly two sons.[33] Since we hear nothing of his beloved wife, we must assume that she was no more. Yet his mind was clear, his thoughts and his speech totally lucid. He had his disciples who watched over him, especially one, Rabbi Joshua HaGarsi, who attended to his every need. Rabban Gamliel II had already passed away. No one officially replaced him, and by now Akiva was in everything but title the intellectual, if not the political, leader of the Jewish people. His knowledge was sought, his opinions were cherished, his methods of study and instruction had formed the basis of Jewish learning. His disciples would go on to cast all Jewish learning into the forms and molds he had determined. No other Sage could compare with the status he had achieved in his own lifetime.[34] Yet he was on the edge of despair.

Perhaps it is true that it is always darkest just before the dawn, even if the dawn proves to be an illusion. For Akiva, at least, light suddenly seemed to emerge from the least expected place. Military actions, armed revolt, were hardly his forte, yet if these would lead to a renewal of Jewish life, a revival of learning and observance, a freeing of Jews and Judaism from the shackles of Roman tyranny, Akiva would embrace them. For Akiva, Rome had always been the enemy predicted in the Torah itself under the name of Edom or Esau. It was Rome he had in mind when he interpreted the verse "The voice is the voice of Jacob, yet the hands are the hands of Esau" (Gen. 27:22) to mean "The voice of Jacob cried out because of what the hands of Esau had done to him."[35] Akiva may well have been the first to identify Rome with Esau.[36] Indeed, the official Roman color, deep red, lent itself easily to the interpretation that Edom—also meaning "red"—referred to Rome. Not for him the doctrines of Yohanan ben Zakkai during the Great Revolt advocating capitulation to the greater force of the Roman Empire. On the contrary, Akiva was ready and anxious to find a leader who could transform the situation. Shimon bar Kosiva, who was later known as Bar Kokhva, appeared on the scene.

Little is known about the history of the man himself. Who was he? Where did he come from? Where did he receive his knowledge of military tactics? What did he look like? This Shimon appeared suddenly out of nowhere, organizing the scattered forces of rebellion into a true guerilla army prepared to take on the legions of Rome. Rabbinic sources are few, generally quite late, and inclined to legendary accounts. Furthermore they are influenced by the fact that the rebellion failed. Had it succeeded, this man would undoubtedly have been praised and seen as another Judah the Maccabee, which is what he probably aspired to be. Other knowledge we have of him, again quite sparse, comes mainly from the second- to third-century Roman historian Cassius Dio and the later Christian source Eusebius.[37]

The only actual accounts extant dating from that time are the famous Bar Kokhva letters found in the Judean desert in the 1950s and later published by Yigal Yadin.[38] Unfortunately the letters are mostly from the last period of the war, though some are dated the first or second year "of the redemption of Israel." They are signed by "Shimon bar KSVA, *nasi* [leader] of Israel at Ein Gedi." They deal with practical matters, supplies, and orders to commanders of how to deal with those who were not ready to fight or who were threats to the army. They contain orders to confiscate lands and supplies and speak of the need for reinforcements. They paint a picture of someone in control of a government, not only of an army. The causes of the rebellion are not mentioned, nor do they tell us anything of Bar Kokhva's background or personal history. We learn that there were non-Jews who fought with him and that there were Jews who did not want to participate.[39] In one famous letter, probably sent in 134, the last year in which the army would have observed Sukkot before the suppression of the rebellion, he ordered the four plant species needed in the *lulav* for the observance of the holiday to be brought to the entire army. The letters reflect a well-organized group, not some rabble. His letters show him to have been an adherent of the religious practices of the Sages and to have a firm hand on everything being done. He managed to forge a kind of Jewish government resisting the domination of Rome. The impression is of a strong and sturdy leader with a commanding presence, a man of the people, not noble and aristocratic but with practical knowledge and a burning desire to lead the people of Judea to victory and freedom, a man to whom the religious traditions of Judaism were important.[40] He took total control of all the forces of rebellion. One scholar has commented, however, that in these letters "he sounds rather like a pious thug, keeping his sacred observances and threatening his men."[41]

How different this was from the situation sixty years earlier, when there was disorganization among the leaders of the Great Revolt, fanatics fought one another, and unity was never achieved. Now one man emerged who somehow attained the allegiance of all those who wanted to fight Rome. The rebellion was well organized and lasted for three and a half years, causing heavy Roman casualties. In hindsight we know that he led the people to disaster, and anyone with knowledge of the reality of the world situation should have known that there could be no other outcome. The Roman Empire led by Hadrian was not about to permit this tiny and insignificant province to outwit and outfight it and would pour as many resources as necessary into defeating this upstart rebellion, as it had in every previous rebellion. But hindsight is always clearer than foresight, and reality could not compete with the memory of ancient victories and a strong belief in ancient prophecies. From the point of view of those beginning the struggle, imbued with a sense of the justice of their cause, nourished by a belief in the power of the God of Israel and the memory of the miracle of the Maccabean rebellion a few hundred years before, Bar Kokhva seemed to hold the promise of a way out of the darkness in which they were living.

To Akiva such an individual would have represented the hope of redemption that he had long cherished, and he made his feelings known to all. There were others who felt differently, but none with the authority that Akiva had earned. There was no Ben Zakkai to say to the rebels, "What you are doing will lead only to further death and despair. Right is on our side, but might is on theirs." If Akiva gave his blessing, we can assume that his followers would have felt the same way, but there is no evidence that the Sages as a whole were enthusiastic supporters of this new revolt.[42] Indeed, even Akiva's role was not as great as some have pictured it in the past, both in scholarly works and in fiction.

All that is recorded is that Akiva proclaimed Shimon bar Kosiva (Bar Kokhva) the Messiah. The Jerusalem Talmud contains a report by Akiva's disciple Shimon bar Yohai that Akiva announced that the verses "A star [*kokhav*] rises from Jacob, a scepter comes forth from Israel. . . . Edom becomes a possession, yea, Seir a possession of its enemies; but Israel is triumphant. A victor issues from Jacob to wipe out what is left of Ir" (Num. 24:17–19) applied to Bar Kosiva.[43] "A star [*kokhav*] rises from Jacob—Kosiva rises from Jacob," said Akiva. "Kosiva" became "Kokhva"—the "star" who would wipe out Edom/Rome. He would destroy "Ir," the Hebrew word for "city," in Latin urbs, the very city of Rome. Since the four consonants of his name were K-S-V-A, all it required to change it to "star" was to substitute one letter and make it K-KH-V-A. With this statement Shimon received not only a new name, Bar Kokhva—a *nom de guerre* that was also a title—but more importantly, the public acknowledgment by the most important Rabbinic authority of the age that he was indeed worthy to lead the rebellion, that he was the long-awaited Messiah. The Talmud then adds, "When Rabbi Akiva saw Bar Kokhva he would say, 'This is the Messianic King.'"[44] That is all we know about Akiva's relationship to Bar Kokhva. The rest is pure speculation.

There was at least one loud voice of dissent to Akiva's messianic proclamation. Rabbi Yohanan ben Torta said, rather crassly but correctly, "Akiva! Grass will grow in your cheeks and the son of David will still not have arrived!"[45] But who was this Yohanan, a relatively unknown Sage, in comparison to Rabbi Akiva, of whom it was commonly said that one who was separated from Akiva was separated from life itself?[46] Such a protest must have been met with derision by all who heard it.

Akiva's statement is found in only one other Rabbinic source, the much later midrash *Lamentations Rabbah*,[47] where it follows a different interpretation of the same verse given generations later by Rabbi Judah the Prince: "Do not read *kokhav* [a star] but *kozev* [a deceiver]"—another play on the name "Kosiva," reflecting the attitude of rejection following the failure of the revolt.[48]

No early tannaitic source mentions Akiva's proclamation of Shimon as the messianic king, but there is good reason to believe that he did so.[49] Considering the terrible consequences of the rebellion and the later Rabbinic denunciation of Bar Kokhva as a false messiah, there would be little reason to ascribe this to Akiva had he not actually done so. But neither is there any evidence that Akiva did more than that, nor that Akiva meant anything more than that this fellow Bar Kosiva could defeat the Romans and bring about Jewish independence.

Although there had always been ideas that depicted the Messiah in mystical and supernatural terms, there were also others that thought of the Messiah very simply as the redeemer, the human being who would lead the people in overcoming the evil empire that enslaved them.[50] Akiva had a very earthly understanding of the Messiah, predicting that the Messianic Age would last for only forty years.[51] This Shimon, rough though he might be, also radiated power. Some have suggested that he was more like one of the bandit leaders Josephus described during the time of the Great Revolt, certainly not messianic in the supernatural sense.[52] Indeed, he himself never seemed to have had such pretensions.[53] Shimon could not have been unhappy to have Akiva's seal of approval, but he very wisely avoided taking the title of Messiah. On his coins and in his letters he styled himself simply *nasi*—leader of Israel, a civil title rather than a religious one.[54] Furthermore it is very telling that in these letters he never used the messianic title of Bar Kokhva, but always his real name, Shimon bar KSVA.[55] Once he had achieved some victories, it seemed indeed possible that he would triumph. For Akiva that had been enough.

There is not a shred of evidence that Akiva joined Bar Kokhva's troops or advised him in any way. The many attempts that have been made to picture Akiva as actively participating in the rebellion, serving as Bar Kokhva's advisor or sending his disciples into battle with him are without any factual basis. Beyond that proclamation, important as it was, Akiva's role in the revolt itself seems to have been negligible. He may have supported it but did not run it. He was, after all, a teacher of Torah and not a general or a politician.[56] There is no evidence that the reported deaths of his many students occurred because they were killed in the fighting. Illness, a plague, is much more likely, to say nothing of the fact that their deaths must have taken place long before the rebellion.[57] The later charges by the Romans against Akiva had nothing to do with the revolt; they concerned his disregard for Roman-decreed prohibitions against gathering multitudes and teaching them Torah.[58] Only one other Sage is said to have been directly connected to Bar Kokhva, Rabbi Eleazar of Modi'in, and that account is legendary.[59]

In short, we know almost nothing about the role that either Akiva or the Sages in general played in the revolt. Some may have seen it as a positive thing, as Akiva evidently did, but it was certainly not originated or driven by the Sages in any organized way. The major contribution that Akiva and the other Sages made to bringing on the revolt may well have been their encouragement concerning the rebuilding of the Temple and their mourning for Jerusalem.[60]

Even later, when it was clear to all that the Messiah had not come and that the revolt had been a disaster, no one blamed Akiva for his enthusiastic endorsement of the man who then came to be called by all "Bar Koziva, the son of falsehood." Eventually the defamation of Bar Kokhva was such that the Babylonian Talmud even claimed, in what is clearly a fabrication, that after two and a half years of the revolt he had said to the Rabbis, "I am the Messiah." They tested him and found that he was not. "They then slew him."[61]

What was it that prompted Akiva to make such a bold determination? One thing is certain, he did not underestimate the power of Rome. As we have seen, he had been there and seen its magnificence. His travels on behalf of the Jews of Judea had taken him to Rome years before as part of a delegation led by Rabban Gamliel, together with Rabbi Joshua and Rabbi Eleazar ben Azariah. It should not be forgotten that at that time, according to the story recorded in the *Sifre*, when the noise of that great city was heard by them while they were still 120 miles away and others began to weep, Akiva burst out laughing. When they asked him why, he turned the question around and asked why they wept. They answered, "These pagans bow down to idols and yet live in security, peace, and serenity while the Temple of our God is in ruins!" "That is why I laughed," said Akiva. "If God has given all this to those who have angered Him, how much more will He give those who fulfill His will."[62]

Many years had passed and the situation had only worsened, but he still believed that. It was not Rome's might that Akiva underestimated. Rather, he trusted that the time had come for God to return Israel to its rightful place, as the Almighty had done in the days of

Nehemiah. Perhaps the very increase in suffering was a sign that things were about to change, that the Messiah would come when things got as bad as they could be. Rabban Gamliel himself had taught that there would be terrible suffering in the Messianic Age.[63] There is a statement in the Talmud that Akiva had interpreted the verses "For thus said the LORD of Hosts: In just a little while longer I will shake the heavens and the earth, the sea and the dry land; I will shake all the nations" (Haggai 2:6–7) incorrectly, most likely seeing this as an immanent prediction of the Messianic Age.[64] He had attempted to calculate the time of the coming of the Messiah and he had been mistaken.[65]

### THE BAR KOKHVA REBELLION

In the summer of 132 CE, after Hadrian had left the Land of Israel, the revolt broke out in all its fury. It has been suggested that Hadrian's visit may have been a contributing factor to the rebellion, since it imposed a great financial burden upon the country. This, together with all the other social, economic, national, and religious difficulties, may have accelerated the breaking out of this rebellion, the main cause of which was the building of Aelia Capitolina.[66] No one knew how long it would last—it was three and a half years before it was put down—but it had great success at first. Shimon's coins proclaimed "the Freedom of Jerusalem," although that was never attained or even attempted.[67] They also showed a picture of the façade of the Temple. In the coins he also proclaimed "the Freedom of Israel," calling himself the "*nasi* of Israel," emphasizing Israel as the name of the nation, a name the Romans had never used.[68]

At the same time, as the fighting went on the Roman authorities, led at first by the governor of the province, Tineius Rufus, enforced more and more restrictions on the observance of Judaism. Among them were forbidding public assemblies and the public teaching of Torah, the eventual cause of Akiva's imprisonment. Other decrees were promulgated during the fighting forbidding some observances of Judaism either as punishment or because these practices were thought to promote rebellion.[69] One of the earliest was against the public proclamation of the *Shma*, "Hear, O Israel, the Lord is our God, the Lord alone!" (Deut. 6:4).[70] For generations Jews had recited those words daily, sometimes in a public ceremony with a leader who recited it as a proclamation of total dedication to the God of Israel. Allegiance to the Lord was exclusive and excluded any human being, even if he proclaimed himself a deity, as did Roman emperors. Even when Jews recited the *Shma* individually, they said it aloud, literally "hearing" what Moses had first proclaimed to Israel more than a thousand years before. In addition there was the ancient practice called *pores al Shma* (proclaiming the *Shma*) in which at a public gathering a leader would proclaim the first line, "Hear, O Israel, the Lord is our God, the Lord alone," and the people would respond, "Blessed is the name of His glorious Majesty for even and ever."[71] This was a public demonstration of exclusive allegiance to the God of Israel and by implication a denial of the authority or divinity of any Roman leader. For the Romans, who had not yet outlawed prayer or study, this vow of allegiance was equivalent to denial of the authority of the Caesar and indeed of the state itself.

For Akiva, the *Shma* was a central pillar of his faith and his life. As the Sages had taught, the first line, "Hear, O Israel," was "the acceptance of the yoke of heaven," the very essence of what it meant to be a Jew. The next words, "You shall love the Lord your God," formed a command that must have spoken deeply to Akiva, for as we have seen, love was the basis of everything that was precious to him. How it must have frustrated him when he once sat with his companions in his house of study and had to recite the *Shma* silently rather than proclaiming it aloud publicly because of the presence there of a Roman spy.[72]

The love that this biblical passage commanded was all-encompassing, all-consuming: love God "with all your heart and with all your soul and with all your might" (Deut. 6:5). According to the Mishnah, "with all your soul" means "even if He takes your soul" (in other words, at the time of death).[73] This is also found in the tannaitic midrash *Sifre Deuteronomy*, which adds in the name of Shimon ben Azzai, "Love Him until the last drop of life is wrung out of you." Akiva had taught that since "with all your soul" means "even if He takes your soul," that would include all of your possessions. If one is willing to give up one's life for the love of God, obviously it is logical that one would be willing to give up one's possessions. Therefore the last part of the verse, "with all your might," cannot mean "with all your possessions," as was commonly taught, but something else. Akiva, playing on the similarity between the Hebrew for "might" (*me'od*) and the word *middah*, meaning "measure," taught that it means that one is to love God regardless of "whatever measure He metes out to you, whether of good or of punishment."[74] He was soon to feel the full meaning of that himself, and his ability to fulfill such a terrible demand would be tested. In the meantime, he went out of his way to find a way to recite the *Sh'ma* without bringing down the wrath of the authorities by saying it silently.

It is quite possible that many of these Roman decrees restricting various religious observances were enacted as a reaction to the revolt, rather than before it, serving as both a punishment and a means of preventing further incitement.[75] Since Judaism, then as today, values life, it faced a dilemma as to whether one was permitted to follow these restrictions and violate the commandments, or was required to fulfill the commandments even though this would risk death. And so it was decided by the Sages in a secret meeting that except for prohibitions against idolatry, incest, and murder, all the other commandments could be violated.[76] Certainly no one was commanded to teach Torah at the cost of sacrificing one's very existence. Surely the aged Akiva would be forgiven for confining himself to his residence and studying quietly or with a few chosen disciples in secret.

### AKIVA DEFIES ROME

More than one friend or colleague urged Akiva to obey the rules of the Roman authorities and live on safely. Eventually this would pass. Either the revolt would succeed and they would be truly free, or it would fail and with defeat would come peace and eventually a return to normalcy, whatever that was to be. For Akiva, however, there was never a moment's hesitation, never a choice. Torah was his whole life. Torah was divine, the word of God. It had to be taught, and taught openly to the masses. In his eyes Torah study was even more important than observance,[77] and so he ignored all warnings and continued to teach Torah in public.

It is recorded that Pappus ben Yehudah, Akiva's ill-tempered contemporary and often Akiva's opponent in biblical interpretation,[78] warned him explicitly of the danger involved in defying the decrees of the Romans, expounding the Torah and collecting an assembly.[79] "Are you not afraid of the government?" he asked. Akiva, who was an excellent teller of tales and Aesop-like parables, answered in the now famous parable of the fox and the fish:

> Walking by the river, the fox saw the fish scurrying from place to place. "Why are you fleeing?" asked the fox. "Because of the nets that men are casting to catch us," answered the fish.
> "Come up to dry land, then, and live with us!" urged the fox.
> "Don't you understand?" said the fish, "If we are not safe in the water, which is the place where we naturally can live, how could we survive on the land, which is not our natural place!"[80]

Depriving Israel of Torah was equivalent to depriving it of life itself, the very air it breathed, the oxygen in the water of the fish. If the rebellion was not successful, Israel would somehow survive, but if Torah was eliminated, Israel had no future. Pappus, like the fox, shook his head in disbelief at Akiva's stubborn insistence on defying the brutal Roman authorities and went on his way. And Akiva continued to teach. Pappus was not the only Sage who warned against defying the Roman authorities. Hananiah ben Teradion warned Yose ben Kisma, "Do you not know that heaven itself has ordained that this nation will rule? It has destroyed the

Temple, slain pious ones, and caused the best to perish, yet it is still firmly established! And you continue to teach Torah and gather assemblies." The reply: "Heaven will have mercy." Sadly, Yose died of illness, and Hananiah, who continued to teach, was caught and burned with a Torah scroll wrapped around him.[81]

Akiva's parable was more than a simple declaration of the importance of Torah study and teaching. It represented a turning point in his life—and one that led to the end of his life. As much as Akiva was dedicated to Torah, so too he was dedicated to the value of life itself and to an optimistic attitude toward whatever happens. The commandments were given to enable us to live through them, not die because of them. As noted above, Akiva himself had earlier acquiesced to reciting the *Sh'ma* quietly when the Romans had forbidden reciting it aloud.[82] He did not run headlong toward martyrdom and death. But soon the situation would drastically change. Forced to choose between the value of life and what he considered necessary for the continued existence of Judaism and the Jewish people, Akiva chose risking his own life to continue Torah teaching and ensure the continuation of Judaism. That was Akiva's message in the parable of the fox and the fish.

We can imagine Akiva coming to a small town and being greeted enthusiastically by a war-weary crowd assembled in the gate to listen to the greatest Sage of the time and a wonderful teller of tales and parables—a man who could not only hold his own in the most complicated discussions on the minutiae of Jewish Law, but could also cast a spell over any group of ordinary men and women. At such a time he might have taught his famous tale based on the verse "This is my God and I shall glorify Him" (Exod. 15:2). Akiva began with a question: "How can I, mere flesh and blood, glorify God, the Maker of heaven and earth?! I can do that by speaking of the praises of He-who-spoke and the world came into being, before all the nations of the world!" Akiva then wove a dialogue between Israel and the nations, a dialogue that immediately addressed the situation Jews were experiencing day by day: persecution and possible martyrdom. It was a dialogue interpreting a section from the Song of Songs and giving it an entirely new meaning:

> The nations of the world ask Israel, "'How is your Beloved better than any other that you adjure us so?' (Song 5:9)—that you die for His sake, that you are slain for His sake! As it says in Psalms, 'For your sake we are killed all day' (Ps. 44:23)."
>
> "Behold—you are lovely, you are mighty—come and merge with us," say the nations.
>
> But Israel answers the nations of the world, "Do you have any idea what He is like? We shall tell you just a bit of His glory—'My Beloved is clear-skinned and ruddy' (Song 5:10)."
>
> As soon as the nations of the world hear this description of He-who-spoke and the world came into being—partial as it is—they say to Israel, "We shall come with you!" as the verse says, "Where has your Beloved gone, O fairest of women? Where has your Beloved turned? Let us seek Him with you!" (Song 6:1).
>
> But Israel says to them, "You have no portion in Him for 'I am my Beloved's and my Beloved is mine!' (Song 6:3)."[83]

A crowd listening to such a midrash would understand his message and appreciate its artistry. So, teaches Akiva at this critical time, the nations have tried to convince us to abandon our God rather than face martyrdom, but even if they were to appreciate that our God is indeed worthy, they would not understand how demanding and how exclusive this relationship is, just like that between man and wife. For them the God of Israel is only one more deity to add to an already crowded pantheon. For us there is no other way. We must love God *ad mavet* (even until death), defying if need be the Roman decrees and never frittering away our heritage by joining with others and demoting the God of Israel to just another deity, lovely as He may be![84] It is a justification of defiance and of martyrdom for the sake of the survival of Judaism.

Akiva continued his teachings in these public gatherings, making no attempt to hide what he was doing. How long this went on we do not know. It seems likely that long before the rebellion was finally and brutally crushed in 135 CE Akiva was already imprisoned and had met his death, most likely toward the very beginning.

The report of his capture is tersely given in the same source that records his retort to Pappus ben Yehudah: "Soon afterward Rabbi Akiva was captured and thrown into prison."[85] Ironically Pappus ben Yehudah was also arrested, and the two were in prison together. When Akiva asked him why he was there, Pappus lamented that his imprisonment was for some unimportant offense, while at least Akiva had been captured for a good cause: teaching Torah. There is no indication that Akiva's imprisonment was in any way related to actual participation in or involvement in the Bar Kokhva Rebellion.[86]

### AKIVA'S IMPRISONMENT

It is not known exactly when Akiva was imprisoned. If the Rabbinic sources are correct that it occurred under the rule of Tineius Rufus, it would have been before 133 CE, since Rufus was replaced by Iulius Severus in that year.[87]

As he sat in the Roman prison, accused of the terrible crime of assembling multitudes while teaching Torah, Akiva surely was prepared for the inevitable end. He had known his teaching could not last forever and that the Romans would not spare him or pity him. He had little hope and he readied himself for the worst. His love of God required no less of him. How often he had taught that loving God "with all your soul" meant being ready to give your soul for the sake of God. "Do not act toward God the way others act toward their gods," he had preached. "When good comes to them they honor their gods, but when calamity comes they curse their gods. If God brings us good we must thank Him, but if He brings suffering, we must also thank Him."[88]

As has been noted earlier in this book, in Akiva's eyes suffering was not without a purpose. Sitting in the darkness of his prison cell perhaps he recalled the time years before when his teacher Rabbi

Eliezer was ill and he, together with others, had gone to visit and comfort him. No matter what the others said, no matter what words of praise they lavished upon him, Eliezer was not comforted. What brought him solace were Akiva's words, "Precious are chastisements. They alone can bring about repentance and forgiveness."[89]

As for death, Rabbi Eliezer, as he lay dying, had also predicted unnatural death for many Sages and told Akiva that his would be the worst of all.[90] Surely those ominous words had haunted Akiva all those years, and now it was only a matter of time until he would learn exactly what they meant.

Time was all that was left to him now. And although he may have thought that his end was imminent, that was not to be the case. For reasons unknown he was not tried and sentenced immediately but languished in jail, although we cannot be certain how long his imprisonment lasted. It is unlikely that it would have been more than a matter of months.[91] At first he was allowed visitors. Many stories are told of that time, although we cannot be certain that all the details are true. It has been said that his faithful disciple Joshua HaGarsi was allowed to bring him food and water daily.[92] Others were permitted to come and spend time with him. One of his most faithful disciples, Shimon bar Yohai, is reported to have come and asked to study with him. Akiva refused to teach him Torah, because he did not want to endanger Shimon and bring calamity upon him as well. Eventually Shimon persuaded, perhaps even forced, him to teach him, and so he did.[93]

As time went by, conditions worsened. Visits were no longer permitted. Once when HaGarsi was bringing him provisions, the guard stopped him and questioned the amount of water that he had with him. The guard suggested that he might be using the water to attempt to weaken a wall so Akiva could escape, and he made him pour out half of it. Akiva was upset because he also needed the water for ritual purposes—to wash his hands—and when he used it for that, there would be nothing left for drinking. But punctilious as he was on matters of ritual, that is what he did, and so he went thirsty that day.[94]

The troubled times were such that the usual practice of discussing and deciding questions of Jewish Law in houses of learning no longer existed and Akiva, imprisoned as he was, served as the final authority on many matters. Although he had never been the head of the academy as had Rabban Gamliel II or Rabbi Eliezer, for all intents and purposes at this time of crises and emergency he now functioned in that capacity. Others turned to him for decisions on weighty matters that required decisive answers. His opinions were so highly valued and so vital on matters concerning marriage and divorce that at least once it was necessary to hire two men at great expense to find a way to get to him in prison in order to obtain his ruling on a particularly complicated case.[95] Another time Yohanan HaSandlar is said to have pretended to be a peddler who walked by Akiva's cell and asked another marriage question by embedding it in his peddler's call.[96]

One of the important matters usually handled by the official Rabbinic court was the intercalation of years. Because the Jewish year is shorter than the solar year, an additional month must be added from time to time prior to Passover, so that the seasons and the holidays will remain in the proper relationship. Akiva took the unusual step of proclaiming three such years in a row from his prison cell, and this was accepted unquestioningly.[97]

A new chapter in this saga began when Akiva was transferred to the prison in Caesarea, the capital of the Roman province, the seat of the governor, Tineius Rufus, who according to a late source took personal control of the case.[98] Considering Akiva's status, that seems quite possible. The ride to Caesarea was to be Akiva's last taste of freedom and the world outside of prison walls. Seeing the buildings of this Roman city must have reminded him of Rome itself. Situated on the shore of the Mediterranean Sea, it was the site of a magnificent harbor, where ships anchored and departed for voyages to Rome, Alexandria, and other distant cities. Although erected by a Jewish ruler, Herod the great builder, it was now a visible symbol of the might of the occupying power and, with its monumental statues and pagan shrines, a refutation of the authority of the God of Israel in the Land of Israel.

## MEETINGS WITH TINEIUS RUFUS

Rabbinic literature contains several accounts of meetings and discussions between Tineius Rufus and Akiva. The earliest of these is found in the fifth-century work *Genesis Rabbah*. Others appear in later midrashic works such as the *Tanhuma* and in the Babylonian Talmud. None are found in any early tannaitic source. On this ground and others scholars today doubt the historicity of these stories. They are seen, rather, as typifying discussions between Jews and non-Jews on matters of Jewish belief.[99] Who would better be presented as conducting such disputes than the highest representatives of each side: the Roman governor and the most popular Sage of the time? Since in the Jerusalem Talmud's account of Akiva's trial Akiva and Rufus are said to carry on a dialogue, these discussions even had historical precedent.

On the other hand some scholars, most prominent among them Saul Lieberman, assert that the stories have a historical basis. As Lieberman put it, Tineius Rufus, commonly referred to as "the wicked," loved to argue with Akiva and met with him often in prison "in order to find out what was causing unrest in Judaea."[100] If Lieberman is correct, these conversations would have taken place as part of ongoing interrogations of Akiva during the period of his imprisonment, although this is not mentioned in any of the sources. All would agree that some details of their relationship are clearly legendary, such as the story that Tineius Rufus's wife became enamored enough of Akiva to convert and actually marry him![101]

In the encounter described in the earliest of these sources and repeated elsewhere, Rufus, "the wicked," wanting to show his cleverness, began with a question that sounded more like a riddle, "What is one day from another?" Akiva, unfazed, retorted immediately, "What is one man from another?" "What did I say to you and what did you say to me?" Rufus asked. "You questioned me about our

Sabbath—why that day should be singled out from other days. I countered by asking why Rufus should be more powerful than any other man," Akiva replied. "I am governor here because my emperor honored me." "So did God wish to honor the Sabbath." "Can you prove that to me?" Tineius Rufus asked. "There is a river called the Sambatyon, which moves great rocks every day but ceases on the Sabbath." "You call that proof? Where is it? Who has seen it?" "Those who conjure up the dead will prove it. Your father's grave will prove it—no smoke arises from it on the Sabbath."[102]

There is nothing in this account that sounds particularly profound and nothing that reflects any attempt to get meaningful information from Akiva. Using popular superstitions to prove something was a familiar device and appears in the well-known story of Rabban Yohanan ben Zakkai explaining the purifying power of the ashes of the Red Heifer (Numbers 19) to a heathen by comparing it to their own way of exorcizing an evil spirit. To his pupils he said that this is not the real reason; it is simply a law decreed by God.[103]

Another incident found in the Babylonian Talmud, recounted by Rabbi Meir, Akiva's student, is more profound; it posed a social and theological question:

> "If your God so loves the poor," Tineius Rufus asked, "why does He not take care of them Himself?"
>
> Akiva answered, "This gives us an opportunity to carry out His work. Thus too we are saved from Gehinnom."
>
> "But if God makes them poor do you not offend Him by giving them food? If a king was angry with his servant and put him in jail and ordered a diet of only bread and water, would he not be angry with a guard who then gave them a meal? And you are called 'servants,' as it is written, 'For it is to Me that the Israelites are servants' (Lev. 25:55)."
>
> Akiva answered, "But what if the prisoner were the king's son who had angered him briefly, would he not send him a

gift? And are we not called 'sons' of God, as it is written, 'You are the sons of the LORD your God' (Deut. 14:1)?"

Rufus then stated that Israelites are called "sons" when they carry out God's wishes and "servants" when they do not. "Now you are not carrying out His wishes."

Akiva then quoted Isaiah to him, "Is it not to share your bread with the hungry and to take the wretched poor into your home?" (58:7).[104]

It seems most unlikely that Tineius Rufus would be quoting Scripture in a discussion with Akiva. Certainly this would be an unusual topic to be brought up when Akiva was a political prisoner. However, considering Akiva's extensive work with the poor, the ideas concerning helping them as part of God's command would reflect his feelings.

Another conversation concerned circumcision:

Tineius Rufus asked, "Which is more pleasing, the work of God or the work of man?"

Akiva understood what was behind the question—circumcision, which was forbidden by Rome. "The work of man is more pleasing," he answered.

"How can you say that? Can you compare the very heavens and earth to anything mere man can do?"

"Of course not—but let us not speak of celestial things that are beyond us and we cannot control but of what is done here on earth."

Tineius Rufus: "Why do you Jews mar the human form—the creation of God—by circumcision—destroying the perfection of the male form?"

"I knew that is what you were hinting at," said Akiva, "and therefore I said that the work of man is more pleasing than that of the Holy One. Think of sheaves of wheat and then consider loaves of bread. Is not the bread a more pleasing creation, more useful to human beings, and is it not the creation of human hands?"

Rufus responded that if God wanted men to be formed like that, why did he not create the child already circumcised at birth? That would surely not be beyond His powers!

Akiva answered with a question: "Why does the child emerge attached to the mother by a cord that a human has to cut? God always leaves something for man to do. Nothing is perfect. All of God's commands are intended to perfect and purify us."[105]

This discussion, focusing on a commandment that was in dispute between Rome and Judaism, would have been in place in a discussion between any Sage and any Roman.

One account has Rufus asking Akiva about the Jewish attitudes toward Rome:

"Why does your God hate us?" and he quoted Malachi 1:3, "I hated Esau."

"I will answer you tomorrow."

On the morrow he asked Akiva, "What did you dream last night?"

Akiva responded that he saw two dogs in his dream, one was called Rufus and one was called Rufina.

Tineius Rufus was of course angry. "You called your dogs by my name and that of my wife?! You should be condemned to death!"

Akiva responded that there is really no difference between Tineius Rufus and the animals; they all eat, drink, procreate, and die—"yet you were angry that I called them by your name. Should not God, Creator of heaven and earth, Giver of life and death, be angry when you call a piece of wood by the name 'God'? Therefore He hates you . . . 'I hated Esau.'"[106]

Again we have the literary convention of the Roman quoting Scripture in his argument with the Jew and the Jew giving the correct answer that justifies either Jewish belief or practice. It is a most dramatic scene, but it is doubtful that such a conversation could have ever taken place. Would Akiva, a prisoner, have asserted to his jailer and judge that he, Rufus, and all of Rome were hated by the Almighty?

All of these incidents deal with matters that non-Jews might question: the importance of the Sabbath to Jews, a day of no work that made no sense to Romans; why an all-powerful God allowed such things as poverty in the world; the oft-derided Jewish practice of circumcision, which to the Greco-Roman civilization always seemed both barbaric and unaesthetic; and finally the Jew's hatred of Rome, identified as Edom and derided by Scripture. Such questions might well have come up in disputes between Jews and Romans in one way or another, but it seems questionable if such meetings actually took place between Tineius Rufus and Akiva. If they ever had meetings, they would more likely have been difficult interrogations about Akiva's actions rather than theological debates.

## THE DEATH OF AKIVA

Just as there are multiple versions of Akiva's marriage and entry into learning, so too there are differing versions of his death. The story is related in two collections. The oldest is found in the Jerusalem Talmud, where it appears twice in virtually the same words. The other version is found in the much later Babylonian Talmud. The one in the Jerusalem Talmud is the simpler of the two and the more believable:

> Rabbi Akiva was being judged before the wicked Tineius Rufus. The time for the recitation of the *Sh'ma* arrived. He began to recite it and smiled. He [Tineius Rufus] said to him, "Old man, old man: either you are deaf[107] or you make light of suffering." He [Akiva] said, "May the soul of that man expire! Neither am I deaf, nor do I make light of suffering, but all of my life I have read the verse "And you shall love the Lord your God with all your heart and with all your soul and with all your possessions."[108] I

loved Him with all my heart and I loved Him with all my wealth, but until now, I was not tested to see if I could love Him with all my soul. But now the opportunity of loving Him with all my soul has come to me. It is now the time of the recital of the *Sh'ma* and I am not deterred from it; and therefore I recite the *Sh'ma* and I smile." [He was not able to complete it before his soul departed.][109]

According to this simple yet profoundly moving, account, Akiva was not executed by the Romans but died while under interrogation. We are not told what Akiva was being accused of at this trial. Perhaps it would not be too much to assume that Tineius Rufus might have said something like this: "You stand accused of violating the decrees of the emperor Hadrian. You have been seen assembling crowds together for forbidden public gatherings in which you were disseminating teachings from the Scripture of the Hebrews—forbidden under Roman law. How do you plead? Are you prepared to acknowledge your guilt? Public gatherings are used to foment more violence against Rome and yet you continued to arrange them—did you not?"

It was early in the morning, the time for recitation of the *Sh'ma*. Akiva knew well that this recitation, proclaiming complete allegiance to the Lord God, was viewed by the Romans as an act of *Lex Majestatis*, the denial of Hadrian's legitimacy as a ruler as well as of his divinity, an act that would not be tolerated. By reciting it in this public forum, the court to which he had been brought, he would be fulfilling his understanding of the command to love God even when dying—his interpretation of "with all your soul"—because he would be endangering his life. Therefore he defied Rome and, in the presence of the very court that was judging him, as the dawn broke, began reciting it with joy.

According to this account, Akiva even had the strength to explain his deed to his judge and interrogator. Whether or not he actually had the opportunity or ability to say that out loud, that was certainly what would have been in his mind and his heart at that moment. Although the story does not specifically say that he was being tortured, the question "Do you make light of suffering?" certainly implies some sort of physical duress, either taking place or being threatened.[110] Perhaps the Romans would have tortured him to stop his recitation, but it is clear that they did not execute him. Had he been executed, the Talmud would undoubtedly have stated that fact. It is more likely, then, that the heart of this elderly man, exhausted after the ordeal of imprisonment and interrogation or because of some torture, simply gave out even before he could complete the recitation.[111]

Later legendary accounts (see below) say that Akiva expired reciting the word *ehad* (one). If it did not happen that way, it is understandable that the tale would have it so, since "one" expresses so much that Akiva lived for—one God, one people, one Torah. As Louis Ginzberg put it, "Pure monotheism was for Akiva the essence of Judaism; he loved, worked, and died for it."[112]

Was Akiva seeking martyrdom? One story states that once when he was being judged by Rufus in the presence of Joshua HaGarsi, a cloud covered them, and HaGarsi said, "It would seem that my master's prayers are not being accepted."[113] Was he praying to be saved from death? That seems to have been the case, an indication that the conveyor of the story thought that he did not actively seek to be a martyr.[114] As Lieberman wrote, "The Jews took their martyrdom calmly and as a matter of course. They tried to avoid it . . . but when they were discovered . . . they submitted to martyrdom quietly."[115] By having Akiva state that he was reciting the *Sh'ma* "with joy," the talmudic account affirms that Akiva saw this as a positive action, as the ultimate fulfillment of the Torah's command of loving God even when in danger. This gives meaning to his death, a death he may not have sought, but which affirmed his devotion to God and to the Torah. Knowing Akiva's positive attitude toward the value of suffering and affliction, it is but a small step to see a martyr's suffering and death as the ultimate expression of love. Thus Heschel wrote, "It is likely that Rabbi Akiva sensed that it was impossible to achieve perfect love of God except through suffering, for a person cannot truly taste of the love of God until he is prepared to mock death itself for the glory of God's name."[116]

How reliable is this account? Do we really know the details of what happened? There is no Roman record of Akiva's trial. The Romans would have been unlikely to relate the story other than to let it be known that Akiva was dead. Perhaps his faithful attendant Joshua HaGarsi managed to be there, although according to a tradition related in a late midrash, he had left Akiva and gone home to observe a holiday and was told of Akiva's death by the prophet Elijah when he was far away.[117] Nor does this account state that any of his disciples were present. Although there is no proof of its historicity, this simple tale is as close as we will ever come to knowing the circumstances of Akiva's death, and it tells us how those nearest in time and place to Akiva understood his death and its religious significance. Anything added in later accounts is most unlikely to have any historical basis but must be seen as an attempt to enlarge and magnify the original story.

## LEGENDARY MARTYRDOM

The story of Akiva's death as originally related was a simple one. Over time it was told and retold and in the retelling has been embellished many times over. Storytellers and dramatists from the time of Homer through Shakespeare, Schiller, and so many others have enhanced the stories of great heroes and villains for their own purposes. So, too, with Rabbi Akiva's death. The most complete, dramatic, and compelling story of his martyrdom, written in fine literary style, is found in the Babylonian Talmud:

> When Rabbi Akiva was being led to execution, it was the time for the recitation of the *Sh'ma*. They [the Romans] were combing his flesh with combs of iron while he was accepting upon himself the kingship of heaven. His disciples said to him, "Our

master—even at this point?" He said to them, "All my life I was troubled by this verse—'with all your soul'—[meaning] even if someone takes your soul! I said, 'When will this come to me and I will fulfill it?' And now that it has come to me, shall I not fulfill it?!" He prolonged the word "one" until his soul departed while uttering the word "one."[118]

Although this is presented in the Talmud as a *baraita* (an early teaching of the Tannaim), this tale does not appear anywhere else in tannaitic literature,[119] and it has been demonstrated that *baraitot* do not always represent an authentic tannaitic tradition.[120] It is a much later literary creation, expanding greatly upon what was known previously, creating the perfect story for Jewish martyrology, and a story that has had a tremendous influence on Jewish life ever since. It glorifies martyrdom, emphasizing that Akiva sought this opportunity. It states that Akiva had always interpreted the words "with all your soul" as "if someone takes your soul," yet we do not find that Akiva ever interpreted the verse in exactly that way. The interpretations—not even specifically in his name—were always, "even if He [God] takes your soul,"[121] which would mean simply at the time of one's death.[122] But this account has expanded it to mean not just continuing to love God even when dying peacefully, but loving Him and accepting God's sovereignty even when others—Romans, killers—are murdering you.[123]

Here, for the first time, a specific connection was made between the first verse of the *Sh'ma*, "Hear, O Israel, the LORD is our God, the LORD is one" (Deut. 6:4), and martyrdom—"his soul departed while uttering the word 'one.'" That which was only implied in the early telling in the Jerusalem Talmud is now made explicit. In order for that to happen, the most important aspect of true martyrdom, which was missing from the story in early sources—execution by the persecuting power—has been added.[124]

According to this version, Akiva had already been specifically condemned to death by the Romans and was being taken out to be executed publicly in a place where his disciples could witness his death. Iron combs were being used to torture and kill him.[125] It was the time of reciting the *Sh'ma*, and he recited it. It is because of this story that, following Akiva's example, the recitation of the *Sh'ma* became the way in which Jews throughout the centuries have met their death. Akiva's disciples appear in this retelling as witnesses to his death, who could pass the story on as an act of *kiddush ha-Shem* (sanctification of God's name). The concept of a martyr's death as the fulfillment of love of God is a powerful combination of love and death.

All of this makes the Akiva of these legends the very perfect martyr, the model for all Jewish martyrs, lending meaning and courage to all those who were called on to sacrifice and die because of their devotion to Torah and to their Judaism from that time until today. The popular saying was "If one sees Rabbi Akiva in his dreams, let him fear calamity."[126]

Later Akiva's death was combined with other tales of martyrdom, in the liturgical poem "The Ten Martyrs," the story of Jews who died for the sanctification of God's name.[127] The midrash to Psalm 9:13—"When He makes inquisition for blood, He remembers them, He does not forget the cry of the afflicted"—mentions specifically that God "demands requital for the blood of Rabbi Akiva" and does not forget "the blood of any one of Israel slain in times of persecution." It then lists "the ten executed by Rome," which became the basis of "The Ten Martyrs." The first are Shimon and Ishmael, the last is Rabbi Akiva.[128] The Holy One inscribes the name of each martyr on His purple robe, and when God judges the nations, He shows them the names there and decrees the doom of the nations.[129]

The story of Akiva the martyr was also important for Judaism's struggle against the spread of Christianity. Early Christianity put much emphasis on martyrdom, a subject that had originated in Maccabean times but was not greatly emphasized in Judaism before the time of the Bar Kokhva Rebellion. Here now was an opportunity to demonstrate that Jews were no less willing to die for their faith than were the early Christians. In a sense Akiva became the answer to Jesus's status as well. Midrashim concerning the sacrifice of Isaac had already implied that there was no need for Jesus to die in order to attain atonement because Isaac, depicted as a willing sacrifice, carrying wood as one carries a cross, had already done that.[130] But the legend of Akiva created a Jewish leader, one born in the same century as Jesus, who also suffered death at the hands of the Roman oppressors and who accepted his fate as the ultimate test of true love of God.

Other legendary aspects of Akiva's life story also added to his stature and importance as a role model for scholars and for devout Jews in general. Stressing his poverty, which may not have been as extreme as depicted, giving him a father-in-law whose objections to his marriage had to be overcome, exaggerating the number of his followers and the years of his separation from his wife were all means of building his image. This is not to say that his image was created out of nothing. He did come from an undistinguished background. He did start his education at an advanced age. He was an extraordinarily intelligent man, with boundless energy. He was a brilliant orator and a wonderful interpreter of Torah. He was obviously charismatic, a great spinner of tales, and devoted to helping others, tireless in his work for the good of others and ingenious in developing and preserving Jewish traditions. What legend later added was just icing on the cake, which made his life story seem even more intriguing, but ultimately can be taken with a grain of salt. Even without it, he was surely worthy of the accolades that tradition has granted him as a second law-giver and one of the "fathers of the world."

It is reported that when the news of Akiva's death reached his disciples and his colleagues, they put on sackcloth and ashes. Some saw this as an ominous sign for the future and for the fortunes of the rebellion. "In a short time from now," said Yehudah ben Betera and Hananiah ben Teradion, who himself was to suffer terrible martyrdom, "no place in the Land of Israel will be found where bodies of the slain have not been cast."[131]

Even Akiva's corpse became the subject of legend. Most likely the guards lifted the lifeless body of the elderly Sage and carried it out of the building to be thrown like refuse on some rubbish heap. Such was the fate of all who dared defy the power of Rome. It seems almost certain that he did not receive a proper burial; the Romans would never have allowed it.[132] Nevertheless legend has it that when Elijah informed Joshua HaGarsi, who had gone home to celebrate a holiday,[133] that Akiva had died, they came together to the prison and entered easily because there was no guard. There they found Akiva's body on his bed, carried it out of Caesarea, and found a place with a bier, a bench, a table, and a lamp. "Happy are you, Akiva, for whom a good resting place has been found at the moment of your death!"[134] In light of what probably happened to his body in reality, there is a bitter irony in this statement.

And there is another, less sanguine legend that says something quite disturbingly different. It recounts that God showed Moses Akiva's academy and when Moses, impressed by Akiva's greatness, asked what Akiva's reward was, God showed him market stalls in which Akiva's flesh was being weighed out for sale. When Moses questioned the justice of this, God replied, "Be silent for such is My decree."[135]

### THE AFTERMATH

The destruction that attended the end of the Bar Kohkva Rebellion was more terrible than anything that Akiva could have imagined. As Tractate Semahot put it, "Not long after Roman armies attacked and put the entire world into chaos. In twelve months the councils of Judea came to an end."[136] Akiva's death spared him the knowledge of the complete failure of the revolt and the fall of the last stronghold of Bar Kokhva, Beitar, seven miles southwest of Jerusalem, in 135 CE.[137] Because the Tenth and Sixth Roman Legions had not been able to quell the rebellion, legions from Syria, Egypt, Arabia, Britain, and the Danube were brought in. Such an array of forces against a rebel band from a godforsaken province was unheard of.[138]

No wonder that the traditional phrase "I and my legions are well" had to be eliminated from Hadrian's proclamation of victory to the Senate. There were no celebrations in Rome, no coins issued, no triumphal parades or monumental arches built there. Later one monumental arch dedicated to Hadrian was built by the Senate far from Rome in Tel Shalem, a sure sign of the great relief that the danger was over. For the first and only time, the Romans changed the name of the province—as if they wanted it to no longer exist. Judea became Syria Palestine, a name that has continued in some variations to this day.[139]

The suffering of the Jews was equally unprecedented. The number of the dead at Beitar was enormous, Bar Kokhva among them. Legends may have exaggerated the numbers, as the sources were wont to do, just as they exaggerated the size of Bar Kokhva's forces and his personal strength.[140] Cassius Dio speaks of 985 villages that were destroyed and 580,000 men killed in the fighting. "Thus nearly the whole of Judaea was made desolate."[141] Draconian anti-Jewish laws were enforced, and many Sages followed Akiva into death and martyrdom. Large numbers of Jews were captured and sold as slaves. Entire cities and villages were destroyed. Jerusalem did not exist as such, only Aelia Capitolina. No Jew was allowed to live there.

A fragment found in the Bar Kokhva letters echoes the feelings that must have prevailed at the end. He writes:

> . . . till the end . . .
> . . . they have no hope . . .
> . . . my brothers in the south . . .
> . . . of these were lost by the sword . . .
> . . . these my brothers . . .[142]

The failure of the uprising put an end to dreams of restoration of Jewish independence and freedom from Rome for centuries to come. It also meant that the possibility that Judaism would replace paganism as the religion of the Roman Empire and the Western world faded from reality. Christianity would do that and would therefore have dominion over Jews in Europe for nearly two millennia, with the tragic consequences that are known all too well. In Jewish tradition Bar Kokhva was no longer Bar Kokhva, "the son of a star" but Bar Koziva, "the son of falsehood," and Judaism adopted the stance that Jews were sworn never to try to "force the end," to bring about the Messiah and the return to Zion. In modern times the consequences of this acquiescence have proved fatal.

And yet for all the suffering, death, and exile that accompanied the end of the Bar Kokhva Rebellion, Jewish life and the spread of Torah did not cease. The center of Jewish life moved to the Galilee, which had suffered much less than Judea.[143] Within seventy years of Akiva's death, under the Severan dynasty that now ruled Rome, relations with the empire improved. Rabbi Judah the Prince (Nasi) was reported to be on good terms with Rome and with its rulers[144] and was able to complete the Mishnah at his Great Court in Bet Shearim in northern Israel. There is something ironic in the fact that instead of calling himself Rabban Judah, Rabbi Judah adopted the title "Nasi," the same title that Bar Kokhva had used for himself, and Rabbi Judah became in many ways the official ruler of the Jews in their own land.

Akiva's work did not stop with his death. By the end of the century the efforts of his loyal disciples Rabbi Meir, Rabbi Nehemiah, Rabbi Yehudah, and Rabbi Shimon led to the creation of the major works of early Rabbinic Judaism, based on Akiva's teachings: the Mishnah and the Tosefta.[145] Within a hundred years after that, the great midrashic works of Akiva and of Ishmael, the midrashim on Exodus, Leviticus, Numbers, and Deuteronomy, known as *Mekhilta*, *Sifra*, and *Sifre*, were published. Imagine Judaism without those tomes. They formed the foundation for the continuation of Jewish life in the harsh conditions that then prevailed, the life-giving water that sustained the Jewish people.

# EPILOGUE

## The Man and His Legacy

Akiva's portrait of the ideal Sage is found in teachings ascribed to him in ancient sources: "An *am ha-aretz* [ignorant person] cannot be pious, the timid cannot learn, and the short-tempered cannot teach."[1] "The ignorant cannot be sin-fearing and those who engage overmuch in business will not attain wisdom."[2] Since these same words are ascribed to Hillel in the Mishnah, it is impossible to know if they originated with Akiva or not.[3] If Hillel said them, Akiva might well have quoted him, for they described his own ideals and his own personality.

### A COMPLEX MAN

Akiva was a man of many contradictions. In a relatively short time he made the leap from lack of knowledge to total mastery of Torah and tradition. On the one hand he was a person of sharp intellect, capable of incisive and complicated legal arguments, often besting his elders with his impeccable logic. On the other hand, he was enthusiastic about using methods of biblical interpretation that defied rational thinking. He practiced mystical exercises to experience transcendent realms but followed logical methodology in organizing legal texts. He derived or linked laws to biblical texts by methods that others found totally unacceptable. He was a master of Midrash and created many collections of biblical interpretations, both legal and literary, but he also favored the mishnaic method of preserving laws according to logical categories, and he provided the basis for the classic Mishnah. He was innovative in his interpretations and ready to change laws that he considered inappropriate, but he was devoted to the preservation of the teachings of the past.

Although sometimes lenient in his rulings, he was strict and fastidious in observance of ritual laws. He always saw the good in whatever happened but believed suffering to be redemptive. He was incisive enough to see what had to be done to preserve the totality of tradition and to use multiple methods of doing so, becoming an expert on law and aggadah as well as in the forms of Midrash and Mishnah. He proclaimed the coming of the Messiah and believed in the imminent restoration of the Temple in defiance of the obvious reality of the situation. He believed that love was the basis of relationship between God and humans and between human beings, even though he extolled the value of suffering. He had boundless energy and was able to teach, study, travel, and engage in community affairs.

### THE UNIQUENESS OF THE TORAH

In view of the many challenges to Jewish life that Akiva encountered in the difficult age in which he lived (not the least of which was the challenge of the teachings of Jewish-Christians), he espoused a theory of the divine origins of the Torah that raised that work far above any human creation. His belief that the Torah was written by God in heaven prior to Creation and that every word, every letter, every sign had meaning and must be interpreted, stood in opposition to that of Ishmael, who contended that the Torah, while divine, used the language of human beings and was the result of prophetic inspiration.

Much of Akiva's way of thinking and acting was based on mystical concepts. Certainly his idea of Torah from heaven—the Torah as a divine document, preexisting in heaven, created and given by God alone—was anchored in mystical thinking. We know that he indulged in active mysticism, "entering paradise." Did he practice mystical methods throughout his lifetime? We cannot be certain, but his frequent references to angels, to an imminent and even a suffering God, certainly played a major part in his thinking and lend credence to that possibility. Yet "he escaped unharmed," remaining a sane individual, very much a part of this world. He was a practical mystic, a mystical intellectual—a unique combination.[4]

Akiva's concept of Torah, the most extreme of all, totally divorcing the Torah from human input, was a major influence on Rabbinic Judaism. It raised the Torah to a level of holiness that was unprecedented.[5] At a time when the Torah's validity was being challenged, this was an important step. Furthermore, Akiva stressed the importance of the study of Torah, even above observance of the commandments, as the basis of Jewish life, something that has remained a critical part of Jewish life.

## THE CENTRALITY OF LOVE

Akiva was moved and motivated by love. He experienced meaningful human love, with his wife, even if the legends concerning his marriage are exaggerated. No wonder that he found in the biblical Song of Songs the supreme description of the relationship of Israel to God and extended that love to the willingness to die for love of the Lord.

Akiva compared the Song of Songs to the Torah itself in its divine origins and in its holiness. This may have influenced the decision of the Sages to accept that scroll as a part of sacred Scripture and certainly determined the way in which it was understood in traditional circles. His interpretation of Song of Songs was an expression of his emphasis on love, rather than fear, as the appropriate relationship to God, and this love was reciprocal, as is the human love depicted in Song of Songs.

Akiva was instrumental in placing love at the center of Judaism's teachings, making it the primary principle of the Torah and the basic motivation of observance of the commandments. He taught that God loves humanity and could and will forgive those who practice repentance and that God suffers together with His people and requires redemption even as they do.

Very much a man of the people, Akiva promoted a Judaism that was accessible to all, one that is based more on love than on fear, on joy rather than on solemnity, on closeness to a living God. His interpretation of Judaism is based on love of God, on God's love of Israel, and on God's love of all humanity. Following in the footsteps of Hillel, who had flourished a century before, Akiva preached and practiced a Judaism that sought adherence not through fear of God's wrath and punishment, but through love and mercy.

## THE COMFORTER

Akiva was passionate about everything, emotional and extreme in his concerns. The frequent refrain "Akiva you have comforted us" emphasized his desire to lift Israel out of despair, to counter the trauma of the disaster of the destruction and defeat of the year 70 CE. In that way he followed in the footsteps of the prophet known as Second Isaiah, whose watchword was "Be comforted, be comforted My people" (Isa. 40:1).

Akiva had the passion of the prophets but not their need to castigate Israel for its faults or question the ways of God. Whatever faults there may have been, whatever the shortcomings of Jews after their defeat in the Great Revolt and during the traumatic postwar period leading up to the Bar Kokhva Rebellion, Akiva did not see it as his task to address sins but rather to bring hope, to emphasize goodness.

An unrepentant optimist, he was able to offer comfort to his fellows and to the entire people by his vision of a redeemed nation, a rebuilt Temple, and a better world (which did not come to be in his lifetime nor for generations to come). This may account for his acceptance of the messianic status of Bar Kokhva. After all, salvation was what he anticipated and predicted all along.

As Heschel has pointed out, Akiva did not question God or God's justice. Regardless of the suffering that Jews had undergone and were still experiencing, Akiva saw God as the Merciful One, as the suffering God, not as a God who punishes. At no time did he question God's actions. When people suffered, he assumed that it was for a reason and even that it was beneficial. The early stories and even the later legends of his own imprisonment and eventual death never depicted him as wondering why this was happening to him. He never asked why he was being martyred nor accused God of abandoning him.

## PRESERVING AND CODIFYING TRADITION

Akiva flourished in the critical period when Rabbinic Judaism was in formation following the destruction of the Second Temple and the Roman victory in 70 CE. With the loss of the Temple, the synagogue and the *beit midrash* (house of study) became the centers of Jewish life and worship. Prayer developed significantly, replacing yet symbolically representing the sacrificial order. Study of the Torah of Moses (the text that had been accepted as sacred and definitive) became as important as worship, and schools, academies of study, flourished. Religious leadership moved from the priesthood to the Sages, whose official title became "Rabbi."

Because of his central role in furthering this Judaism, Akiva was considered one of the "fathers of the world." He did not create the forms of Mishnah or Midrash—they were already in existence in a less complex manner—but he made significant contributions to their further development and to Rabbinic Judaism's ability to flourish and shape the Jewish world.

His most significant contribution was the codification of all the unwritten traditions of both aggadah and halakhah that had developed over the centuries and were in danger of being lost. He found the way to preserve them, together with the current decisions being made by his colleagues regarding Jewish Law and practice, both attaching them to scriptural texts and arranging them in logical collections. This led to the corpus of Rabbinic texts we have today and that form the very basis of Rabbinic Judaism.

Akiva collected the traditions, sifted them, arranged them logically, and thus created the basic unwritten text that eventually became the Mishnah of Rabbi Judah the Prince (c. 200 CE). This Mishnah became the basis for elaborate discussions that resulted in the Jerusalem Talmud and the Babylonian Talmud, the medieval codes and the vast literature of responsa that continues to this day. None of that could have come into being without the Mishnah.

Akiva's influence on Jewish Law was so great that the Babylonian Talmud even ruled that although the law followed the majority when there was a case in which an individual was lenient and the majority was strict, if the lenient opinion was in accord with the teachings of Akiva, that was followed rather than the opinion of the majority.[6] In view of the fact that Akiva was responsible for the basic makeup of the Mishnah and that he was accepted as a major authority, many of the laws appearing there represent his opinion. The law as codified did not always follow his opinion, but certainly many of the laws cited without a name were those he initiated or supported.

The works that became the foundation of Jewish Law, legend, and study for all time were largely his doing. Akiva contributed to the corpus of tannaitic midrashim based on the books of the Torah. Akiva's approach to midrashic material was based on two things: his desire to connect as much oral material to biblical texts as possible to ensure their continuance and his belief that every word, letter, and mark in the Torah had meaning. This opened many more opportunities for creative interpretations.

## CREATIVITY AND INNOVATION IN LAW AND TRADITION

Although Akiva was concerned to preserve ancient traditions and rulings, there are times when he boldly overruled what had been previously taught to bring about a change he deemed necessary. He was often willing, even eager, to change long-held practices in order to innovate and to give far-reaching rulings that had profound effects, easing certain ritual requirements. Thus many practices are described as existing "until Rabbi Akiva came" and changed them.[7] Akiva's reinterpretation of Jewish Law in light of current developments and needs remains an important principle for those who see Judaism as changing and evolving with the times.

## THE MAVERICK

What seems to characterize many of the various stories, sayings, and rulings of Akiva that are recounted in this volume is that Akiva emerged so often as someone who was unusual, who did the unexpected. He was a source of surprise to his colleagues and to his students, both in his reactions and in his legal rulings. Akiva frequently surprised and astonished others with his actions and his words. Many stories describe him doing or saying something unexpected. He laughed when others cried. He gave a ruling that made his students wonder what he was doing. He seemed impulsive, "jumping in" to controversies, performing some act that seemed to defy good manners or proper conduct. "Why do you put your head in between great ones?" he was asked.[8]

Akiva could not easily be fit into an accepted mold. The one word that best sums up this aspect of him is "maverick." He delighted in saying things that caused astonishment. He spoke of God's appearance as a slave and of God's exile and redemption. He did not hesitate to ascribe a controversial meaning to a verse, saying, "Were it not written in Scripture it would be impossible to utter it—as it were—Israel said to God, 'You have redeemed Yourself!'"[9] Both when experiencing the greatness of the city of Rome[10] and when seeing the ruins of the Temple in Jerusalem he laughed when everyone else wept, and he interpreted these calamities as positive signs of redemption and glory for Israel.[11] When he visited the suffering Rabbi Eliezer, he rejoiced because that was a sign of the reward awaiting him, and when others praised Eliezer to comfort him, Akiva comforted him by telling him how much suffering was to be welcomed! "Precious are chastisements. They alone can bring about repentance and forgiveness." He taught, "One should rejoice more in chastisement than in prosperity."[12] Even the last act of his life, when he was about to die, continued this motif. "The time of the recital of the *Sh'ma* has now come, and I am not deterred from it; and therefore I recite the *Sh'ma* and I smile."[13] To smile when suffering and about to die—that is the ultimate irony.

## SUFFERING AND MARTYRDOM

Akiva placed great importance on human suffering, which in his theology brought with it benefits such as forgiveness and eternal reward. The stories of his death, which was viewed as the epitome of martyrdom, influenced Jewish thought and ritual, seeing martyrdom as the ultimate test of one's loyalty to Judaism and to one's love of God. As the third-century *amora* Shimon ben Lakish said, "'This is the book of the generations of Adam' (Gen. 5:1). This teaches that the Holy One showed Primal Adam each generation and its expositors, each generation and its Sages, each generation and its leaders. When He came to the generation of Rabbi Akiva, He rejoiced in his Torah and grieved in his death, saying, 'How precious are Your dear ones, O God' (Ps. 139:17)."[14]

Akiva also contributed the concept that God so identified with Israel and with humanity that God suffered with them, was in some way enslaved with them, and required redemption, which would only come with their redemption. His concept of God emphasized God's nearness to humanity, God's presence in the world, and God's concern for people.

## SCHOLAR AND ACTIVIST

Akiva functioned on many different levels throughout his career. On the highest intellectual level, he participated in discussions of the Yavneh Sanhedrin and in decisions of the Rabbinic courts. He worked to systematize learning and to preserve the tradition through Mishnah and Midrash. He headed his own academy and raised numerous disciples who followed his words and his methods. He also worked outside of the academy for the good of the community, traveling to Rome on political missions and elsewhere to raise funds and care for the needy. He cared for the poor and devoted much effort to raising money and helping them, interpreting many laws in such a way as to favor them. But he was strict in court, adhering to the conviction that justice must always be done with no favoritism, even to those in need. He was scornful of those who would take charity when they did not need it or pretend to be disabled in order to beg alms.[15]

Hardly the elitist, he took his teaching outside of the classroom and taught the general public as well as aspiring sages, preaching and spreading Torah. Although a controversial figure to many of his peers, he was admired for his intellect and his erudition. His disciples followed him and respected his dedication and brilliance as a teacher. The general public appreciated his devotion to them and admired his skill as a preacher and a teller of parables. He remained always a man of the people, not an aristocrat, never forgetting his humble origins.

It may be said that in some ways Akiva resembled the classic eighteenth-century Hasidic rebbe whose followers (Hasidim), like Akiva's students, were constantly amazed by what he said and did. There too one finds the tendency to say the opposite of what is expected, to surprise and astonish people with an unusual interpretation or statement, to overrule things that have been taken for granted, and to relax certain strictures. The staid and the usual are put aside in favor of the unexpected and the surprising. Unlike the Hasidic rebbe, however, Akiva was first and foremost a scholar, an expert in Jewish Law, and one who put the study of Torah and careful observance of all mitzvot at the top of his priorities. Nor did Akiva attempt to set himself up as a leader who had to be followed, was above all others, or had special divine powers or the ability to heal or perform miracles or wondrous deeds.

Akiva disdained paganism and often warned Jews not to do things that might lead them into idolatry. He denied the teachings of Christianity that spoke of God in human form, regarded the

Torah as "old law," and promoted the emergence of a "new law," as well as its attitude concerning salvation. He devoted himself to the promotion of belief in the One God, the Merciful One, the Just One, and in the sacredness of the Torah, the study of which was his primary concern. He saw Rome as the enemy of the Jewish people and believed with certainty in its eventual overthrow. Although Akiva supported Bar Kokhva as the leader of the rebellion, he did not involve himself in the conduct of the war.

### THE ROLE OF LEGEND

Akiva has assumed a major role in Jewish tradition. Possibly the legends that grew up about him contributed to that. Without the stories of his marriage to Rachel and the legends about his death, would he have assumed as central a role in the popular mind as he has? No one can know. But aside from the obviously legendary material, all the very admirable (and colorful) character traits and the many important accomplishments attributed to him in the early literature had already made him a popular figure and folk hero, and the teachings and opinions given in his name had a major influence during his life and later on all the generations after him. It was on this basis that legends expanded on these themes grew and flourished. Therefore Akiva outshone Ishmael in both popular imagination and influence on Jewish tradition.

In conclusion, Akiva ben Yosef was undoubtedly one of the most influential Rabbinic figures of the tannaitic period, a Sage who made contributions of lasting importance to Judaism. Akiva was not the originator of Rabbinic Judaism, nor was he the only teacher of importance. Ishmael must be given great credit for his contribution to the creation of important tannaitic midrashim and to the Rabbinic discourse. He too was one of "the fathers of the world," the one who gave legitimacy to a more logical and rational approach to biblical interpretation. Those who led the new Sanhedrin, Yohanan ben Zakkai, Rabban Gamliel II, and Rabban Shimon ben Gamliel, played an enormous role in creating forms that molded

Jewish life and in the organization of a new Jewish polity, as did Rabbi Judah the Prince. Nevertheless, one cannot exaggerate the impact of Akiva on the formation of Rabbinic Judaism.

That one man could have accomplished so much is astonishing, and even more so if the tradition is correct that Akiva attained Jewish knowledge and practice only as an adult, an adult who previously could neither read nor write. No wonder that a midrash quotes Moses, when given the opportunity to listen to Akiva's lesson in his house of learning, as saying to God, "You have such a man, yet you give the Torah through me?!"[16]

# NOTES

**PREFACE**

1. Ginzberg, "Akiba ben Joseph," 1:304.
2. Goldin, "Toward a Profile," 299.
3. Yadin-Israel, "Rabbi Akiva's Youth." All the most current works concerning the unreliability of our sources are cited there in the footnote. See also Friedman, "A Good Story," for a discussion of problematic sources.
4. Shinan, "Three Wives," 22.

**1. AKIVA'S EARLY LIFE**

1. *Tannaim* is the Hebrew term used to denote the Sages who lived from the time of Hillel and Shammai, first century BCE, until the completion of the Mishnah, c. 200 CE. Akiva belonged to the third generation of these teachers, which concluded in 135 CE.
2. Ginzberg, "Akiba ben Joseph," 304.
3. Ginzberg, "Akiba ben Joseph," 304.
4. Y. *Shekalim* 3, 47b.
5. *Sifre D.* 48.
6. *Sanhedrin* 36a.
7. *Kiddushin* 72b.
8. See, for example, Aleksandrov, "Role of 'Aqiba," 431; Oppenheimer, *Galilee in the Mishnaic Period*, 60.
9. Goldin, "Toward a Profile," 299.
10. Sarna, JPS Torah Commentary: Genesis, in his commentary to Genesis 25:26 suggests that the real meaning is "to protect," from the Semitic root *'-k-v*.
11. *Berakhot* 27b. Although some interpreted this to mean he was descended from converts, the meaning is more likely that his ancestry was not from learned or distinguished people.
12. *Pesahim* 49b.

13. See the discussion of these sources in chapter 2.

14. *ARN-A* 21.

15. *ARN-A* 6.

16. Yadin-Israel, "Rabbi Akiva's Youth," 577, believes otherwise and takes an extreme view. There is nothing, he states, to suggest that Akiva was an *am ha-aretz* or that his poverty was anything other than the result of his going to study, and no indication how late in life that was.

17. *Semahot* 8.

18. *ARN-B* 12. Lod (Lydda) was the chief town of one of the districts (toparchies) but was not a city. M. Stern, in Ben-Sasson, *History of the Jewish People*, 260.

19. *Pesahim* 49b.

20. See S. Cohen, *From the Maccabees*, 143–73, for a comprehensive discussion of the sects in Judaism during this period.

21. See Louis Ginzberg, "The Significance of the Halachah for Jewish History," in *On Jewish Law and Lore*.

22. Cohen, *From the Maccabees*, 172.

23. Finkelstein, *The Pharisees*, 1:25, 2:754–61. See also Baron, *Social and Religious History* 2:47.

24. *Sotah* 22a. Other definitions there include one who does not put on tefillin (phylacteries) and one who does not wear tzitzit (fringes) as well as one who does not recite the *Sh'ma*.

25. M. Stern, in Ben-Sasson, *History of the Jewish People*, 259.

26. *Gittin* 57b.

27. *Sotah* 3:4.

28. *Sotah* 22b.

29. Zeitlin, *Rise and Fall*, 3:219 and 3:143.

30. S. Safrai in Ben-Sasson, *History of the Jewish People*, 319–22.

31. Baron, *Social and Religious History*, 2:120.

32. Baron, *Social and Religious History*, 2:56.

33. See S. Cohen, "Significance of Yavneh," 27–53.

34. Baron, *Social and Religious History*, 2:120.

### 2. BECOMING A SAGE

1. See Hammer, "A Rabbinic Response," for similar views expressed somewhat later.

2. S. Cohen, "Significance of Yavneh."

3. *ARN-A* 4.

4. Alon, *Jews in Their Land*, 1:482, 2:472.

5. *Sifre D.* 357.

6. Mss London.

7. Yadin-Israel, "Rabbi Akiva's Youth," beginning with 590.

8. *Gen. R.* 100, 1295, ed. Theodor-Albeck.

9. On the antiquity of this work, see Goldin, *The Fathers*, xxi. See also Friedman, "A Good Story," 71.

10. *ARN*-A 6, translation by Goldin, in *The Fathers*. A similar version is found in *ARN*-B 29. Scholars differ regarding the age of this work. Goldin and others believe it to be of tannaitic origin. Others think the final version was edited later than that but contained older material.

11. Goldin, *The Fathers*, xxii.

12. *ARN*-B 12.

13. It was customary for children to begin the study of the Torah with Leviticus. See *Lev. R.* 7:3, "Those who are pure should study laws of purity."

14. *ARN*-A 6.

15. *ARN*-B 12.

16. *ARN*-A 6.

17. *ARN*-B 12.

18. *ARN*-B 12. Had he done so he would have had no time to study (Schechter).

19. *ARN*-A 6; *ARN*-B 12.

20. *ARN*-A 6.

21. *Sanhedrin* 32b. See also *Sifre D.* 144, where his academy is mentioned but without specification of a place.

22. See Ginzberg, "Akiba ben Joseph."

23. *Sanhedrin* 32b; see Alon, *Jews in Their Land*, 1:179.

24. Zeitlin, *Rise and Fall*, 3:180.

25. *ARN*-A 6.

26. *Gittin* 56a.

27. *Sanhedrin* 32b.

28. *ARN*-A 6.

29. Y. *Pesahim* 6, 33b.

30. *Sanhedrin* 86a. The Mishnah was transmitted by his student Rabbi Meir.

31. *ARN*-A 6.

32. *ARN*-B 12.

33. See Ilan, *Mine and Yours*; Shinan, "Three Wives."

34. Safrai, *Eretz Yisrael*, 172–77.

35. Y. *shabbat* 6:1, 7d; Y. *sotah* 9:15, 24c.

36. *ARN*-A 6; *ARN*-B 13.

37. *Ketubot* 62b–63a; *Nedarim* 50a.

38. *Gittin* 56a; *ARN*-A 6; *ARN*-B 13.

39. See Friedman, "A Good Story," 65, for a detailed analysis of the two stories and their differences.
40. *Ketubot* 62b.
41. *Nedarim* 50a.
42. Or wood, in some versions.
43. *ARN-A* 6.
44. *Gittin* 56a.
45. Chronologically it is also unlikely. See Ilan, "Quest for the Historical."
46. *Yadayim* 3:5.
47. *Yadayim* 3:5.
48. See *Ketubot* 5:6; Ilan, Mine and Yours, 207, 274, 277; Shinan, "Three Wives," 21.
49. See Ilan, Mine and Yours, 80.
50. *ARN-A* 6.
51. See Schechter's note on 29.
52. Ilan, "Quest for the Historical," 9.
53. Friedman, "A Good Story," 72–73.
54. *Ketubot* 63a.
55. Ilan, Mine and Yours, 290; "Quest for the Historical," 10. Ilan assumes that *ARN-A* was edited after the Babylonian Talmud and that the name was added there then. Others believe that *ARN* was edited earlier, but the adding of a name to printed versions could have been done at any time.
56. Y. *Shabbat* 6:1, 7d.
57. *Shabbat* 59a.
58. Y. *Shabbat* 6:1, 7d; Y. *Sotah* 9:16, 24c; *ARN-A* 6.
59. See Ilan, Mine and Yours, 108.
60. *Avodah Zarah* 20a.
61. *Song R.* 1:20.
62. *Mekh. Be-shallah* 6, i 235; T. *Berakhot* 4:16–17. See Lieberman's comments.
63. *Song R.* 1:20.
64. *Ketubot* 84b. There is a disagreement over whether Tarfon was a colleague or a master. He is generally treated as an older colleague.
65. *ARN-A* 6.
66. Y. *Yoma* 1:1, 38d; *Sifre N.* Be-ha'alotekha 75. The two versions differ as to exactly what occasion Tarfon saw his crippled uncle blowing the trumpet. *Sifra* 6:2 contains another dispute between the two in which Akiva is able to disprove Tarfon's arguments so that Tarfon agrees with him and swears that "anyone who separates himself from you is like one who separates himself from life."

67. *Pesahim* 6:1–2, Y. *Pesahim* 6:3–4 33b–c.

68. *Pesahim* 6:2.

69. *ARN-A* 25.

70. Y. *Sanhedrin* 1:2,19:a.

71. Y. *Sanhedrin* 1:2,19:a.

72. *Berakhot* 62a, where he follows him into a privy. Ben Azzai similarly followed Akiva into a privy to learn proper conduct, which he (and Akiva) called "a matter of Torah."

73. *Hagigah* 14b.

74. Y. *Nazir* 7:1, 56a–b.

75. Ilan, Mine and Yours, 275.

76. *Hagigah* 12a–b.

77. *Ta'anit* 21a.

78. *Berakhot* 60b.

79. *Menahot* 29b.

80. *Sifre D.* 1. See also Piska 16 on the work of the proctor.

81. *Sanhedrin* 32b.

82. See Paul, "Jerusalem."

### 3. THE NEW SAGE AND PUBLIC FIGURE

1. Hillel, the great Sage who lived in the first century BCE, was the founder of a dynasty of leaders. Hillel's son, Rabban Gamliel I was the grandfather of Rabban Gamliel II.

2. Ben-Sasson, *History of the Jewish People*, 310ff.

3. *Eduyot* 7:7.

4. Y. *Horayot* 3:7, 48a; *Lev. R.* 5:4. See Levine, *The Rabbinic Class*, 43.

5. Ben-Sasson, *History of the Jewish People*, 322–30.

6. Y. *Peah* 4:6 describes Akiva as being a parnas—someone charged with the welfare of the poor. The source also reiterates that Akiva had been poor and then became rich.

7. Y. *Yevamot* 1:6, 3a.

8. *Yevamot* 16a.

9. Zeitlin, *Rise and Fall*, 3:184.

10. *ARN-A* 3.

11. Zeitlin, *Rise and Fall*, 3:185.

12. Y. *Sanhedrin* 7:19, 25d.

13. Schafer, "Rabbi Aqiva and Bar Kokhba," 114.

14. *Min* sometimes denotes a Christian, which is possible here but not certain.

15. *Exod. R.* 30:9. On the Sabbath one is not allowed to move things from one's personal property into the public arena. Since "the earth

is the Lord's" all the world is God's private preserve and therefore the
Lord can move things—wind and rain—wherever God wants without
violating the Sabbath.

16. *Avodah Zarah* 4:7. See also the discussion in *Avodah Zarah* 54b–55a.

17. *Avodah Zarah* 55a.

18. *Eccles. R.* 10:7.

19. *ARN-A* 16.

20. Schafer, "Rabbi Aqiva and Bar Kokhba," 115–16.

21. *Sifre D.* 43; *Makkot* 24a; *Lam. R.* 5:19. See also *Ma'aser Sheni* 5:9, where
the Sages are on a boat on the sea.

22. *Sifra*, Emor 16:2.

23. Y. *Eruvin* 1:1, 19b; Y. *Sukkah* 2:4, 52d. In *Sukkah* 23a the remark is
attributed to Rabban Gamliel, who declared that a sukkah built on a
ship was invalid.

24. *Eruvin* 4:1.

25. *Rosh Hashanah* 26a.

26. See also Y. *Yevamot* 16:1, 15d; *Yevamot* 121a. Schafer, "Rabbi Aqiva and
Bar Kokhba," 117, "Aqiva's journeys, if they took place, were to various
Jewish communities and served such internal purposes as the settling
of halakhic problems, collections, questions of self-government and
the rest."

27. Y. *Horayot* 3:7, 48a; *Lev. R.* 5:4.

28. T. *Berakhot* 1:2.

29. *Bava Kamma* 8:6.

30. *Peah* 3:2.

31. *Peah* 3:7. See also *Peah* 1:6.

32. *Peah* 7:7. *Sifre D.* 285. When Akiva says in *Peah* 4:5 that the rule that
the poor can come and take their portion three times during the day
is "so that they will not come more often," he is explaining the rule
and not changing it. The other explanation, that it is stated so that
they will not come less, also sets the limit to three times. Having them
all through the day would make farming work impossible.

33. Y. *Peah* 7:1, 20a. He connects the word *aharekha* in Deut. 24:20–21.

34. See Deut. 26:12.

35. *Sifre D.* 303. See also *Sifre D.* 110; T. *Peah* 4:2.

36. *ARN-A* 3.

37. *Sanhedrin* 32b.

38. S. Safrai, in Ben-Sasson, *History of the Jewish People*, 329.

39. Aleksandrov, "Role of 'Aqiba," 429.

40. *Gen. R.* 61:3, 660; *Yevamot* 62b; *Nedarim* 50a.

41. *Gen. R.* 61:3, 660.

42. T. *Berakhot* 4:18.

43. *Eruvin* 13a.

44. *Lev. R.* 21:8.

45. *Pesahim* 109a.

46. The story is found in the Haggadah as an illustration of the idea that the more one discusses the Exodus, the better.

47. T. *Berakhot* 4:18.

48. *Nedarim* 40a.

49. *Sifra, Tazria* 1:2, ed. Weiss 58a–b.

50. *Shevuot* 6a.

51. *Sifre D.* 46. Some versions, however, read not "ben Akiva" but "ben Akavya." See *Sifre D.*, ed. Finkelstein 104.

52. *Ketubot* 63a.

53. T. *Ketubot* 4:7.

54. *Shevuot* 6a.

55. T. *Ketubot* 4:7.

56. *Midrash Psalms* 59:3. Ruth Calderon includes this tale from the Talmud, along with her own modern version of it and her commentary, in *A Bride for One Night: Talmud Tales* (Philadelphia: Jewish Publication Society, 2014).

57. *Pesahim* 112a.

58. *Semahot* 8. In *Mo'ed Katan* 21b no names are mentioned, but it is said that two sons died while in their young manhood.

59. The last phrase is from *Mo'ed Katan*; the rest is the version in *Semahot*.

60. Y. *Ma'aser Sheni* 5:6, 56:c.

61. *Lev. R.* 35;6. The same phrase appears in *Hagigah* 9b in the name of Rabbi Yosef.

62. See *Nedarim* 50a, where six incidents are related as having contributed to his wealth. None of them are credible.

63. T. *Ketubot* 4:7.

64. Friedman, "A Good Story," 84.

65. ARN-B 12.

66. *Nedarim* 50a–b.

67. *Sifre D.* 133.

68. *Sifre D.* 205. See also *Sotah* 9:3.

69. *Sifre D.* 212, 213. See also 291, where they disagree concerning the ceremony of *halitzah*; and 303, concerning the meaning of Deut. 26:14.

70. *Sifre N.* 95.

71. T. *Berakhot* 4:15.

72. The reference to Rome is missing in manuscripts and may not be correct. See Lieberman, *TK*, part 5, 955.

73. T. *Yom Tov* 2:12. See also *Beitzah* 2:5, where this is listed as one of three matters where Gamliel followed the strict rulings of the School of Shammai rather than the more lenient teachings of the School of Hillel. See also *Beitzah* 22a.

74. Oppenheimer, *Galilee in the Mishnaic Period*, 26.

75. T. *Demai* 5:24.

76. *Sifre D.* 61.

77. *Pesahim* 48b.

78. *Rosh Hashanah* 2:9–10.

79. Y. *Berakhot* 4:1 (end), 7:d, *Berakhot* 27b. See Zeitlin, *Rise and Fall*, 194.

80. T. *Hullin* 2:24; *Avodah Zarah* 16b–17a. See Boyarin, *Dying For God*, 33.

81. Y. *Mo'ed Katan* 3:1, 81c–d; *Bava Metzi'a* 59a–b.

82. *ARN*-A 25; *Sanhedrin* 68a.

83. *Sifra*, ed. Weiss 79c; *Shabbat* 64b.

84. *Nedarim* 9:6.

85. T. *Mo'ed Katan* 2:14.

86. T. *Demai* 4:13.

87. T. *Bava Kamma* 10:17; Y. *Bava Kamma* 9:15, 7a. See Finkelstein, *Akiba*, 118.

88. See Ginzberg, "Akiba ben Joseph."

89. *Gen. R.* 58:3 and parallels.

90. *Gen. R.* 33:7. It is not clear what the story was, and some texts read "Job" rather than "raven." See notes in Theodor-Albeck ed., 1:310.

91. Y. *Sotah* 9:10, 24a, *eshkolot*, "cluster of grapes," i.e., containing great amounts of material.

92. *ARN*-A 6.

### 4. THE MYSTICAL INTERPRETER OF TORAH

1. Nehemiah 8–10.

2. Y. *Peah* 1:1, 15a.

3. Y. *Peah* 2:6, 17a.

4. See Romans 3:19–31; 7:1–25; Hebrews 8:1–13.

5. *Shabbat* 116a.

6. *Sifre N.* 7.

7. The midrash contains verses to prove each point. They have been omitted here.

8. *Sifre D.* 48.

9. Ilan, "Daughters of Israel," 20–21.

10. Y. *Shekalim* 3:1, 47b.

11. *Gittin* 58a; *Ketubot* 105b; T. *Hallah* 1:10.

12. *Shevuot* 26a; *Hagigah* 12a.

13. Heschel, *Heavenly Torah*, 32–39.

14. In a discussion in *Sanhedrin* 51b Akiva refers to Ishmael as "my brother." This was a common way of referring to other Sages, as we see in *Yadayim* 4:3, where Eleazar ben Azariah calls both Ishmael and Tarfon "my brother" and Joshua calls Tarfon "my brother" as well.

15. ARN-A 37, T. *Sanhedrin* 7:11.

16. *Sifra* introduction, 1:7.

17. Lieberman, *Hellenism in Jewish Palestine*; David Daube, "Rabbinic Methods of Interpretation."

18. Jacobs, Hermeneutics, 8:366; Hammer, *Or Hadash*, xxxvii.

19. See *Sifre D.* 103, for example, where Akiva uses the rule of the *gezera shava*—comparing similar phrases in two verses.

20. *Sifra*, ed. Weiss 79c.

21. *Sifre N.* 112. See Jacobs, "Hermeneutics."

22. *Nedarim* 9:10; Ilan, "Daughters of Israel," 30.

23. T. *Hagigah* 2:3; *Hagigah* 14b; Y. *Hagigah* 2:1, 77b. See Lieberman, TK on the passage; Scholem, *Major Trends*, 43.

24. The biblical term *pardes* means "an orchard," but it became a technical term for the heavenly paradise and is used in texts as early as those found in Qumran. See Scholem, *Jewish Gnosticism*, 16.

25. *Aher*, "the other," a term indicating that he had left the Jewish fold. Some texts have *ahor*, meaning "having gone backward." See Lieberman, TK to the passage.

26. T. *Hagigah* 2:2–4.

27. T. *Hagigah* 2:3.

28. *Song R.* 1:28 (to verse 1:4).

29. *Hagigah* 14b.

30. Scholem, *Jewish Gnosticism*, 50–52.

31. T. *Hagigah* 2:1.

32. Y. *Hagigah* 2:1, 77a; T. *Hagigah* 2:1–2.

33. T. *Hagigah* 2:2.

34. Ginzberg translates *pardes* as "paradise" and states, "There is no doubt that the journey of the 'four' to paradise . . . is to be taken literally and not allegorically" (JE 5:138).

35. Scholem, *Major Trends*, 49.

36. *Ketubot* 63a.

37. T. *Yevamot* 8:4; Y. *Sotah* 1:2, 16c. This is also found in *Yevamot* 63b. See Ilan, "Quest for the Historical," 10.

38. *Lev. R.* 16:4.

39. Y. *Hagigah* 2:1, 77a.

40. Found there and in Y. *Hagigah* 2:1, 77b. Elisha frequently quotes the teachings of Rabbi Akiva.

41. Y. *Hagigah* 2:1, 77b.

42. *Avot* 4:20.

43. *ARN-A* 24; *ARN-B* 35.

44. See Scholem, *Jewish Gnosticism*, chapter 3. This literature is quite old and reflects mystical teachings that existed at the time of the Tannaim and are also reflected in Paul's second epistle to the Corinthians. See Scholem, *Jewish Gnosticism*, 16.

45. Scholem, *Major Trends*, 57.

46. Scholem *Major Trends*, 45.

47. The other possibility, of course, is that Ishmael too practiced mysticism and therefore is so prominent in the *Hekhalot* literature. If so, it is strange that there is no hint of this in early Rabbinic writings. Although some of these mystical tracts go back to the second century, they were not edited until the sixth century, sufficient time for unhistorical traditions to develop. See Scholem, *Major Trends*, 45 and 42n356.

48. Scholem records that in the *Hekhalot* literature, which was written after the time of the Tannaim, Rabbi Ishmael and Rabbi Akiva were the heroes of *Merkavah* mysticism (*Major Trends*, 68). There is no record of Ishmael in this regard, however, in Tannaitic literature.

49. See Heschel, *Heavenly Torah*, for a complete discussion of the differences between Akiva and Ishmael on the origins of the Torah and its nature.

50. Heschel, *Heavenly Torah*, 379.

51. *Tanhuma*, Ha'azinu to the verse.

52. Heschel, *Heavenly Torah*, 351.

53. *Sanhedrin* 99a. See also *Sanhedrin* 10:1.

54. *Sifre D.* 357.

55. Mystical thought envisions seven different levels in the heavenly sphere, the highest being the seventh, the sacred number. It is there that the presence of God can be found.

56. *Avot* 3:15.

57. Heschel, *Heavenly Torah*, 39.

58. See also *Sanhedrin* 74a, where a discussion is described in the same place on the question of what mitzvot a Jew could transgress rather than be killed. It has been suggested that these discussions took place in secret during the time of the Hadrianic persecutions.

59. *Kiddushin* 40b.

60. *Mekh. Bahodesh* 9, ii 266.

61. *Mekh. Bahodesh* 9, ii 275–76.

62. *Menahot* 29b.

63. Zeitlin, *Rise and Fall*, 3:348.

64. *Pesahim* 22b.

65. Y. *Berakhot* 9:7 (end), 14b.

66. *Gen. R.* 1:14. See also Y. *Kiddushin* 1:2, 59a; Y. *Shabbat* 19:1 17a for other examples of the different methods of Akiva and Yishmael.

67. *Sifre N.* 2.

68. Y. *Berakhot* 9:7 end, 14b.

69. *Sifre N.* 112.

70. *Sifre N.* 7.

71. *Sanhedrin* 51b.

72. *Sifra*, Tzav 33a; *Zevahim* 82a.

73. *Menahot* 89a; *Niddah* 72b.

74. *Mekh. Shabbata* 1, iii 197.

75. But they reason from different examples. Akiva's method here is no different from that of Ishmael.

76. Y. *Yevamot* 8:1, 8c.

77. *Sifre N.* 75.

78. *Midrash Psalms* 104:9.

79. *Yoma* 75b.

80. Flusser, *Judaism of Second Temple Period*, 266n20, thinks that this is not Akiva's interpretation because it does not accord with Akiva's view of the Messiah, since he identifies the Messiah "with the very human figure of Bar Kosiba."

81. *Sanhedrin* 38b.

82. *Shabbat* 96b–97a.

83. *Mekh. Nezikin* 9, iii 53.

84. See, for example, *Sifre D.* 107, where Akiva interprets the word *v'tzarta* in Deut. 14:25, which means "bind up," as "something with a figure in it." From that he learns that money with no figure may not be used. Ishmael says it simply means money that can be bound up.

85. *Sifre N.* 112 toward the end.

86. *Sifre D.* 197.

87. Heschel, *Heavenly Torah*, 709–19.

### 5. THE ORGANIZER OF TORAH

1. *ARN-A* 18. "Rings" refers to general rules. See Lieberman, *Hellenism in Jewish Palestine*, 95.

2. *Kiddushin* 72b.

3. Lieberman, *Hellenism in Jewish Palestine*, 95.

4. *Sifre D.* 48.

5. *Gittin* 60b; *Temurah* 14b. See also Y. *Peah* 2:6, 17a; Y. *Megillah* 4:1, 74c.

6. Y. *Peah* 2:6, 17a.

7. Y. *Peah* 2:6, 17a; Y. *Megillah* 4:1, 74c.

8. Baron, *Social and Religious History*, 2:143.

9. *Megillah* 3a; Y. *Kiddushin* 1:1, 59a.

10. Zeitlin, *Rise and Fall*, 3:200. The name "Onkelos" was an Aramaic distortion of Aquilas. It is unlikely that "Aquilas" translated both into Greek and into Aramaic. The Aramaic translation known by the Aramaic version of his name was written by unknown translators.

11. Y. *Shekalim* 5:1, 48c.

12. *Shabbat* 19:1. See also *Shevi'it* 6:2.

13. T. *Zavim* 1:5. See Lieberman, *Hellenism in Jewish Palestine*, 91.

14. *Sanhedrin* 86a.

15. See Judah Goldin's preface and the introduction by the author in Reuven Hammer, *The Classic Midrash*.

16. Halivni, *Midrash, Mishnah, and Gemara*, 60–61.

17. The *Sh'ma* is the central creed found in the Jewish prayer book, a declaration of faith in one God consisting of three paragraphs from the Torah recited morning and evening. *Berakhot* 1:6.

18. See *Eruvin* 54b, where Moses and Aaron are depicted teaching in the same way that the Sages must have done. Moses receives instruction from God and teaches it to Aaron. It is then passed on to Aaron's sons, then to the elders, who in turn teach the people.

19. *Sotah* 22a.

20. Lieberman, *Hellenism in Jewish Palestine*, 87.

21. Lieberman, *Hellenism in Jewish Palestine*, 93.

22. Lieberman, *Hellenism in Jewish Palestine*, 96. See also Halivni, *Midrash, Mishnah, and Gemara*, 59.

23. Halivni, *Midrash, Mishnah, and Gemara*, 144n27.

24. *Sotah* 9:15; *Sotah* 49b.

25. *Sotah* 5:2. Actually Akiva was not his pupil and had probably never even met Ben Zakkai, but he was a disciple of Ben Zakkai's disciple Joshua.

26. *Sifre D.* 351. The general may have been Marcus Antonius Julianus, procurator of Jordan at the time the Temple was destroyed.

27. *Sifra* 112c.

28. Finkelstein, *New Light*, 86.

29. *Avot* 1:1. ARN-A–B 1 also uses the word "Torah" rather than "the Torah" in a parallel passage.

30. *Sotah* 37b.
31. Y. *Kiddushin* 1:2, 59d. See Heschel, *Heavenly Torah*, 49. See also *Sotah* 16a. Another one of these instances, the fact that any instrument may be used to pierce the ear of a perpetual slave, while the Torah specifies an awl (Exod. 21:6) appears in *Mekh. Nezikin* 2, iii 16.
32. *Berakhot* 27b–28a. Some have suggested that "on that day" here simply means that these were taught on the same day that Akiva gave his ruling concerning the *Sotah* in the previous mishnah, 5:1. See Albeck's edition of the Mishnah, *Nashim* 384–85.
33. *Sotah* 5:2–4.
34. *Sotah* 5:5.
35. Rosen-Zvi, "Who Will Uncover."
36. Rosen-Zvi, "Who Will Uncover," 102–3.
37. *Hallel* is a collection of psalms praising God that is recited on Jewish festivals. Since people had no written text to follow, the leader would recite a verse and the people would then repeat it. The *Sh'ma* was well-known, and the leader would recite one part of a verse, which the people would complete.
38. Rosen-Zvi, "Who Will Uncover," 114.
39. Rosen-Zvi, "Who Will Uncover," 127.
40. Rosen-Zvi, "Who Will Uncover," 116.

### 6. AKIVA AND THE SONG OF SONGS

1. *Yadayim* 3:6.
2. The acceptance of the Torah as God's word had been proclaimed at the time of Ezra, as recorded in Nehemiah 8. There is no record of exactly when the books of the Prophets were officially accepted. Perhaps it was simply a matter of general consensus rather than any official decision. As for the other books that are today part of the third section of the Bible, the Writings, this was exactly the matter under discussion in the academy on "that day." See the discussion in Eissgeldt, *Old Testament*, 562–71.
3. T. *Yadayim* 2:14, where the contention is that Ecclesiastes was simply Solomon's wisdom and not uttered under the influence of the Holy Spirit.
4. *Eduyot* 5:3.
5. Alter, *Wisdom Books*, 342. See also Gordis, *Koheleth*, 41.
6. T. *Yadayim* 2:14.
7. *Yadayim* 3:6. See also *Song R.* 1:1.
8. *Yadayim* 3:5, 6.
9. The Tosefta also states that at some unspecified time a decision was made that "the Gospels and books of *Minim* [sectarians] [works that

were written by Christians and other Jewish groups considered heretical] are not sacred and Ben Sira and all books written from now on are not sacred." Perhaps that too happened "on that day." T. *Yadayim* 2:13.

10. See Eissgeldt, *Old Testament*, 568.

11. See Gordis, *Song of Songs*, 2–4, 8–9.

12. *ARN-A–B* 1. Some texts erroneously have "the men of the Great Assembly." They bring examples of passages that seem to be against biblical teachings and required correct interpretation.

13. *ARN-A* 17.

14. *Mekh. Bahodesh* 3, ii 219–20. See Lieberman, "Teaching of Song of Songs," 118–19.

15. T. *Sanhedrin* 12:10.

16. *Song R.* 1:1.

17. Lieberman, "Teaching of Song of Songs," 118.

18. This allegorical interpretation went so far that the description of the physical attributes of the lover in Song 5:10–16—clear-skinned and ruddy, curled hair, black as a raven's, eyes like doves, cheeks like beds of spices, lips like lilies, hands of gold, ivory belly, legs like marble pillars—served as the basis for a mystical poem describing all of the limbs of the Holy One, the famous "Shiur Komah." See Lieberman, "Teaching of Song of Songs," 123, 126.

19. *Song R.* 1:1.

20. Goldin, "Toward a Profile," 307.

21. See G. Cohen, "Song of Songs," 3–18.

22. Heschel, *The Prophets*, 44.

23. *Sifre D.* 32.

24. *Berakhot* 61b.

25. *Sifre D.* 32 end. The midrashic interpretations of the story of Abraham and Isaac, unlike the biblical tale, turn Isaac into a willing martyr, ready and prepared to give his life for God.

26. *Sifre D.* 32.

27. *Sifre D.* 32.

28. *Berakhot* 61b. See discussion of his death in chapter 8.

29. *Mekh. Shirata* 3, ii 26. See also *Song R.* to the verse (1:22), where it is connected to the generation that endured the Hadrianic persecutions.

30. *Deut. R.,* Va-ethannan.

31. Goldin, "Toward a Profile," 309.

32. *Sotah* 17a.

33. This is the position taken by Goldin in "Toward a Profile." The examples cited here are brought by him.

34. *ARN-A* 26. See also T. *Sotah* 5:11, where this is cited in the name of Akiva's disciple, Rabbi Meir.

35. *Sifre D.* 269 and the last mishnah of *Gittin.*

36. Goldin, "Toward a Profile," 314. See the detailed discussion beginning on 310.

37. *Sifre* 79c; *Shabbat* 64b.

38. *Sotah* 3a.

39. Hauptman, *Rereading the Rabbis,* 153.

40. *Niddah* 8:3.

41. Hauptman, *Rereading the Rabbis,* 155; *Zavim* 2:2.

42. *Ketubot* 5:2.

43. *Nedarim* 9:5.

44. Ilan, "Daughters of Israel."

45. *Sifre N.*, Hukkat 124. See Ilan, "Daughters of Israel," 22.

46. *Sifre D.* 122, 143, 157; *Sifre N.* 39, 70, 11, 115. See Ilan, "Daughters of Israel," 23–24.

47. *Sifre D.* 46.

48. *Sifre N.*115.

49. *Yevamot* 16:7.

50. *Nedarim* 9:11, Ilan, "Daughters of Israel," 30.

51. *Sifra* 89b. See the full discussion in chapter 7.

### 7. ASPECTS OF AKIVA'S THEOLOGY

1. Kadushin, *The Rabbinic Mind.*

2. See *ARN-A* 39, where one statement beings with "He" rather than any name, and *ARN-B* 44, where another is attributed to Rabbi Eliezer the son of Rabbi Yose HaG'lili.

3. *Avot* 3:15.

4. See chapter 4.

5. *Sifra* 89b.

6. *Gen. R.* 24:5. The order is reversed there, with Ben Azzai giving his verse first and Akiva saying that his verse is even greater. That is due to the fact that here the entire discussion is attached to the verse from Genesis, which is then interpreted by Ben Azzai. See Theodor-Albeck ed., 237.

7. *Avot* 3:15.

8. See Goldin, "Toward a Profile," 323.

9. *Shabbat* 31a. See Flusser, *Judaism of Second Temple Period,* 178.

10. *Avot* 1:12.

11. *Mekh. Pisha* 8, i 37. Heschel has also pointed out that in the School of Ishmael, the one commandment that was the basis for everything was

not love of humans but the denial of idolatry, a much less appealing subject. See Heschel, *Heavenly Torah*, 75.

12. See chapter 4.
13. *Sifra* 89b.
14. T. *Yevamot* 8:7.
15. Flusser, *Judaism of Second Temple Period*, 160.
16. *Makkot* 1:11.
17. *Makkot* 1:11.
18. *Sifre D.* 154; *Sanhedrin* 11:4.
19. *Sifra*, 90b
20. *Makkot* 1:7.
21. *Sifra*, 109c; *Bava Metzi'a* 62a.
22. T. *Berakhot* 3:3. This same statement, however, is found in *Avot* 3:11 in the name of Hanina ben Dosa.
23. *Sifre D.* 79.
24. *Bava Kamma* 113a.
25. *Bava Kamma* 113a.
26. *Sifre D.* 81.
27. *Sifre D.* 61.
28. *Sifre D.* 31. This was one of four passages that Shimon bar Yohai interpreted differently from his teacher and of which he said, "I prefer my interpretation to his." Shimon says that Ishmael was quarreling with Isaac over who would get more of the fields and the vineyards. *Gen. R.* 43:13, a later source than the *Sifre*, has Ishmael explaining it as idolatry, while Akiva says it was sexual misconduct. T. *Sotah* 6:6 has the same version as the *Sifre*.
29. *Sifre D.* 84.
30. *ARN-B* 33.
31. *Ta'anit* 25b.
32. *Sifre D.* 43; *Makkot* 24b.
33. *Pesahim* 10:6.
34. *ARN-A* 36.
35. *ARN-A* 26.
36. *ARN-A* 26.
37. *Lev. R.* 13:2.
38. *Avot* 3:16.
39. Y. *Kiddushin* 1:10, 61:d.
40. *Ketubot* 9:2–3.
41. *Yoma* 8:7.
42. *Avot* 3:17.
43. *Berakhot* 61b.

44. Heschel suggests that the idea of the net represents the angel of death and is borrowed from Ecclesiastes 9:12, "And a man cannot know his time. As fishes are enmeshed in a fatal net, and as birds are trapped in a snare, so men are caught at a time of calamity." Heschel, *Heavenly Torah*, 175.
45. *Avot* 3:17.
46. *Gen. R.* 26:3.
47. *Sifre Zuta* 248.
48. *ARN*-A 30.
49. *Sanhedrin* 110b; *Sanhedrin* 10:3.
50. *Sanhedrin* 110b.
51. *Sifre D.* 32. The discussions on suffering that follow are all from that section.
52. *Gen. R.* 33:1. See Sanders, "Rabbi Akiva's View of Suffering," 332–51.
53. *Sanhedrin* 101a.
54. *Sifre D.* 32.
55. See Heschel, *Heavenly Torah*, 35.
56. *Semahot* 14.
57. *Mekh. Nezikin* 18, iii 142.
58. *Berakhot* 60b.
59. *Mekh. Bahodesh* 10, ii 279.
60. The verse is usually translated as "With Me, therefore, you shall not make any gods of silver." Akiva takes the phrase out of context for his purpose of interpretation.
61. *Mekh. Bahodesh* 10, ii 277.
62. See chapter 8.
63. *Mekh. Shirata* 3, ii 24–25.
64. *Sifra* 4:a–b.
65. *Exod. R.* 29:9.
66. See Heschel, *The Prophets*.
67. The usual reading of the verse is "nations and their gods."
68. *Mekh. Pisha* 14, i 114.
69. *Y. Sukkah* 54:c. 4:3.
70. *Exod. R.* 15:12.
71. *Exod. R.* 42:3. See also *Num. R.* 2:2, where Exodus 14:30 is read as meaning that God was saved together with Israel. See Heschel, *Heavenly Torah*, 107–8.
72. *Mekh. Pisha* 14, i 115.
73. From the word *lavan* (white), the place that whitens the sins of Israel.
74. This same midrash is found in the Talmud (*Megillah* 29a), where it is ascribed to Akiva's disciple Shimon bar Yohai.

75. The usual translation is "a pavement of sapphire."
76. *Mekh. Pisha* 14, i 113. This entire midrash is also found in *Sifre N.*, 84. See also *Lev. R.* 23:8 and *Song R.* 4:17 to verse 4:8.
77. See Heschel, *Heavenly Torah*, 35 and Flusser, *Judaism of Second Temple Period*, 103n110.
78. See Held, *Abraham Joshua Heschel*, 145.
79. *Sifre D.* 319, interpreting Deut. 32:18, "God that bore you," *meholele-kha*, as "travailed," *hehil.*
80. See, for example, Habakkuk 1:13, "Why do You countenance treachery, and stand by idle while the one in the wrong devours the one in the right?"
81. For example, Psalm 44, especially verses 24–27.
82. *Mekh. Bahodesh* 10, ii 277.
83. Heschel, *Heavenly Torah*, 36.
84. *Megillah* 17b. See Hammer, *Entering Jewish Prayer*, 86–88.
85. *Sanhedrin* 86a.
86. *Sifre D.* 32.
87. *Berakhot* 9:5.
88. *Megillah* 1:1; *Megillah* 2a.
89. This is not mentioned in the Jerusalem Talmud.
90. *Berakhot* 5:2. These decisions were frequently not indicated in the Mishnah itself, which merely records the various opinions. Decisions were made by later authorities, as recorded in the Talmud.
91. T. *Megillah* 3:11.
92. *Megillah* 4:2.
93. Liebeman, *TK* 1175.
94. *Berakhot* 31a.
95. *Sukkah* 3:4; *Sifra*, 103d.
96. *Sukkah* 34b.
97. *Sukkah* 3:9.
98. *Rosh Hashanah* 18b.
99. *Berakhot* 4:3.
100. These sections were originally in the morning service and later were moved to *Musaf.* See Hammer, *Entering the High Holy Days*, 76.
101. *Rosh Hashanah* 4:5.
102. Y. *Rosh Hashanah* 4:6, 59c; Y. *Pesahim* 10:6, 37d.
103. T. *Kippurim* 4:14; Y. *Yoma* 8:9, 45c. The formulas currently in use were not decided on before the gaonic period in the ninth and tenth centuries.
104. Yoma 86b.
105. See Hammer, *Entering the High Holy Days*, 135–41.

106. *Yoma* 8:4.
107. T. *Kippurim* 4:2. See TK 812. See also *Pesahim* 109a.
108. *Pesahim* 109a.
109. *Ta'anit* 25b.
110. Y. *Ta'anit* 34, 66c–d.
111. *Pesahim* 10:6.

## 8. AKIVA—RESISTANCE, IMPRISONMENT, AND DEATH

1. Goodman, *Rome and Jerusalem*, 482.
2. Baron, *Social and Religious History*, 2:94.
3. The daily *Amidah* is a prayer asking for the restoration of the pre-destruction situation, the return of exiles, the restoration of the Davidic kingship, and the rebuilding of Jerusalem and of the Temple. See Hammer, *Entering Jewish Prayer*, 174–81.
4. Eck, "Bar Kokhba Revolt," 76.
5. Goodman, *Rome and Jerusalem*, 464.
6. Goodman, *Rome and Jerusalem*, 486.
7. *Bava Batra* 60b.
8. *Ta'anit* 30b.
9. *Pesahim* 10:6.
10. This must have been before the year 115 CE, since that is when Rabban Gamliel II died.
11. *Sifre D.* 43; *Makkot* 24a.
12. *Berakhot* 61b; Y. *Berakhot* 9:6, 14:c.
13. T. *Yoma* 2:7.
14. *Rosh Hashanah* 31a, reported by Rabbi Judah in the name of Rabbi Akiva.
15. Safrai in Ben-Sasson, *A History*, 331ff.; M. D. Herr, in Oppenheimer, *Bar-Kokhba Revolt*.
16. *Gen. R.* 64:29. Some have seen this midrash as merely another attempt to rail against the Samaritans (see Mor, "New Factors," 161, 163). Indeed the story seems to reiterate the events concerning the rebuilding of the Second Temple after the return from Babylonia in the fifth century BCE when the Samaritans interfered, combining them with the legacy of Ben Zakkai in opposing rebellion against Rome. This is exactly the kind of story that the disillusioned Sages might well have told retroactively after the failure of the revolt.
17. Schafer, *Bar Kokhba War Reconsidered*, 7. Some have suggested that the priesthood may have been more actively involved, as suggested by the fact that the name Eleazar the Priest appears on a Bar Kokhva coin.

18. Not the famous Ishmael, according to Lieberman, in Oppenheimer, *Bar-Kohba Revolt*, 219. Heschel, on the other hand, assumed it was the well-known Ishmael.

19. Lieberman, in Oppenheimer, *Bar-Kokhba Revolt*, 219.

20. *Mekh. Nezikin* 18, iii 142; T. Sotah 13:4. See also ARN-A 38, where Shimon is identified incorrectly as Shimon ben Gamliel. Finkelstein, however, identified him as Shimon ben Netanel (*Akiba*, 229).

21. *Sanhedrin* 65b.

22. *Bava Batra* 60b.

23. Baron, *Social and Religious History*, 2:97.

24. Personal communication from Prof. Gavriel Barkai. Some other archeologists prefer other sites for it, but this seems the most likely.

25. See accounts of new archaeological findings in *Haaretz* and the *Jerusalem Post*, October 22, 2014.

26. Hasson, "Construction Work."

27. This was immortalized by Rembrandt in his painting *The Conspiracy of Claudius Civilis*.

28. *Mekh. Bahodesh* 6, ii 247.

29. Mor, "New Factors," 171.

30. Goodman, *Rome and Jerusalem*, 485.

31. Dio Cassius, *Roman History* 69.12–14, Loeb Classical Library; Y. Yadin, *Bar-Kokhba*, 257; Goodman, *Rome and Jerusalem*, 484.

32. Hasson, "Construction Work."

33. *Mo'ed Katan* 21b.

34. This should not be taken to imply that the Sages had achieved complete hegemony over the Jews. It is doubtful if the majority of the people considered themselves to be true Pharisees now, any more than they had before the year 70. Nevertheless in the absence of any other group, religious or political, claiming leadership, their opinions surely carried great weight, and within that group there was none with greater authority than Akiva. On this issue see Aleksandrov, " Role of 'Aqiba," 429.

35. *Gen. R.* 65:22, 740. See notes there concerning the reading "Akiva my Master would expound. . . ."

36. See G. Cohen, "Song of Songs," 245.

37. According to Eusebius, Bar Kokhva killed the Christians when they refused to help him in his war with the Romans. These sources have been published in Y. Yadin, *Bar-Kokhba*, 255–59.

38. Y. Yadin, *Bar-Kokhba*, 124–84. In the Hebrew version of Yadin's book 124–84.

39. Y. Yadin, *Bar-Kokhba*, 125, 126, 137.

40. Observance of the Sabbath is mentioned in the letters. Y. Yadin, *Bar-Kokhba*, 139.

41. G. W. Boersock, "A Roman Perspective on the Bar Kochba War," in *Approaches to Ancient Judaism* (Chico CA: Scholars Press, 1980), 2:131.

42. See Aleksandrov, "Role of 'Aqiba," 430. He feels that most of the Sages saw Rome as another Babylon, divinely ordained, and therefore did not support the rebellion. Akiva was the exception.

43. Y. *Ta'anit* 4:7, 68d. Schafer (*Bar Kokhba War Reconsidered*, 2) contends that even this statement may not be reliable, since a similar saying is attributed to Rabbi Judah the Prince in *Lam. R.* 2:4. It should be pointed out, however, that Rabbi's saying is explicitly framed to say the opposite, namely that the one called Bar Kokhva (star) was really Kozev (false), while Akiva's is that the "star" was Ben Kosiva and then—in both places—states specifically that he was the Messiah. Schafer believes that this was added later to emphasize "Bar Kokhba's role as the messiah" and attributed to Akiva because he was so well known and died during the revolt (*Bar Kokhba War Reconsidered*, 4). However it makes no sense after the revolt had failed and the Sages were already calling him the false one to attribute that to the leading Sage of the time.

44. Y. *Ta'anit* 4:7, 68d.

45. Y. *Ta'anit* 4:7, 67d.

46. *Zevahim* 13a.

47. *Lam. R.* 2:4; *Lam. R.*, ed. Buber 101.

48. Akiva's words are reported here by Yohanan ben Torta, the same person who then goes on to say that Akiva was mistaken. This later source is obviously based on the Jerusalem Talmud. See Schafer, "Rabbi Aqiva and Bar Kokhba," 118.

49. Schafer ("Rabbi Aqiva and Bar Kokhba," 119) states that if these sources are authentic, nevertheless this is "by no means a solemn proclamation of Bar Kokhba as the Messiah," but does not explain why not. On the contrary, that is exactly what it is and would have been important in rallying support for Bar Kosiva. See also Mor, "New Factors," 182.

50. See *Midrash Psalms* 90:15; *Sanhedrin* 93a–97b; Cohen, *The Synoptic Problem*, 433.

51. *Midrash Psalms* 90:17. Others cited there have much greater numbers, up to four thousand.

52. Mor, "New Factors," 185.

53. Schafer, *Bar Kokhba War Reconsidered*, 18.

54. Mor, "New Factors," 182, 185, and further references there to the

opinions of M. D. Herr and Israel Lee Levine. Schafer, however, believes that the term *nasi* did in fact refer to kingship, since it is found in that context in Ezekiel 37:25, "with My servant David as their *nasi* for all time" (*Bar Kokhba War Reconsidered*, 15). It seems much more likely that *nasi* was borrowed from its usage in the Torah, where it indeed means something less than a king, as in Numbers 7, where it refers to heads of tribes, rather from Ezekiel's usage. When Rabbi Judah was called *nasi* some time later, it hardly meant "king" and certainly not "messiah."

55. Y. Yadin, *Bar-Kokhba*, 124–39.

56. Aleksandrov, "Role of 'Aqiba," 422ff.

57. Alon, *Jews in Their Land*, 2:631ff.

58. Isaac and Oppenheimer, "The Revolt of Bar Kokhba," 52, also demonstrate that the many travels of Akiva had no connection whatsoever to the revolt.

59. The Jerusalem Talmud, in a long and probably legendary account of the siege of Beitar and the death of Bar Kokhva, records that Rabbi Eleazar of Modi'in was there during the entire siege, lamenting, and that Bar Kokhva suspected him of wanting to surrender to the Romans and therefore killed him—and that was the reason why Bar Kokhva himself was killed. Only a decree from heaven would have permitted the Romans to kill him. Since the name "Eleazar the Priest" occurs on Bar Kokhva coins, it has been suggested that this refers to Rabbi Eleazar of Modi'in. This is pure speculation, since it is not known if he was a *kohen* or not. It should be noted, moreover, that on the coin this person is identified as "the Priest" and not as "Rabbi." What was important to Bar Kokhva was to invoke the prestige of the Priesthood, not of the rabbinate. This was so since it follows ancient precedent, going as far back as the joint leadership of Moses and Aaron and of Zerubbabel of the house of David and Joshua the High Priest at the time of the return from the Babylonian exile, as reported in Zechariah 3:1, 4:6–7. In any case, it is Eleazar—whoever he was—whose name is on the coin, not Akiva. Oppenheimer, *Bar-Kokhba Revolt*, 176; Y. *Ta'anit* 4:68d; Alon, *Jews in Their Land*, 2:623. Because of the legend that Eleazar was at Beitar, Alon assumes "as an informed guess" that he is the Eleazar whose name appears on the coin.

60. Isaac and Oppenheimer, "The Revolt of Bar Kokhba," 49.

61. *Sanhedrin* 93b.

62. *Sifre D.* 43.

63. *Derekh Eretz Zuta* 10.

64. *Sanhedrin* 97b.

65. Schafer, "Rabbi Aqiva and Bar Kokhba," 120.

66. Mor, "New Factors," 186.

67. Goodman, *Rome and Jerusalem*, 490.

68. Y. Yadin, *Bar-Kokhba*, 24.

69. Schafer, *Bar Kokhba War Reconsidered*, 84.

70. See Lieberman, "Redifat Dat Yisrael," 206ff. and 220, for a full list of the decrees and the sources in Rabbinic literature.

71. Hammer, *Entering Jewish Prayer*, 129.

72. T. *Berakhot* 2:13.

73. *Berakhot* 9:5.

74. *Sifre D.* 32.

75. Isaac and Oppenheimer, "The Revolt of Bar Kokhba," 59. See also Baron, *Social and Religious History*, 2:107.

76. *Sanhedrin* 74a.

77. *Kiddushin* 40b.

78. *Gen. R.* 21:5, 200. See *Mekh. Be-shallah* 7, i 247, where there is an entire series of interpretations of biblical verses given by Pappus to each of which Akiva says, "Enough, Pappus!" and offers a different interpretation. Akiva's interpretations here are often further from the plain sense of the verse than are those of Pappus.

79. Lieberman, "Martyrs of Caesarea," 425.

80. *Berakhot* 61b.

81. *Avodah Zarah* 18a for this and other stories of martyrdom.

82. T. *Berakhot* 2:13.

83. *Mekh. Shirata* 3, ii 26.

84. Goldin, "Toward a Profile," 321. Heschel sees this rejection as a result of Akiva's depression at what is happening, a time when he abandoned his usual generosity and universal love of man. See Heschel, *Heavenly Torah*, 198. For a completely different interpretation of this parable see Boyarin, *Dying for God*, 114. Boyarin believes that this parable was a later invention, ascribed to Akiva because he had become the prototype of the martyr. The "nations" here are Christians. They see themselves as the true martyrs.

85. *Berakhot* 61b.

86. Cohen, "The Synoptic Problem," 431. Ginzberg, in his seminal article "Akiba ben Joseph "in *JE*, is most emphatic that Akiva played no actual role in the revolt.

87. The assumption has been that this was because Rufus had failed to control the rebellion and had to be replaced by a better general, but this is not certain. He may have died. See Eck, "Bar Kokhba Revolt," 79.

88. *Mekh. Bahodesh* 10, ii 277.

89. *Mekh. Bahodesh* 10. ii 280.

90. *ARN-A* 25.

91. The length of time is not certain. It may have even been one or two years. See Lieberman, "Redifat Dat Yisrael," 222.

92. *Eruvin* 21b.

93. *Pesahim* 112a.

94. *Eruvin* 21b.

95. *Yevamot* 108b.

96. *Yevamot* 105b.

97. *Sanhedrin* 12a. Some have suggested that his imprisonment lasted for two or three years, largely based on the account that he proclaimed three different leap years while in prison; however he could have done those calculations over a shorter period of time and did not have to do it only once per year. Such a long prison time is highly unlikely.

98. *Lam. R.* 3:60. Although Caesarea is not mentioned specifically in the earliest sources, the presence of the Roman governor Tineius Rufus at Akiva's death, according to the Jerusalem Talmud, would seem to indicate that that is where it took place, since it was the seat of the Roman government.

99. Schafer, "Rabbi Aqiva and Bar Kokhba," 120.

100. Lieberman, "Redifat Dat Yisrael," 217, 223.

101. *Avodah Zarah* 20a. See Shinan, "Three Wives," 22.

102. *Gen. R.* 11:5 (92); *Sanhedrin* 65b; *Tanhuma*, Ki Tissa 33; *Pesikta Rabbati* 23; *Num. R.* 19.

103. *Num. R.* 19:8.

104. *Bava Batra* 10a.

105. *Tanhuma*, Tazria, 5.

106. *Tanhuma*, Terumah 3.

107. Or: a wizard.

108. "Possessions" is the Rabbinic understanding of the Hebrew word *me'od*, which is usually translated "might."

109. Y. *Berakhot* 9:7, 14b; Y. *Sotah* 5:7, 20c (based on translation of Boyarin, *Dying for God*, 127). The words "He was not able to complete it before his soul departed" found in the printed text are in brackets because there is a question as to whether or not they are original. While they are found in the Leiden manuscript of the Jerusalem Talmud, they do not appear in others, such as Vatican 113. It is important to note, however, that whatever their origin, they are not simply copied from the text of the Babylonian

Talmud, since there, on the contrary, the point is made that he did finish the first line of the *Sh'ma*, dying while saying the word *ehad*, "one." See *Berakhot* 61b.

110. According to Lieberman, "Martyrs of Caesarea," 427, Akiva may have already been sentenced to death by the sword for these offenses, but he recited the *Sh'ma* before the execution was to be carried out and died when they tried to stop him with iron combs.

111. Lieberman, "Redifat Dat Yisrael," 217ff.

112. Ginzberg, "Akiba ben Joseph," 308.

113. *Lam. R.* 3:60.

114. Oppenheimer, *Galilee in the Mishnaic Period*, 142.

115. Lieberman, "Martyrs of Caesarea," 416.

116. Heschel, *Heavenly Torah*, 134–35. See also Boyarin, *Dying for God*, 95, who states that martyrdom as an expression of fulfilling the command to love the Lord was new to Judaism and started with Akiva.

117. *Midrash Proverbs* 9.

118. *Berakhot* 61b.

119. Tropper, *Like Clay*, 113.

120. S. Friedman, "Concerning the Nature of *Beritot*."

121. *Sifre D.* 32. See also *Tanhuma*, Ki Tavo 2.

122. *Sifre D.* 32; *Berakhot* 9:5.

123. Tropper, *Like Clay*, 113.

124. See Frankel, "Iyunim b'Olamo haruhani," 50, 167.

125. According to *Eccles. R.* 3:17, he was taken up to the gallows. See also *Lam. R.* 3:60.

126. *ARN-A* 40.

127. See Finkelstein, "Ten Martyrs."

128. *Midrash Psalms* 9:13. See also *Lam. R.* 2:2, 4.

129. *Midrash Psalms* 9:13.

130. See Shalom Spiegel, *The Last Trial* (New York: Pantheon Books, 1967), 86–89.

131. *Semahot* 8:9.

132. Lieberman, "Martyrs of Caesarea," 216.

133. The *Ge'onim* believed that Akiva died on the fifth of Tishrei, so HaGarsi would have left for the observance of Rosh Hashanah or Yom Kippur. See Safrai, *R. Akiva ben Yosef*, 32.

134. *Midrash Proverbs* 9. On the basis of this midrash, Baron wrote that indeed Akiva was buried in Caesarea. Baron, *Social and Religious History*, 2:371.

135. *Menahot* 29b.

136. *Semahot* 8:9.

137. Some believe that Akiva died after the revolt was quashed and not before. See Safrai, *R. Akiva ben Yosef*, 31.
138. Eck, "Bar Kokhba Revolt," 81.
139. Eck, "Bar Kokhba Revolt," 87–89.
140. See *Lam. R.* 3:51.
141. Dio Cassius, *Roman History* 69.12–14, Loeb Classical Library; Y. Yadin, *Bar Kokhba*, 257.
142. Y. Yadin, *Bar Kokhba*, 139.
143. Isaac and Oppenheimer, "The Revolt of Bar Kokhba," 59.
144. Goodman, *Rome and Jerusalem*, 505.
145. *Sanhedrin* 86a.

### EPILOGUE

1. *ARN-A* 26
2. *ARN-B* 33.
3. *Avot* 2:6.
4. For Heschel's view of Akiva's personality, see *Heavenly Torah*, 33–42
5. See Heschel, *Heavenly Torah*, chapters 17–20.
6. *Eruvin* 46a.
7. See Ginzberg, "Akiba ben Joseph," 1:307, for examples.
8. T. *Berakhot* 4:15.
9. *Mekh. Pisha* 14, i 114.
10. *Sifre D.* 43.
11. *Sifre D.* 32.
12. *Sifre D.* 32.
13. Y. *Berakhot* 9:7, 14b.
14. *Avodah Zarah* 5a.
15. *ARN-A* 3.
16. *Menahot* 29b.

# BIBLIOGRAPHY

Alexandrov, G. S. "The Role of 'Aqiba in the Bar Kokhba Rebellion." In
  *Eliezer Ben Hyrcanus*, part 2, edited by Jacob Neusner, 422–36. Leiden:
  Brill, 1973.
Alon, Gedaliah. *The Jews in Their Land in the Talmudic Age.* Jerusalem:
  Magnes Press, 1984.
Alter, Robert. *The Wisdom Books.* New York: Norton, 2010.
Baron, Salo Wittmayer. *A Social and Religious History of the Jews.* Vol. 2.
  New York: Columbia University Press, 1952.
Ben-Sasson, H. H., ed. *A History of the Jewish People.* Cambridge MA: Har-
  vard University Press, 1976.
Bickerman, Elias. *The Maccabees.* New York: Schocken Books, 1947.
Boersock, G. W. "A Roman Perspective on the Bar Kochba War." In
  *Approaches to Ancient Judaism* (Chico CA: Scholars Press, 1980).
Boyarin, Daniel. *Dying for God.* Stanford CA: Stanford University Press,
  1999.
———. *Intertextuality and the Reading of Midrash.* Bloomington: Indiana
  University Press, 1990.
Cohen, Gerson D. "The Song of Songs and the Jewish Religious Mental-
  ity." In *Studies in the Variety of Rabbinic Cultures.* Philadelphia: Jewish
  Publication Society, 1991.
Cohen, Shaye J. D. *From the Maccabees to the Mishnah.* Philadelphia: West-
  minster Press, 1987.
———. "The Significance of Yavneh." *Hebrew Union College Annual* 55
  (1984): 22–53.
———, ed. *The Synoptic Problem in Rabbinic Literature.* Providence RI:
  Brown Judaic Studies, 2000.
Daube, David. "Rabbinic Methods of Interpretation and Hellenistic Rheto-
  ric." *Hebrew Union College Annual* 22 (1949): 239–64.
Eck, Werner. "The Bar Kockba Revolt: The Roman Point of View." *Journal
  of Roman Studies* 85 (1999): 76–89.
Eissgeldt, Otto. *The Old Testament.* New York: Harper and Row, 1965.

Elbaum, Y. "Linguistic and Conceptual Patterns." *Proceedings of the 7th World Congress of Jewish Studies* 3 (1981): 71–77.

Finkelstein, Louis. *Akiba*. Philadelphia: Jewish Publication Society of America, 1962.

———. *New Light from the Prophets*. London: Valentine, Mitchell, 1969.

———. *The Pharisees*. 2nd ed. Philadelphia: Jewish Publication Society of America, 1962.

———. "The Ten Martyrs." In *Essays and Studies in Memory of Linda R. Miller*, edited by Israel Davidson, 29–55. New York: Jewish Theological Seminary of America, 1938.

Flusser, David. *Judaism of the Second Temple Period*. Jerusalem: Magnes Press, 2009.

Frankel, Yonah. "ha-Ruhani shel Sipur ha-Agada" [Hebrew]. *Iyunim*, 1981.

Friedman, Shamma. "Concerning the Nature of *Beritot*" [in Hebrew]. In *Jubilee Volume in Honor of David HaLivni*. Jerusalem: Orhot, 2005.

———. "A Good Story Deserves Retelling: The Unfolding of the Akiva Legend." *Jewish Studies Internet Journal* 3 (2004): 55–93.

Gafni, Isaiah. "Eretz Yisrael in the Period of the Mishnah and the Talmud" [in Hebrew]. *Cathedra* 100 (2001): 199–226.

Gereboff, Joel. *Rabbi Tarfon: The Tradition, the Man, and Early Rabbinic Judaism*. Brown Judaic Studies 7. Missoula, MT: Scholars Press, 1979.

Ginzberg, Louis. "Akiba ben Joseph." In *Jewish Encyclopedia*, 1:304–10. New York: Funk & Wagnalls, 1901.

———. *The Legends of the Jews*. Vol. 1. Philadelphia: Jewish Publication Society of America, 1954.

———. *On Jewish Law and Lore*. Philadelphia: Jewish Publication Society of America, 1955.

Goldin, Judah. *The Fathers according to Rabbi Nathan*. New Haven CT: Yale University Press, 1955.

———. "Toward a Profile of the Tanna, Aqiba ben Josef." In *Studies in Midrash and Related Literature*, 299–324. Philadelphia: Jewish Publication Society of America, 1988.

Goodblatt, D. "The Beruriah Tradition." *Journal of Jewish Studies* 26 (1975): 68–85.

Goodman, Martin. *Rome and Jerusalem*. London: Allan Lane, 2007.

Gordis, Robert. *Koheleth—The Man and His World*. New York: Jewish Theological Seminary, 1951.

———. *The Song of Songs*. New York: Jewish Theological Seminary, 1954.

Halivni, David Weiss. *Midrash, Mishnah, and Gemara*. Cambridge MA: Harvard University Press, 1986.

Hammer, Reuven. *The Classic Midrash*. New York: Paulist Press, 1995.

————. Entering Jewish Prayer. New York: Schocken Books, 1994.

————. *Or Hadash*. New York: Rabbinical Assembly, 2003.

————. "A Rabbinic Response to the Post Bar Kochba Era." *Proceedings of the American Academy for Jewish Research* 52 (1985): 37–53.

Hasson, Nir. "The Construction Work That Triggered the Bar Kokhba Revolt." *Haaretz*, May 18, 2014, http://www.haaretz.com/jewish-world /jewish-world-features/.premium-1.591302.

Hauptman, Judith. *Rereading the Rabbis: A Woman's Voice*. Boulder CO: Westview Press, 1998.

Held, Shai. *Abraham Joshua Heschel: The Call of Transcendence*. Bloomington: Indiana University Press, 2013.

Heschel, Abraham Joshua. *Heavenly Torah as Refracted through the Generations*. Edited and translated by Gordon Tucker with Leonard Levin. New York: Continuum, 2005.

————. *The Prophets*. Philadelphia: Jewish Publication Society, 1962.

Ilan, Tal. "'Daughters of Israel, Weep for Rabbi Ishmael': The Schools of Rabbi Akiba and Rabbi Ishmael on Women." *Nashim: A Journal of Jewish Women's Studies and Gender Issues* 4 (Fall 2001): 15–34.

————. *Mine and Yours Are Hers*. Leiden: Brill, 1997.

————. "The Quest for the Historical Beruriah, Rachel, and Imma Shalom." *AJS Review* 22, no. 1 (1997): 1–17.

Isaac, Benjamin and Aharon Oppenheimer. "The Revolt of Bar Kokhba." *Journal of Jewish Studies* 36 (1985): 33–60.

Jacobs, Louis. "Hermeneutics." In *Encyclopaedia Judaica*, vol. 8. Jerusalem: Keter, 1972.

Kadushin, Max. *The Rabbinic Mind*. New York: Jewish Theological Seminary, 1952.

Levine, Lee I. *The Rabbinic Class in Palestine during the Talmudic Period* [in Hebrew]. Jerusalem: Yad Izhak Ben Zvi Institute, 1985.

Lieberman, Saul. *Hellenism in Jewish Palestine*. New York: Jewish Theological Seminary, 1994.

————. "The Martyrs of Caesarea." *Annuaire de l'Institute de Philologie et d'Histoire Orientales et Slaves* 7 (1939–44): 395–446.

————. "Redifat Dat Yisrael" [Hebrew]. In *The Bar-Kokhba Revolt* [in Hebrew], edited by Aharon Oppenheimer. Jerusalem: Zalman Shazar Center for Jewish History, 1980.

————. "The Teaching of Song of Songs" [in Hebrew]. In Gershom Scholem, *Jewish Gnosticism, Merkabah Mysticism and Talmudic Tradition*. New York: Jewish Theological Seminary, 1965.

Mor, Menahem. "Are There Any New Factors concerning the Bar-Kokhba Revolt?" *Studia Antiqua et Archaeologica* 18 (2012): 161–93.

Oppenheimer, Aharon, ed. *The Bar-Kokhba Revolt* [in Hebrew]. Jerusalem: Zalman Shazar Center for Jewish History, 1980.

———. *Galilee in the Mishnaic Period* [in Hebrew]. Jerusalem: Zalman Shazar Center for Jewish History, 1991.

Paul, Shalom. "Jerusalem: A City of Gold." *Israel Exploration Journal* 17 (1967): 259–63.

———. "Jerusalem of Gold-Revisited." In *I Will Speak the Riddles of Ancient Times*, edited by Aren M. Maeir and Pierre De Miroschedji. Winona Lake IN: Eisenbrauns, 2006.

Rosen-Zvi, Y. "Who Will Uncover Dust from Your Eyes?" [in Hebrew]. *Tarbiz* 75 (5766): 95–128.

Safrai, Shmuel. *R. Akiva ben-Yosef: Hayyav u'Mishnato* [Hebrew]. Jerusalem: Mosad Bialek, 1970.

———. *Eretz Yisrael v'hokhmeha b'tekifat haMishnah v'haTalmud* [Hebrew]. Jerusalem: Hakibbutz Hameuchad, 1983.

Sanders, E. "Rabbi Akiba's View of Suffering." *Jewish Quarterly Review* 63 (1972–73): 332–51.

Sarna, Nahum. The JPS Torah Commentary: Genesis. Philadelphia: Jewish Publication Society, 1989.

Schafer, Peter, ed. *The Bar Kokhba War Reconsidered*. Philadelphia: Coronet Books, 2003.

———. "Rabbi Aqiva and Bar Kokhba." In *Approaches to Ancient Judaism*, 2:113–30. Chico CA: Scholars Press, 1980.

Scholem, Gershom. *Jewish Gnosticism, Merkabah Mysticism and Talmudic Tradition*. New York: Jewish Theological Seminary, 1965.

———. *Major Trends in Jewish Mysticism*. New York: Schocken Books, 1941.

Shinan, Avigdor. "The Three Wives of Rabbi Akiva" [in Hebrew]. *Masekbet* 2 (2004): 11–23.

Tropper, Amram. *Like Clay in the Hands of the Potter* [in Hebrew]. Jerusalem: Zalman Shazar Center for Jewish History, 2011.

Yadin, Yigal. *Bar-Kokhba*. London: Weidenfeld and Nicolson, 1971.

Yadin-Israel, Azzan. "Rabbi Akiva's Youth." *Jewish Quarterly Review* 100, no. 4 (Fall 2010): 573–97.

———. *Scripture and Tradition: Rabbi Akiva and the Triumph of Midrash*. Philadelphia: University of Pennsylvania Press, 2014.

———. *Scripture as Logos: Rabbi Ishmael and the Origins of Midrash*. Philadelphia: University of Pennsylvania Press, 2004.

Zeitlin, Solomon. *The Rise and Fall of the Judean State*. Vol. 3. Philadelphia: Jewish Publication Society of America, 1978.

# INDEX TO
# CLASSICAL SOURCES

# GENERAL INDEX

Midrash refers to the books known as Midrash—such as *Sifre*, *Sifra*, *Mekhilta*, etc.; "midrash" refers to the method of interpretation of Biblical texts used by the Sages.

Aaron (biblical figure), 62, 110, 200n18

adultery, 72, 86

Aelia Capitolina, xxii, 145, 146, 147, 154

aggadah, 74–75, 83, 93

agricultural laws, 40–41, 55, 194nn32, 33

*aher* (Elisha ben Abuya), 64, 66–67, 197n25, 198n40

Akiva ben Yosef: academy at B'nai Brak founded by, xxi, 32, 42–43; accuracy of attributions to, 108, 203n2; *am ha-aretz*, 3, 5, 6, 11, 190n16; anti-Roman sentiments of, 7, 114, 147, 148, 157–60, 166–68; *Avinu Malkeinu* attributed to, 115, 136; Blessing after Meals in a house of mourning, 123; blessing before Passover seder meal, 115, 136–37, 141; builds Sukkah on boat, 39, 194n23; on capital punishment, 111, 112; on children's welfare and education, 105, 135; codification of unwritten traditions, 79–82, 83–88, 90–91, 181–82; as comforter, 38,

56, 101, 117, 120–22, 126, 133, 142, 180, 183; concern for the poor, 39–42, 185, 194n32; death of, 89, 167–68, 173–74, 212n109; death of his son Shimon, 46, 195n58; as decisor of Jewish law, 48–51; decorative crowns on letters in Torah, 31, 70, 77; on divorce, 102, 104–5; on Eleazar ben Azariah's appointment as *nasi*, 52; exaltation of Torah by, 59–60; on the execution of Sages, 123–24, 144; on the existence of two Torahs, 90; on God's judgment (*tziduk ha-din*), 116–19, 205n44; Hillel's influence on, 110; on human accountability, 116, 117, 119–20; identification with patient Job, 130; on idolatry, 37, 113, 204n28; on impurity, 103–4; as judge, xxi, 34–35; leap years calculated by, 162, 212n97; love in thought of, 99–101, 106, 109–10, 120, 179–80, 203n11; marriage and marital love, 17–18, 21–22, 101–2, 103–5; martyrdom of, 100, 168–72, 184, 213n116; Messianic

Akiva ben Yosef (*cont.*)

Age predicted by, 150–51, 153–54, 199n80, 209n43; *middah k'neged middah*, 42; monotheism of, 125, 130–31, 169, 212n109; mystical experiences of, 65, 66, 67, 68, 98, 198n48; Nahum of Gimzo as teacher of, 31, 61, 71; on observance of commandments, 112–13; optimism of, 3, 38, 115, 117–19, 124, 140, 142, 144, 158, 180; parables of, 118, 205n44; Pharisees viewed by, 5, 9; on the priesthood, 28–29; profile of, 1–13, 15–18, 34–35, 37, 46–48, 189n11; on prophecy, 114; relations with non-Jews, 54–55, 59, 112–14; relations with Rabbi Joshua, 30; relations with Rabbi Tarfon, 19–20, 28–29, 73–74, 117, 192n64, 192n66; on the revelation at Sinai, 69–70, 97–98; in Rome, xxi, 35–38, 153, 185; sanctity of the Land of Israel, 115–16; on saying *Sh'ma*, 155–56, 167–69, 212n109; seder with Rabbi Joshua and Rabbi Eleazar, 44; seven-year agricultural cycles, 41; on spread of Christian doctrine, 82; status of, 147, 208n34; on the status of captive women, 49; as storyteller and preacher, 56, 59–60, 112, 118, 157–59, 168, 185, 196n90, 205n44; strictness of ritual observance, 39; students of, 21, 22, 23; teachers of, 18, 28; on the Temple in Jerusalem, 13, 38, 115, 141, 142, 153; Tineus Rufus, conversations with, 154, 160, 162–69, 211n87, 212n98; on Torah from heaven, 68–70, 76, 79, 178–79; Tosefta

on heavenly ascent of, 65–66, 197n34; traditions overturned by, 54–55; on translations of the Bible, 83; travels of, 39–40, 124, 194nn21,22,23, 194n26; willingness to die for God, 100, 101; witnesses, testimony of, 112. *See also* Bar Kokhva; Bar Kokhva Rebellion; Eliezer, Rabbi (Eliezer ben Hyrkanus); Gamliel II, Rabban; Ishmael ben Elisha, Rabbi; Joshua, Rabbi; Mishnah; Song of Songs; *individual disciples* (e.g. Shimon bar Yohai)

—anecdotes: community involvement of, 40; on the death of his son Shimon, 46; on disagreements between Akiva and Rabban Gamliel, 51; discussions with son, 45–46; on God's mercy, 124; on his students, 43–44; on man uncovering woman's hair in the marketplace, 34–35; on marital love, 101; on marrying off daughters, 43–44; the night that Akiva slept outside, 124; on poverty, 46, 195n61; proper observances of mitzvot, 39–40; respect for authority, 51; separation from wife during years of study, 23–24; stone motifs in, 15, 16, 28, 56; on studying Torah, 14–17, 20, 24, 30–31, 193n72; as tireless teacher, 43

—education: adult beginnings of, 3–4, 14–15, 17; at Lod, 18; motivation for, 13, 17–18, 21, 30–31; ordination, xxi, 30, 32; separation from wife during years of study, 23–24; wife's support for, 21–22, 25; years devoted to, 14–15

—hermeneutics: on aggadah, 74–75; Aquila's Greek translation of the Bible reflecting, 83; "At first they used to say . . . until Rabbi Akiva came and taught," 54; biblical prooftexts for oral law, 85, 86, 87, 89–94, 102–3, 108, 121, 155; connecting oral traditions to biblical verses, 31, 73, 86–88, 89–93; durability of, 76–77; God's suffering, 127–28, 129–30; *kivyakhol* in describing God, 127–28, 130; methodology of, 29–30, 31, 70–74, 77, 83–84, 92–94, 108, 112–13, 197n19, 199n75, 205n60; modern scholarship on, 76–77; *nakeh lo y'nakeh*, 119; on the nature of Torah, 62, 76–77, 90–91, 107; opposition to, 72–75; permissibility of saving a life on Shabat, 73; on the phrase "to be cut off," 72; Rome identified with Esau, 148; rules of extension in, 71; Sabbath observances, 83; sacrifices, 73; on sitting on a bench belonging to a non-Jew on Shabat, 54–55; *tziduk ha-din* (God's judgment), 116–19; on women's dignity, 34–35, 49, 54, 72, 86, 102, 103, 104–5; words in, 72–73, 75, 92, 101, 110, 112–13, 117, 126–27, 194n33, 199n84; on the world to come, 120–23

—personal life: children of, 17, 18, 23, 45–46, 195n58; family background, 3–5; financial standing of, 3–5, 21–22, 24, 25, 46–47, 173; straw gathering, 18, 22, 23, 25. *See also* wife of Akiva

Aknai, oven of, 52–53

*Al Het* (Yom Kippur liturgy), 135

"The All Merciful does what is best," 124, 125

Alon, Gedaliah, 210n59

*am ha-aretz/amei ha-aretz*, 3, 5, 6, 177, 190n24

*Amidah*, 131–35, 132–33, 207n3

Amoraim, 111

apostasy of Elisha ben Abuya (*aher*), 64, 66–67, 197n25

Aquila, 83, 200n10

Aramaic translations, 83, 200n10

archaeological discoveries, 145, 148–49

ARN-A (*Avot de-Rabbi Natan* A): Akiva's deathbed visit to Rabbi Eliezer, 53–54; Akiva's desire to study Torah, 16–17, 19, 24, 28; on Akiva's determination to learn Torah, 15–16, 191n10; on Akiva's personal wealth, 30; dating of, 192n55; Jerusalem of Gold motif in accounts of Akiva's betrothal to daughter of Kalba Savua, 20; Rachel as name of Akiva's wife, 26; on reward and punishment, 119–20; water allegory, 16

ARN-B (*Avot de-Rabbi Natan* B): on Akiva as literate, 16–17; on Akiva's determination to learn Torah, 16, 191n10; on Akiva's personal wealth, 3–5, 30; Jerusalem of Gold motif in accounts of Akiva's betrothal to daughter of Kalba Savua, 20; on life of Akiva ben Yosef, 2; rope allegory, 16

*Ashamnu* (Yom Kippur liturgy), 135

atonement, efficacy of, 117

*Avinu Malkeinu* (Our Father, Our Sovereign), 115, 136

*Avot* (Tractate). See *Pirke Avot*

*Avot de-Rabbi Natan* (ARN): Akiva's deathbed visit to Rabbi Eliezer, 53–54; on Akiva's role as judge, 34–35; attempted seduction of Akiva in Rome, 37; Elisha ben Abuya in, 67; man uncovering woman's hair in the market-place, 34–35; mentions of Akiva's wife, 24; reliability of accounts of Akiva, 24; on sanctity of Proverbs, Song of Songs and Ecclesiastes, 97; on taking unneeded charity, 42, 185

Barkai, Gavriel, 208n24
Bar Kokhva: Akiva's support for, 150–51; defeat of, xxii, 210n59; history of, 148–49, 208n37; as *kozev* (deceiver), 151, 153, 209n43; letters of, 148–49; as messiah, xxii, 150–52, 176, 199n80, 209n43, 209nn48, 49; as *nasi,* 148, 152, 209n54; scriptural precedents for, 150–51, 209n43
Bar Kokhva Rebellion: Akiva's role in, 152; causes of, 146; coinage of, 147, 152, 154, 207n17, 210n59; death of Akiva ben Yosef, 2; destruction after, 174–76; failure of, 151, 207n16, 209n43; legendary accounts of, 151, 209n43; Roman restrictions on Jewish observances, 154–56; support for, 143, 207n17
Baron, Salo, 9, 213n134
Beitar, siege of, 210n59
Ben Patura, 112
*b'khol me'odekha* (with all your might), 100
"Blessed is the true Judge," 123
Blessing after Meals, 123

blessing before Passover seder meal, 115, 136–37, 141
B'nai Brak academy, xxi, 32, 42–43
bodily discharge, 103–4
Boyarin, Daniel, 211n84, 213n116
*Brit ha-Hadashah* (New Covenant), 59, 81, 82

Caesaria, 162, 212n98
Cairo Geniza, 16
Calderon, Ruth, 195n56
calendar, calculation of, 52–53, 162, 212n97
capital punishment, 111–12
chastisements, 122, 123, 161, 183–84
Christianity: atonement in, 117; *Brit ha-Hadashah*, 81, 82, 83, 185–86; canonization of Scripture, 6, 201n9; development of Midrash and the Mishnah, 82; on God's suffering, 129, 130; Gospels, 59, 201n9; Jesus, 7, 53, 59, 117, 120; Jewish-Christians, 11, 58; Marcionism in, 120; martyr-dom, 172–73, 211n84; negative stereotypes of Judaism, 120; oral tradition lacking in, 82, 91; Pauline Christianity, 59, 82; Septuagint as standard Bible text, 83; Torah and the rise of, 53, 59, 76, 77, 82, 120
circumcision, 146, 165–66, 167
cities of refuge, 93
Cohen, Gerson, 99
Cyrus of Persia, 139, 141

daughter of Kalba Savua (Akiva's wife). *See* wife of Akiva
David (biblical figure), 98
Dead Sea Sect, 5, 81
death, 99–100, 125, 130, 159, 202n25

deathbed visit to Rabbi Eliezer, 53–54, 122, 123, 161, 183

death penalty, 111–12

deposition of Rabban Gamliel II ("that day"), 3, 52, 92, 95, 201n2, 201n32

Dio, Cassius, 145, 146

divine love, 97–100, 108

divorce, 54, 91, 102–3, 104–5

Dosa, Rabbi, 34, 204n22

Eleazar ben Arakh, Rabbi, 65

Eleazar of Modi'in, Rabbi (Eleazar the Priest), 152, 207n17, 210n59

Eleazer ben Matya, 43

Eliezer, Rabbi (Eliezer ben Hyrkanus): academic career of, 19, 27, 32, 191n21; Akiva's deathbed visit to, 53–54, 122, 123, 161, 183; Akiva's relations with, 18, 19–20, 22, 29–31, 48–49, 52, 195n69; Akiva's view of the world to come, 120–21; alleged Christian beliefs of, 53; attempted seduction of, 38; delegations to Rome, 35–37, 153; excommunication of, 52–55; on idol of Micah, 128; on the mitzvah of *Peah*, 41; oven of Aknai incident, 52–53; physical manifestations of God, 126–27; prayers in time of drought, 136; as Sanhedrin member, 32; on the status of captive women, 49; as student of Yohanan ben Zakkai, 19, 52. *See also* Lod, academy at

Eliezer ben Azariah, Rabbi: on Akiva's interpretations, 39, 73, 194n23; deposition of Gamliel II ("that day"), 52, 92, 95, 201n2, 201n32; on excommunication of Rabbi Eliezer, 54; Gamliel

replaced by, 52, 92, 95; as *nasi,* 52; relations with Tarfon and Joshua, 197n14; on religious observances at sea, 39, 194n23; trips to Rome, 35–36; visit to the Temple ruins, 142

Eliezer ben Yose HaG'lili, 93, 203n2

Elijah (biblical figure), 22, 23, 170, 174

Elisha ben Abuya (*aher*), 64, 66–67, 197n25, 198n40

engagement of a woman to a man who is a *kohen*, 104–5

Esau (biblical figure), 148

Esther, Queen (scriptural figure), 56

Eusebius, 148, 208n37

excommunication of Rabbi Eliezer, 52–53

Ezra the Scribe, 1, 57

fast of the tenth month, 134

Finkelstein, Louis, xiii, 90–91, 208n20

Flusser, David, 111, 199n80

"forgotten things," law of, 41

forgotten things law, 41, 194n33

four Sages entering paradise (*pardes*), 64–66, 69, 197n25, 197n34

four species for Sukkot, 133–34

fox and the fish parable, 118, 157, 158, 205n44

free will (doctrine), 116, 119–20

fringes (tzitzit), 105, 190n24

Gamliel II, Rabban, xxi; Akiva as emissary for, 33–34, 39–42, 193n6; Akiva as student of, xxi, 32; Akiva's arguments with, 50–51, 121, 196n73; on Akiva's view of the death penalty, 111; authority

Heschel, Abraham Joshua: acceptance of God's justice, 180–81; Akiva on love of God, 211n84; on Akiva's doctrine, 76; God's love for man, 99; Ishmael on idolatry, 203n11; the net (fox and the fish parable), 205n44; on Rabbi Ishmael's exegetical method, 61; on suffering, 127, 129, 170, 180–81; on Torah from heaven, 68, 69, 77

Hezekiah (biblical figure), 97, 98

Hillel, School of, 6, 30, 33, 84, 86, 96, 102, 134, 193n1, 196n73

Hillel the Elder, 110

*hillul ha-Shem*, 113

Hosea (biblical figure), 13, 99

human life, sanctity of, 73, 99–101, 108–13, 116–20, 184, 198n58, 203n11

idolatry, 37, 114, 116, 128, 145, 204n28

Ilan, Tal, 192n55

imprisonment of Akiva: conversations with Tineus Rufus, 162–69, 211n87, 212n98; death of Akiva, 167–68, 173–74, 212n109; leap years calculated during, 162, 212n97; *Shʿma*, recitated before his death, 167–68, 169–72, 212n109

Isaac (biblical figure), 100, 125, 173, 202n25, 204n28

Ishmael (biblical figure), 114, 204n28

Ishmael ben Elisha, Rabbi: on burning of Christian books, 59; four species for Sukkot, 134; hermeneutics of, 71, 72–73, 113, 203n11; interpretation of letter *vav*, 72; Kfar Aziz, 42; law anchored in the Bible, 89; love and fear of God, 100; on love of humans, 203n11; methodology of, 61, 68, 73, 75, 199n75, 199n84; Midrash compiled by, 84–86; mourning for, 105–6; mystical practices of, 68, 198nn47, 48; Nehunia ben Hakana as mentor of, 60; opposition to the Mishnah, 86; personality of, 63; on the phrase "to be cut off," 72; relations with Akiva, 72–73, 86–87, 197n14; on Roman oppression, 144; sanctity of Song of Songs, 97; thirteen rules of textual interpretation, 61–62; Torah as divine revelation, 68, 76; "the Torah speaks in human language," 61–62, 74, 75, 77; on the transmission of Torah, 91; on the use of the word *et*, 71; women in rulings of, 105

Jacob (biblical figure), 26

Jacob of Kefar-Sekniah, 53

Jannai, King, 7–8

Jeremiah (biblical figure), 98, 99

Jerusalem: as Aelia Capitolina, xxii, 145, 146, 147, 154; after the Great Revolt, 8; seat of power relocated to Yavneh, 8–9. *See also* Hadrian; Second Temple; Temple in Jerusalem

Jerusalem of Gold motif, 20, 22, 25–26, 26–27, 47

Jesus, 7, 53, 59, 117, 120, 173

Jewish calendar, 51–52, 162

Jewish-Christians, 11, 58

"Love your fellow as yourself," 106, 109–10, 120, 203n11
*lulav*, 37, 132, 133–34, 149

*Mahzor Vitri*, 117
male emissions (*zavim*), 103–4, 203n41
Marcion, 120
marriage and marital love, 17, 21–22, 45, 54, 63, 101–2, 103–5
martyrdom, 100, 125–26, 155–56, 159–60, 168–72, 184, 202n25, 213n116
Meir, Rabbi: account of Tineius Rufus's conversation with Rabbi Akiva, 164; as Akiva's disciple, 43; "all your might" taught by, 100; Elisha ben Abuya and, 66–67; on "God" in 2 Sam. 7:23, 128; ordination of, 30; origins of Mishnah, 80, 84, 88; on suffering, 125, 130; on Torah from heaven, 69
*Mekhilta de-Rabbi Yishmael*, 69–70, 73, 128
Men of the Great Assembly, 98, 202n12
*Merkavah* mysticism, 65, 66, 68–69, 98, 198n48, 198n55
messianism, 59, 82, 116, 151–52, 154, 176, 199n80, 209n43
Midrash: Akiva's systemization of, 77, 83; biblical prooftexts in, 31, 73, 86–88, 89–94, 102–3, 108, 121, 155; compilation of, 82–84, 86; defined, 81, 84; Sages' citations in, 61; on Solomon's authorship of Song of Songs, 98. See also *Sifra*; *Sifre*
midrash: Akiva's exaltation of Torah, 59–60; Akiva's mystical

inclination in, 67, 69–70, 77; biblical prooftexts in, 84, 85, 86, 87, 89–94, 102–3, 108, 121, 155; defined, 81, 82; play on words in, 72–73, 75, 92, 101, 110, 112–13, 117, 126–27, 151, 153, 194n33, 199n84, 209n43; return from exile in, 128–30, 205n74; rules of textual interpretation, 61–62; on Sinaitic revelation, 69–70; *Song of Songs Rabbah*, 28, 97, 202n29. See also *Sifra*; *Sifre*
Milgrom, Jacob, 77
*min* (sectarian), 36–37, 193n14
Mishnah: agricultural laws in, 41; Akiba and the development of, 20, 41, 63, 80, 83–85, 182; Akiva on women's dignity, 102, 103, 104–5; Akiva's views on liturgy, 132–37; biblical prooftexts for, 85, 86, 87, 89–94, 102–3, 108, 121, 155; connecting oral traditions to biblical verses, 86, 87, 89–90; on the death of Ishmael, 63; death penalty in, 111–12; defined, 20, 84; discussion on which scrolls are considered sacred, 95, 96, 201n2; Ecclesiastes and Song of Songs as sacred scripture, 96; on Ishmael's character, 63; "Joshua" as father-in-law of Akiva, 23; of Judah the Prince, 80, 85, 87, 88, 176, 182; Midrash compared with, 86–87; organization of law into logical categories, 86–87; origins of, 84; on Pharisees, 7; Rabbi Joshua's calendar dispute with Rabban Gamliel II, 52–53; respect for Rabban Gamliel's authority, 51–52; Sabbath observance, 83; the world to come, 97, 120–23. See also *Pirke Avot*; Tosefta

Moses (biblical figure), 31, 58, 69–70, 73, 77, 90, 173, 187, 200n18
mourning customs, xv, 123
Muffs Yohanan, 77
mysticism and mystical experiences: of Akiva, 65, 66, 67, 68, 98, 198n48; dangers of, 67; four Sages entering paradise (*pardes*), 64–66, 69, 197n25, 197n34; heavenly chariot, mysteries of, 65, 66, 68–69, 98, 198n48, 198n55; *Hekhalot* literature, 67, 68, 198nn47, 48, 198n44; preparations for, 66; scriptural interpretation, 67

Nahum of Gimzo, 31, 61, 71
*nakeh lo y'nakeh*, 119
Nathan, Rabbi. See *Avot de-Rabbi Natan*
Nehemiah, Rabbi, 84, 93
Nehunia ben Hakana, 60
New Covenant (*Brit ha-Hadashah*), 59, 81, 82
ninth of Av (fast day), 141
non-Jews, 37, 54–55, 113–14, 164–67
Noy, Dov, 24

*olelet* (defective grape cluster), 41
Oppenheimer, Aharon, 146
oral law: Akiva's systemization of, 86–88; biblical prooftexts for, 31, 73, 86–88, 89–94, 102–3, 108, 121, 155; codification of, 79–82, 83–88, 90–91, 181–82; sanctity of, 58; Sinaitic revelation of, 58, 90; transmission of, 87
Our Father, Our Sovereign (*Avinu Malkeinu*), 115, 136
oven of Aknai, 52–53

paganism, 114, 130, 185–86, 204n28

Pappus ben Yehudah, 157, 160, 211n78
*pardes*, 64–66, 69, 197n24, 197n25, 197n34
Passover, 29, 44, 48, 115, 135–37, 141, 195n46
Paul, Shalom, 77
Pauline Christianity, 59, 82
*peah*, 41
Pharisees, 5–6, 7–8, 9, 12, 208n34. See also Hillel, School of; Shammai, School of
phylacteries (tefillin), 190n24
*Pirke Avot*: Akiva's teachings in, 108–9, 110–11, 115, 118; fox and the fish parable, 118, 157, 158, 205n44; God's judgment, 118; God's parent-child relationship with Israel, 115; love of your fellow human, 110; on studying Torah, 177; three-fold structure of, 108–9, 116; on the transmission of the Law, 58, 91; *tzafui*, use of term in, 116
the poor: Akiva's concern for, 39–42, 193n6, 194n32
*pores al Sh'ma* (proclaiming the Sh'ma), 155
"Precious are chastisements," 122, 123, 161, 183–84
priesthood, 8, 28–29, 104, 192n66, 207n17
punishment for adulterous daughter of priest, 72–73
purity laws, 92, 117, 135

Quietus, Lucius, 140
Qumran, 96

Rabbi (use of term), 9, 30, 58
Rabbinic court at Yavneh, xxi, 8–9, 19, 33, 111

of, 96, 179; divine origin of, 107, 179; God's love for Israel as depicted in, 97, 98–99, 108; as the Holy of Holies, 96–97, 98–99; the lover described in, 202n18; as mystical work, 98, 202n18; sanctity of, 95, 96; Sinaitic revelation of, 97–98; Solomon as author of, 96, 97, 98, 201n3; willingness to die for God, 100

*Song of Songs Rabbah*, 28, 97, 202n29

*Sotah*, law of, 72, 86, 102

suffering, 93–94, 121–25, 127–28, 129–30, 160, 168–69, 184

Sukkot, 39, 133–34, 149, 194n23

Tannaim (reciters), 87, 189n1. *See also individual headings* (e.g. Meir, Rabbi; Tarfon, Rabbi); *Sifra*

Tarfon, Rabbi: blessing before Passover seder meal, 115, 136, 137; on burning of Christian books, 59; on the death penalty, 111; on the importance of study v. practice, 69; learning the law from precedents, 74–75; on the priesthood, 28–29; relations with Akiva, 19–20, 28–29, 56, 73–74, 117, 192n64, 192n66; relations with Rabbi Joshua, 197n14; sanctity of human life, 111

*Targum Onkelos* (Aramaic translation), 83, 200n10

tefillin (phylacteries), 190n24

Temple in Jerusalem: in blessing before Passover seder meal, 115, 136–37, 141; Christianity after the destruction of the Second

Temple, 76, 79, 81–82; destruction of, 141; Hadrian's rebuilding of, 140–41, 142, 143–46; hopes for restoration of, 38, 115, 130, 137, 141, 180; Jewish law after the destruction of Second Temple, 57–59, 81–82, 85, 104; Lebanon as reference to, 129, 130, 205n74; messianism and restoration of, 154, 178; mourning for, 13, 38, 129, 141, 142, 153, 158, 183; pagan temple on site of, 145–46; prayer after, 131–32; priesthood, 8, 28–29; on the sacredness of, 142; sacrifices, 29, 73; Samaritans and, 143, 207n16; Torah study after destruction of, 8–9, 12, 33, 43, 181

"The Ten Martyrs" (liturgical poem), 172

"that day" (deposition of Rabban Gamliel II), 3, 52, 95, 201n2

Tigay, Jeffrey, 77

tithing, 41, 50

Torah: after the destruction of the Second Temple, 57–59; agricultural laws in, 40–41; Akiva's exaltation of, 59–60; authority of, 1, 82; biblical prooftexts for the Mishnah, 85, 86, 87, 89–94, 102–3, 108, 121, 155; *Brit ha-Hadashah*, 59, 81, 82; death penalty in, 111; decorative crowns on letters in, 31, 70, 77; as divine document, 68–70, 76, 79, 90, 97–98, 178–79; existence of two Torahs, 90; liturgical practices in, 29, 39, 44, 48, 51, 115, 132–37, 141, 149, 194n23, 195n46; love as principle of, 99, 100, 106, 108, 109–10, 203n11; "Love your fellow as yourself" as principle of,

Torah (*cont.*)
106, 109–10, 120, 203n11; modern scholarship on, 76–77, 90–91, 99, 102, 103; mystical interpretations on, 69–70, 198n55; oral tradition of, 31, 73, 86–88, 89–93; as preexisting instrument, 68–69; Red Heifer, burning of, 105, 164; resolution of contradictions in, 62; and the rise of Christianity, 53, 59, 76, 77, 82, 120; rules of interpretation, 61–62; sacredness of, 57, 76, 81, 82; sectarian exegesis of, 5–6, 7–8, 9, 12; Sinaitic revelation of, 58, 69–70, 90, 97–98; *Sotah,* law of, 72, 86, 102; study in defiance of Rome, 156, 157–60; study of, 6, 8–12, 14–17, 23–24, 30–31, 33, 43, 46, 156, 157–60, 181, 193n72; in the time of Ezra the Scribe, 57; translations of, 83. See also *Sh'ma*; Song of Songs; individual academies (e.g. Yavneh)
Torah from heaven doctrine, 68–69, 79, 178–79
"the Torah speaks in human language" (Ishmael ben Elisha), 61–62, 74, 75, 77
Tosefta: Akiva enters *pardes*, 64–66; Akiva on Jewish law in, 54–55, 83–84; on Akiva's collection of traditions, 83–84, 88; Akiva's preparations for the rebuilding of the Temple, 142; on canonicity of sectarian writings, 201n9; on confession of sins (*Vidui*), 135, 206n103; on disagreements between Akiva and Rabban Gamliel, 51; on the four Sages entering paradise (*pardes*),

64–65; Gamliel's relationship with Akiva, 51; on heavenly ascent, 65–66, 197n34; on human kindness, 112–13, 204n22; on the Sages' observances of mitzvot, 40, 50, 133; on the Song of Songs, 97
Trajan, 140
two thousand cubits (walking distance on the Sabbath), 93
*tzafui*, use of term in *Pirke Avot*, 116
*tziduk ha-din* (God's judgment), 116–19, 130
tzitzit (fringes), 105, 190n24

*Vidui* (Yom Kippur liturgy), 135, 206n103
vows, 63

water in the desert (parable on sanctity of human life), 112
Wexler-Bedolah, Shlomit, 145
wife of Akiva: Akiva's gratitude toward, 20, 25, 26; gold diadem given to, 20, 25–26, 32, 47, 101; her role in making him a sage, 20, 21, 22, 23, 24; Kalba Savua as father of, 21–23, 25–26, 47; name of, 21, 25–26; Rachel, source of name, 26; romantic love in marriage to, 101; wife of Tineus Rufus as second wife of, 27
witnesses, 105, 112
women: Akiva on determining a women's state of impurity, 103; divorce, 54, 102, 104–5; education of, 105; fine levied for uncovering woman's hair in the marketplace, 34–35; law of *Sotah*, 72, 86, 102; marriage and marital love, 17, 21–22, 45, 54, 63, 101–2,

## Other works by Reuven Hammer

*The Other Child in Jewish Education*

*Sifre: A Tannaitic Commentary on the Book of Deuteronomy*
(NATIONAL JEWISH BOOK AWARD WINNER)

*Entering Jewish Prayer*

*The Classic Midrash*

*Entering the High Holy Days: A Complete Guide to the History, Prayers, and Themes*
(NATIONAL JEWISH BOOK AWARD WINNER)

*The Jerusalem Anthology*

*Or Hadash: A Commentary on Siddur Sim Shalom Shabbat and Festivals*

*Or Hadash: A Commentary on Siddur Sim Shalom Weekdays*

*Entering Torah*

*The Torah Revolution*